Known for My Work

UNIVERSITY PRESS OF FLORIDA

Florida A&M University, Tallahassee
Florida Atlantic University, Boca Raton
Florida Gulf Coast University, Ft. Myers
Florida International University, Miami
Florida State University, Tallahassee
New College of Florida, Sarasota
University of Central Florida, Orlando
University of Florida, Gainesville
University of North Florida, Jacksonville
University of South Florida, Tampa
University of West Florida, Pensacola

KNOWN FOR MY WORK

African American Ethics from Slavery to Freedom

LYNDA J. MORGAN

University Press of Florida
Gainesville · Tallahassee · Tampa · Boca Raton
Pensacola · Orlando · Miami · Jacksonville · Ft. Myers · Sarasota

This book may be available in an electronic edition.

First cloth printing, 2016
First paperback printing, 2018

23 22 21 20 19 18   6 5 4 3 2 1

Library of Congress Cataloging-in-Publication Data
Names: Morgan, Lynda J., author.
Title: Known for my work : African American ethics from slavery to freedom /
   Lynda J. Morgan.
Description: Gainesville : University Press of Florida, [2016] | Includes
bibliographical references and index.
Identifiers: LCCN 2016004126 | ISBN 9780813062730 (cloth : alk. paper)
ISBN 9780813064697 (pbk.)
Subjects: LCSH: African Americans—Social conditions. | Ethics—United
   States. | African American philosophy. | African Americans—Intellectual
   life. | African Americans—Psychology. | United States—Race
   relations—Moral and ethical aspects. | Slavery—Moral and ethical
   aspects—United States. | United States—Moral conditions.
Classification: LCC E185.86 .M365 2016 | DDC 305.896/073—dc23
LC record available at http://lccn.loc.gov/2016004126

The University Press of Florida is the scholarly publishing agency for the State University
System of Florida, comprising Florida A&M University, Florida Atlantic University, Florida
Gulf Coast University, Florida International University, Florida State University, New
College of Florida, University of Central Florida, University of Florida, University of North
Florida, University of South Florida, and University of West Florida.

University Press of Florida
15 Northwest 15th Street
Gainesville, FL 32611-2079
http://upress.ufl.edu

Contents

Preface and Acknowledgments

Growing up in western North Carolina during the death throes of formal Jim Crow in the late 1960s, I wondered why so many whites treated African Americans with such hostility. As I worked on finishing this book in the summers of 2014 and 2015, I observed similar yet different hostilities from my youth. The death of Michael Brown in Ferguson, Missouri, in August 2014 galvanized debates about race and violence and brought a resurgence of protest culminating in the Black Lives Matter movement. The deaths of several other African Americans in that year also gained national attention: Eric Garner in New York in July 2014; John Crawford in Beavercreek, Ohio, in August; Tanisha Anderson and Tamir Rice, both in Cleveland, in November. Then came the summer of 2015, dominated by the assassination of nine Emanuel African Methodist Episcopal Church members, including Pastor Clementa Pinckney, in Charleston, South Carolina, in June. This event spawned debates about the Confederate flag and its meaning. Even though the murders led directly to the removal of the flag from the statehouse grounds, legions of private individuals continue to venerate this proslavery symbol. Earlier, in March, Tony Robinson lost his life in Madison, Wisconsin, as did Walter Scott in North Charleston, South Carolina, and Freddie Gray in Baltimore in April. In June, police in McKinney, Texas, attacked a group of teens at a pool party. One month later, Sandra Bland died mysteriously in a Waller County, Texas, jail.

These are just a few of the better known contemporary cases of violence against African Americans. But the numbers are, of course, much higher, and the patterns have a long history in America, going back to slavery. Thousands of African Americans, female and male, young and old, have met death, injury, and terror at the hands of the state or of individuals who were, and still are, rarely brought to justice. One immigration defense lawyer in California's Alameda County Public Defender's Office, Raha Jorjani, recently argued that African Americans qualify for asylum status based on oppressions stemming from race.[1]

These attacks are part of a larger effort to negate African American achievements. The Supreme Court's 2013 undermining of the Voting Rights Act of 1965, the numbers of African American men and women caught in the penal system, and the contempt that President Barack Obama and his family have endured during his tenure are additional evidence that such assaults on families and communities, the backbone of the social ethics I address within, are actions directed against a democratic humanism that defines the ethos.[2] Comparing these current attacks with, say, ones that occurred in such abundance and with such terroristic intent during Reconstruction and Jim Crow is difficult. They nonetheless have similar causes and effects, reminding us that Reconstruction is indeed, in the words of historian Eric Foner, an unfinished revolution in whose arc we remain fixed.[3]

African Americans are among the foremost guardians of democratic impulses, which they have defended since the days of slavery and have transmitted to their descendants. For centuries, African Americans from all walks of life have struggled to have their views on ethics, morality, democracy, and labor gain an equal hearing. Often, they have been drowned out. This book is a partial effort to correct that ongoing historical problem and to document that slavery produced an ethos we do not often recognize: a profound desire to make the country a stronger, more equal place with an emphasis on justice for all. As we continue the national debate on race, I hope that the material here will contribute to the discussion about our ongoing freedom project.

I owe a particular debt to the African American voices that guided me through this project, and I dedicate this work to them. The final chapter, based on an article published in the Fall 2014 issue of the *Journal of African American History*, is a call for reparations for these centuries of injustice. I thank the anonymous readers of the *JAAH* article and the journal editor, V. P. Franklin, for their careful reading and helpful suggestions that made both the article and the book stronger. I also thank the anonymous reader at the University Press of Florida, who patiently and carefully read the manuscript twice, each time delivering thoughtful remarks, critical information, and a most fruitful critique that greatly improved the whole. Other readers, including Justin Behrend, Joye Bowman, Jane Gerhard, Holly Hanson, Peter Rachleff, Manisha Sinha, and Nan Woodruff also strengthened my arguments. Holly Sharac and Dawn Larder have provided invaluable and good-natured administrative assistance and technical support. Colleagues past and present in Mount Holyoke's History Department, the Africana Studies Program, and the Five College Consortium have created a vibrant intellectual environment and encouraged me to press onward, while the college itself has provided crucial financial support. Sian Hunter and Stephanye Hunter, editors at the University Press of Florida, have given me superb guidance and support. I owe special thanks to copyeditor extraordinaire, Kirsteen E. Anderson, who saved me from numerous infelicities and made this book far better.

I owe a great many debts to friends who have supported me, not only in this endeavor but over the years of my career. They include Paul Gaston and the late Armstead Robinson, my professors and profound intellectual influences in graduate school; Charlie Bright; Malaika Chehab; Imani Higginson, John Higginson, and John Higginson Jr.; Bruce Ragsdale; Diana Rhodes; Denise Rone-Johnson; Stephanie Shaw; and Pat and Donny Williams. My friends at the Taber Pool—especially my swim coach, Kerry Cordis, and all the wonderful lifeguards and swim buddies over the years—have helped me stay on track more than they realize. At home, Huey and Jazz always keep it real.

INTRODUCTION

The Social and Intellectual Gifts of Black Folk

Foundations and Legacies of a Humanistic Democratic Ethos

> What do we mean by democracy? Do we mean democracy of the white races
> and the subjection of the colored races? Or do we mean the gradual working
> forward to a time when all men will have a voice in government and industry
> and will be intelligent enough to express that voice? It is this latter thesis for
> which the American Negro stands and has stood, and more than any other
> element in the modern world it has slowly but continuously forced America
> toward that point and is still forcing. . . . The emancipation of the Negro
> Slave in America becomes through his own determined effort simply one
> step toward the emancipation of all men.
>
> —W.E.B. Du Bois, *The Gift of Black Folk*

Frederick Douglass observed in 1850 that "only when we contemplate
the slave *as a moral and intellectual being* . . . can [we] adequately compre-
hend the unparalleled enormity of slavery, and the intense criminality of
the slaveholder."[1] He thereby condensed, as W.E.B. Du Bois did almost
seventy-five years later, the fundamental ethical principles born of the collective historical experience of two and a half centuries of slavery. The pursuit of equality and freedom for all was the most enduring intellectual and
ethical legacy for slaves, free blacks, and their descendants. It derived from
their experiences with and analysis of bondage itself. After the Civil War
and emancipation, that ethos united the bulk of the heterogeneous ex-slave
population in articulating the pressing need for democratic social reform.

These aspirations were on full display during Reconstruction. Theirs
was a vision so egalitarian as to provoke the consistent violent opposition
of elites, culminating in the 1890s in an implacable terroristic counterrevolution that entailed disfranchisement and segregation.[2] These measures,

designed to silence threats against capitalistic excess, paved the way for decades of extraordinary abuse of not only black laborers but their poor white and immigrant counterparts as well. In addition to enduring grisly working conditions, people were hanged, burned and dismembered alive, raped, and placed on chain gangs for minor offenses. This epidemic of terrorism was concentrated in the South but occurred throughout the nation. The counterrevolution between the 1890s and the mid-twentieth century was so vicious that it has become known as the nadir of postemancipation African American history.[3] Despite the pitiless ferocity of the counterrevolution, the democratic visions of the emancipation generation continued to inform African American resistance strategies into the twentieth century. To preserve and transmit the history, lessons, and meanings of slavery and Reconstruction to subsequent generations, and thereby provide them with intellectual and moral armament, was a vital imperative for the emancipation generation.

When we consider the oft-posed question about slavery's continued influence on the present, the answers typically focus on the many deleterious results that the institution has had on racial and economic disparities. It also remains common to hear arguments that posit long-term residual effects of slavery on African American cultures—alleging poor work ethic, indifference to education, and disordered family life. Rarely do we acknowledge the rich ethical legacy slaves bequeathed not just to their descendants but to the nation, an ethics that fueled one of the most radical democratic and egalitarian movements in American history.[4] These insights remain applicable to many of our most troubling current problems, including, for example, poverty, unequal educational access, the mass incarceration of black men, and the rise in vigilante justice.

The fulcrum of freedpeople's ethical views pivoted on the interdependence of political economy and morality, which to them meant a universal human responsibility to work for the common good. This emphasis on community placed them far from the individualistic ethics that were ascendant in nineteenth-century America.[5] Slaves employed the foundational nexus they identified between work and ethics as the springboard for multifaceted deliberations about human nature, oppression, liberation, fairness, justice, and opportunity. Their moral economy was not a derivative or a simple assimilation of "white" or "American" beliefs, though American they surely were. Numerous overlaps with the cosmologies of other free Americans, especially the nascent antebellum working class and small landholders, certainly existed.[6] But on balance, the experience of slavery itself formed the primary material context from which slaves' and freedpeople's ethical codes emerged. Enslavement had been no abstract metaphor for freedpeople, as it often was for the emerging working class; for slaves, the lessons of bondage were unique and visceral.[7]

This egalitarian ethos had long permeated African American religious rhetoric. By the early nineteenth century African American religions were the syncretized products of West and Central African animistic religions, West African Islam, the experiences of slavery, and a redefined Christianity. Many precolonial West and Central African religions, particularly among lineage societies, were profoundly egalitarian, humanistic, communal, and spiritualistic, and blurred separations between the sacred and the secular. Such populations as the Igbo in the Bight of Biafra and peoples in West Central Africa were particularly vulnerable to slave raids, accounting for 25 and 40 percent, respectively, of the Africans enslaved in Virginia and South Carolina.[8] Their ethics survived the Middle Passage intact, establishing the foundation for the eventual Africanization of Christianity, which began to take shape in the mid-eighteenth century and matured in the early nineteenth century.[9] Africanized western religions were notable for their refutation of proslavery ideology, firm embrace of equality and humanism, and rejection of race as a primal cause of slavery or status. Slavery was immoral, as were most whites; slaveholder Christianity was blasphemous. Pre–Civil War African Americans generally believed that salvation and emancipation were both spiritually and temporally inevitable, hence their widespread use of the biblical story of Exodus. When emancipation occurred in 1865, many took it as a fulfillment of prophecy.[10]

A central feature of Africanized Christianity was its insistence that religion was as much or more concerned about life on earth as in heaven, and should be used to address injustices in the here and now. Regarded by many scholars as fundamentally a protest religion, Africanized Christianity placed stress on what slaves called "honest labor"—the divine imperative for all to labor toward the common good. Freedman John Quincy Adams reflected the views of many when he observed that living off the labor of others violated a divine edict. "Who ever heard of such a thing," he asked, "as a man working for another for nothing and he sitting down doing nothing, but only violating the laws of God and the just laws of the land, and then say it is right."[11] Born into slavery in Delaware in 1760, Bishop Richard Allen, founder of the African Methodist Episcopal Church in Philadelphia in 1794, preached a gospel and led a life that exemplified the connections among activism, morality, and religious rhetoric. Among his many political involvements, he helped organize the first National Convention of Colored Persons in 1830 to serve as an opportunity to discuss activist agendas, and was a prominent supporter of the Free Produce Society, which joined moral with economic arguments in its attack on slavery. Allen's was a liberation Christianity that posited the United States could be rescued from racial and economic immorality by recognizing black experiences as revolutionary and redemptive, capable of creating a true democracy. Allen thus utilized religion to generate a moral critique of the state, a critique that subsequent generations continued to venerate.[12] During disfranchisement and segregation, religious protest rhetoric continued to inform African American critiques of the United States as a Christian nation. Frederick Douglass, Frances E. W. Harper, Ida B. Wells, W.E.B. Du Bois, and Martin Luther King Jr., among others, identified segregation and lynching as the moral, economic, and spiritual matters that they were, thereby lengthening the antebellum legacy of utilizing religion as a vital instrument of protest against earthly injustices.[13]

This recognizable ethos did not mean that their views were homogenous or static, nor that slaves, freedpeople, and their descendants possessed innate goodness, were ethically infallible, or were uniformly humane. What it did mean was that their debates about a better future were grounded in the experience of slavery and the role of labor in human society, and that this perspective persisted in subsequent generations. As with any group of humans who shared a common historical experience, slaves' analysis of their predicament posed particular questions, which spawned multiple answers and some widely recognized truths. Generating a history of slavery and a definition of freedom were fundamental responsibilities for those whose experiences were shaped by bondage.[14]

Following emancipation, growing class divisions among African Americans made debates about the nature of the interface between work and morality more contentious, and changing historical circumstances required that the tactics of earlier generations be reshaped—but not jettisoned.[15] Divergent approaches on how best to use, or not use, the memories of slavery, and even on what those memories were about, fostered rifts about how best to attack disfranchisement and segregation, the pre-eminent products of advancing capitalism.[16] But irrespective of African Americans' approach, the enduring philosophical touchstone remained the fundamental connection between work and an ethical existence, and the centrality of labor to the human experience.[17]

Douglass's insistence upon seeing slaves as people, and independently insightful ones at that, is now a reflexive habit among most historians.[18] Nonetheless, the intellectual history *writ large* of the enslaved population, and the influence that body of thought exerted well into the future, remains somewhat disjointed. Unless they became well-known published fugitives on the abolitionist circuit, enslaved people typically lacked intellectual history until after emancipation. Historian Lawrence W. Levine was the first among modern historians to caution against dismissing slave cosmologies as frail, imitative, or nonexistent. His *Black Culture and Black Consciousness: Afro-American Folk Thought from Slavery to Freedom* (1977) argued, "Those who would restrict intellectual history to the educated, the intelligentsia, the elite, would do well to look carefully at the richness of expression, the sharpness of perception, the uninhibited imagination, the complex imagery" of those who lived with limited access to formal trappings of power. Levine relied heavily on tales and songs to document his study of folk expression. The chief message of the intellectual history he traced was that "despite the . . . social, economic, and cultural diversity that marked them," slaves "were bound together by a common identity and a shared heritage" and insisted upon being "accepted in American society not merely as Americans but as black Americans, not merely as individuals but as a people."[19]

In Levine's day and since, a massive outpouring of literature on slave and free black labor has transformed the way historians understand many fundamental nineteenth-century historical problems. These include the causes, course, and consequences of the Civil War, slave resistance, free black experiences, the abolitionist movement, the mechanics of the Atlantic and interstate slave trades, the intersections of race and gender, class stratification among whites and blacks, the sizzling political contests of the antebellum and postwar worlds, and diplomatic and global history, to list but a few.[20] We know a tremendous amount about the work that slaves and freedpeople performed, about the material worlds that formed the bedrock of their cultures, the oppressions they faced, the coercion and terror that defined their everyday lives, their challenges and accomplishments as they flexed their political muscle during Reconstruction, and the grim obstacles they confronted when Reconstruction failed in 1877. Even our ability to match the West and Central African origins of slaves with their ultimate western hemispheric locations has expanded dramatically.[21] We take them seriously as people. But the point to be made here is that they took themselves seriously as people too; were confident in their own analyses of slavery, democracy, and freedom; and understood much of what historians have taken decades to establish.[22]

This study thus seeks to add a long-range view of the ethical outcomes and legacies produced by slaves and freedpeople who intellectualized their labor experiences, drew political and moral lessons from them, and employed that body of thought to approach the problems and opportunities of the post–Civil War world and beyond. Shrouding that ethos causes us to underappreciate that the civil rights movement has an even longer history than the long civil rights movement school recognizes in placing the movement's basic historical roots in the 1930s.[23] Connecting the dots between slave ethics and the strategists of the modern civil rights movement allows us to hear not a distant echo but a thunderous shout from the emancipation generation, whose moral economists identified a range of policies and behaviors befitting a strong democracy.

Since this study seeks to analyze the thoughts and beliefs of slaves and freedpeople and their descendants, my chief primary sources have been autobiographical accounts—narratives, speeches, pamphlets, and some historical fiction—that specifically address the chief themes that concern me. While I have used some narratives collected in the 1930s under the auspices of the Federal Writers' Project, these sources, on balance, tend to focus more on folklore, family life, and recollections about Civil War military history than on connections between labor and ethics. As a recent student of the collection has observed, these Depression-era narratives are a more reliable source for African American life in the 1930s than in the antebellum and postwar eras, and sometimes the nature of the questions interviewers asked jeopardized the narratives' quality.[24] Others have concluded that because most interviewees were youngsters at the time of emancipation, they had had little direct experience with slavery, but that caveat is less of a concern for my purposes given that people who were young at the time of emancipation and beyond clearly listened to their forebears' tales about slavery's history and incorporated those lessons into their own lives.[25] By contrast, the fugitive slave narratives, whose authors not only knew about slavery but had the opportunity to advance their analysis of it, and as members of the abolitionist movement could influence abolitionist strategies, have been more revealing sources of information.

Debates among historians about the usefulness of different genres of slave narratives have been lengthy and conflicted. For decades, most historians shunned the Works Progress Administration (WPA) narratives on the basis that they were oral histories, and thus subject to corruption and narrative control. Today they are far more widely used, and different historians use various narrative categories in ways that they feel are best suited to their investigations.

Mirroring the lengthy neglect that the WPA narratives met, many scholars prior to the 1960s dismissed pre- and post-emancipation slave and ex-slave narratives based upon the charge of collaboration with white abolitionists, who allegedly set the tone and content of these works, even though hundreds were written without assistance. But dated arguments that dismiss these works as tainted by white abolitionists fail to recognize the historical context of their production. It strikes me as unsurprising that activists against slavery of whatever color or historical background wisely chose narrative formats designed to garner more (white) adherents to the cause of abolition. These formats were not unique to slave narratives but characterized a wide variety of nineteenth-century writings. Moreover, the narratives were fundamentally political and written with the express intention of advancing the abolition movement and, in some cases—notably with Douglass—improving the condition of free blacks in the North and West. I would also argue that fugitive slaves were pleased to find people with whom they could collaborate on the weighty and dangerous issue of abolition, and who could offer them assistance in writing and publishing when many of them had had limited access to literacy, to say nothing of the world of editors. It is also important to recall that many if not most fugitive slaves were resourceful and exceptional people. They were hardly dupes or puppets, nor was the information they provided compromised. African American authors had little trouble relating diverse lives within the frameworks that typified most such narratives.[26]

Douglass, for example, was initially overwhelmed that he had found an ally in William Lloyd Garrison when he first met him at a Nantucket antislavery lecture in 1838. With Garrison's help, Douglass subsequently published his first narrative in 1845. Garrison urged Douglass to hew closely to his life as a slave and to eschew strategic analysis of abolitionist methods. But as he grew intellectually, Douglass no longer embraced Garrison's emphasis on moral suasion as the proper path to abolition. He then produced a second 1855 autobiography, which expanded the 1845 edition, to make his independent thoughts known. Similarly, John Brown took issue with moral suasion in his 1854 narrative. Harriet Jacobs is another ex-slave who chose her editors, dismissing Harriet Beecher Stowe as intrusive but finding Lydia Maria Child a person with whom she could work. Her narrative, unlike Douglass's, appeared under a pseudonym and languished in the academy until 1987, when Jean Fagan Yellin conducted extensive research proving that Jacobs was in fact the author of her autobiography. David Walker, an outspoken abolitionist and author of *An Appeal to the Coloured Citizens of the World* (1829), likewise addressed many of the themes common to the narratives under discussion, and is now regarded not as an intellectual outlier in the northern African American community but typical of it. Walker also lived much of his early life in the slave states and had frequent contact with fugitives after he moved to Boston. Solomon Northup's *Twelve Years a Slave* (1853) had the assistance of a white abolitionist, but in their 1968 edition of the book, historians Sue Eakin and Joseph Logsdon painstakingly researched the details of Northup's story and provided proof that Northup's memories about time, place, and people in Louisiana were remarkably sharp; no assistant would have been able to produce such a level of detail. And what of the collaborations among whites, whether abolitionists or not? Or of the many collaborations that contemporary scholars seek out as they complete their works? The suggestion that to be a viable slave or ex-slave narrative it must have been completed in isolation, or perhaps only with African American assistance, seems unhelpful. As C. Vann Woodward observed in 1974, these sources must be approached the same way as any other primary materials, by establishing their purpose, context, and significance.[27]

A growing number of lesser-known narratives housed in manuscript repositories are now being made available online, and these have proved very useful. The University of North Carolina–Chapel Hill *American Documents* site, and the American Memory Project at the Library of Congress, in the *From Slavery to Freedom: The African-American Pamphlet Collection*, are two such collections of note. I have also found Freedmen's Bureau papers useful, along with the observations of some northern free blacks, when applicable. Evidence on the longevity and applicability of the black humanistic ethos into the twentieth century also depends upon autobiographical accounts, as well as an interpretation of the links between the thought of the emancipation generation and the tactics of the modern civil rights movement. Material on the reparations debate comes chiefly from a large secondary historical literature, although staying abreast of newspaper announcements on the steady stream of apologies, regrets, and reparations efforts recently and currently issued has sometimes proved a near-daily exercise. I have also benefited from the works of a host of other historians who have toiled diligently in African American history, particularly since the 1970s.[28]

To illustrate the foundational character of the emancipation generation's reimagined democracy, I have analyzed some basic themes that appeared in their philosophy and reappeared in subsequent generations. Chief among them was the cornerstone belief that labor was quintessential to the human condition and that people were entitled to the fruits of their labor. They also strongly insisted that slavery was a national institution that corrupted the integrity of everyone in the land and, indeed, internationally. They did not lack for evidence in constructing this ethos. Careful examination of slaveholders' character and the effects of slavery on whites generally facilitated another key investigation: the nature of race. Here again, data was plentiful, plainly written within the social relations in their environments, which easily enabled them to grasp that race was a human rather than a divine or natural creation, or in current language, was a social construction. What was natural to them was the very opposite of proslavery racial rhetoric: human equality. Racism was an economic and social disease that thrived on the expropriation of labor. Because racism was enshrined in law, it followed that only political and economic power could destroy it. Only then would their kinship- and community-based culture profit from the natural connections between individual accumulation and the good of the whole. Their analysis of the significance of the violence, torture, and terror employed against them reinforced their belief that the institution of slavery could hardly be considered natural or permanent. This awareness left a particularly abiding stress on the right to self-defense, which they sharply distinguished from violence, violent behaviors being far more characteristic of whites. This was the substantive core of the ethos that the emancipation generation embraced and bequeathed.

Many emancipation-era whites, some well-meaning and many not, assumed that freedpeople at emancipation utterly lacked any understanding of freedom. This study seeks to amplify the findings of many historians who have demonstrated that nothing could have been further from the truth.[29] Precisely *because* they possessed two and a half cumulative centuries of experience as slaves in a country allegedly founded to promote human freedom to its fullest, they collectively contemplated liberty's meaning extensively. This moral economy burst onto the emancipation scene with an immediacy and earnestness of purpose that took many people, both allies and opponents, by surprise. Most striking to these contemporaries was the robust egalitarian and humanistic bent that characterized black political and social activism. Their intellectual and social property aptly reflected, in Lawrence Levine's words, a "style of life" or a "world view" that freedpeople utilized as an agenda for a more justly ordered society.

In the late 1870s and 1880s, the enemies of these Reconstruction-era gains grew ever more determined to rein them in, if not destroy them. The federal government, under Republican administrations, steadily began to withdraw legal and military protections from freedpeople and focused attention instead on promoting the Industrial Revolution. The conditions for workers of all backgrounds worsened, but none so much as southern African Americans. Freedpeople's opponents at the state and local levels grew in number and power, and took violence against blacks and their allies to new and more vicious heights. The setbacks freedpeople confronted resulted directly from the success with which they had used political power to check mounting capitalist excess, safeguard the rights of workers, and promote democracy.[30] W.E.B. Du Bois understood the dynamics of this counterrevolution perfectly. He opened his chapter on this topic in *Black Reconstruction* with, "It must be remembered and never forgotten that the civil war in the South which overthrew Reconstruction was a determined effort to reduce black labor as nearly as possible to a condition of unlimited exploitation and build a new class of capitalists on this foundation. . . . This program had to be carried out in open defiance of the clear letter of the law."[31]

These battles and their influence on subsequent generations speak to our own problems with poverty, inequality, and economic injustice. The current gap between the rich and the poor rivals those of the Gilded Age and the late 1920s, the heydays of the Industrial Revolution, disfranchisement, and segregation.[32] As we tackle these issues, many Americans retain an abiding belief that cultural factors—a people's "values" or "attitudes"—explain the causes of poverty. Economic inequality, in this view, results from individual failings born of a poor work ethic, bad family values, and an embrace of dependency and irresponsibility, the very charges levied against slaves, freedpeople, and the industrial-era working class. Slavery is frequently invoked as the chief factor that instilled these negative purported values, which were then habitually handed down over generations with the inevitable result of economic marginality for a disproportionate number. Proponents of such ahistorical formulas believe that the alleged moral deficiencies have become so culturally ingrained in most African Americans that they have become permanent. These beliefs in no small part feed the vigilante violence against African Americans that we witness today.[33]

The historical record tells a very different, powerful, and often unrecognized story about the moral and ethical universe of slaves and freedpeople. The evidence demonstrates that, though equally vulnerable to moral ambiguity and failure as other mortals, slaves and freedpeople collectively valued honest toil, family, community, education, self-reliance, self-defense, justice, and equality dearly. They did not see vengeance as the path to those ends. They rejected greed, fraud, and personal gain as deleterious to community welfare, and believed they were uniquely suited to help redeem the nation from these ills. Toward those ends, they charted a course of vigorous political participation and the enactment and enforcement of legislation aimed at leveling the economic playing field. The charge they left their heirs was an obligation to be vigilant about maintaining a humanitarian balance between labor and morality, the fulcrum of any society devoted to ending poverty and discrimination. We could do worse than to heed their experiences and what they made of them.

We are currently in the midst of a renewed investigation about how best to respond to crimes against humanity during the U.S. slavery and segregation eras. These debates often resemble the ethical arguments that occurred among earlier generations of African Americans experiencing Reconstruction and its demise. The recent spate of apologies—or, more often, statements of regret—for slavery and the many race-related injustices that occurred during the nadir often resonate with the fund of knowledge that the emancipation and Jim Crow generations assembled. One student of reparations has noted that the movement's linkage of political economy and moral principles constitutes its "philosophical and tactical brilliance."[34] I would add that such a pairing likewise reflects the ethos of the emancipation generation. Many recognize reparations as the historically logical outcome of the civil rights movement, or of the "Third Reconstruction" that addresses economic human rights, the unfinished business of both Reconstruction and the civil rights movement. This call for economic justice has had, of course, a long and complex history, and exactly what constitutes economic justice remains unsettled. Envisioning reparations as a process of individual payments to slave descendants sparks by far the most heated and polemical opposition. The most visionary proposals recommend sweeping reforms in many realms of social and economic life, including centralized funds for education and child care, retraining of workers, universal health care, prison reform, and tax subsidies, to name but a few. Were reparations advocates able to advance the cause using this last approach, they would be fulfilling the revolutionary agenda of the emancipation generation at this, the 150th anniversary of their legal liberation.[35]

1

"There Will Be a Day of Reckoning"

What Is a Slave?

Four months after emancipation, in Dayton, Ohio, Jourdon Anderson responded to a request from his former owner, Colonel P. H. Anderson of Big Spring, Tennessee, to return with his family to work on the plantation. With controlled sarcasm, Jourdon Anderson made short work of the Colonel's "promise to do better for me than anybody else can. . . . I want to know particularly what the good chance is you propose," responded freedman Anderson, asking how life in Big Spring could outstrip the opportunity of Dayton, where the family was "tolerably well" and "kindly treated." He made twenty-five dollars a month, plus food and clothing, and lived in a "comfortable home" with his wife, Mandy—"the folks call her Mrs. Anderson"—and children, Milly, Jane, and Grundy, all enrolled in school. The family attended church regularly. The colonel promised the family their freedom, but Anderson tartly observed that "there is nothing to be gained on that score, as I got my free papers in 1864" from a Union provost marshal in Nashville.

Mandy was loath to return without irrefutable evidence that they would be treated fairly. So Anderson offered a proposal that would allow them to make a clear judgment: "We have concluded to test your sincerity," Anderson explained, "by asking you to send us our wages for the time we served you. This will make us forget and forgive old scores, and rely on your justice and friendship in the future." He calculated that his thirty-two years of enslavement, and Mandy's twenty, at twenty-five dollars per week for him and two dollars weekly for Mandy, adding interest but deducting for clothing and three doctor's and one dentist's visit, meant their back pay amounted to $11,680. This "balance will show what we are in justice entitled to," he concluded, furnishing an address where the money could be sent. "If you fail to pay us for faithful labors in the past," Anderson explained, "we can have little faith in your promises in the future. . . . Surely there will be a day of reckoning for those who defraud the laborer of his hire."

Back wages were not the sum of the matter. The Anderson family had to weigh the safety of daughters Milly and Jane, "both good-looking girls." "You know how it was with poor Matilda and Catherine. I would rather . . . starve—and die . . . than have my girls brought to the same by the violence and wickedness of their young masters." And, they asked, did Tennessee have schools open for freed children? "The great desire of my life now is to give my children an education, and have them form virtuous habits." In conclusion, Anderson bade the colonel to give his regards to George Carter, "and thank him for taking the pistol from you when you were shooting at me."[1]

The colonel's comeuppance was based on distinct elements of the moral economy that former slaves embraced by the time of emancipation. The centerpiece of Anderson's demands was reparation for stolen labor. His precise calculation of the dollars justly due him and his wife was meant to underscore how his labor and that of his family had enriched the colonel's coffers while leaving the family destitute. Respect for women also figured in Anderson's demands for restitution, even if equal wages did not. Finally, the proper education of children was vital for full freedom.

An end to violence rounded out Anderson's requests for settlement. Pointedly, Anderson reminded the colonel that emancipation occurred not through any post-emancipation Rebel generosity but from the barrel of a gun, many of those guns wielded by former slaves. African American military and civic alliances with the Union Army, which contained some 200,000 African American troops in the final two years of the war, proved decisive in overpowering slavery. Anderson's letter resonated with the optimism, assertiveness, dignity, and intellectual independence—backed by an ethical diagnosis of the slave past—that typified the emancipation generation.

The chief principle of slave ethics held that producers were entitled to the fruits of their own labor.[2] It is hardly difficult to understand why such a belief would become a philosophical centerpiece, since the experience of rarely if ever reaping any profits from labor united all formerly enslaved people. This one overarching feature of slavery dramatized the extent to which bondage inverted the Protestant work ethic: slave labor generated prosperity and leisure for people who employed terror, torture, and tyranny to get those benefits, leaving slaves impecunious and demonized as lazy, intractable barbarians. Indeed, numerous related ironies born of the juxta-positions of proslavery rhetoric and actual material conditions littered the experiential, and thus the intellectual and ethical, landscape of slaves. En-slaved people studied these antipodal conditions carefully, as we shall see, in order to defend themselves against psychological intimidation and violence and to construct a cosmology that rejected proslavery and capitalist pro-paganda—the values of the rich—in favor of promotion of legitimate gain for hard work in a world that was honest, just, and generous to all.

Multiple streams of belief flowed from these intellectual headwaters, all grounded in the certainty that to steal the labor of others was to com-mit a crime so heinous that none were spared. Its effects rippled across space, gender, class, race, and time. Numerous slaves held the conviction that because slavery was a national, not a uniquely southern, institution, the effects of its degradation were boundless. Slavery corrupted all labor—not just slave labor—because it undermined production and efficiency and hence the general welfare. Simultaneously, slavery promoted a level of materialism and unchecked greed that bondspeople and many of their descendants found deplorable. They remarked at length on the negative social consequences resulting from exploitation and acquisitive excess.

Another striking feature of slaves' moral universe was their apprecia-tion for the power of law, especially its ability to mold people's thoughts and actions. Slaveholders' power required an elaborate legal edifice that helped them instill racial ideologies among whites of all backgrounds and regions. Everyday life proved how statecraft joined to racial rhetoric, or racecraft, enabled planters to persuade non-slaveholders that but for slav-ery and color their lives would be on a quite different trajectory, and that the preservation of yeomen's freedom hinged on their political support for the aristocracy. Law was the force that sanctioned beatings, maimings, sell-ings, rapes, theft, and even murder. Law was the reason why slave testimony was not admitted into the courts, unless against other slaves.

Surely, slaves reasoned, law could also be used well and wisely, if transformed into a flexible and dynamic guardian rather than a rigid and punitive exploiter of human life. Slaves, of course, were hardly unique in appreciating the rule of law, but they did stand out for their forthright conviction that law should be divested of racial disparities, could reset damaged moral compasses, and was absolutely essential in bringing an end to slavery. Law was an essential tool of social engineering.

Such ambitious goals required hard work. Slaves and free blacks believed they knew more about hard work than anyone in nineteenth-century America. Many took pride in their prowess as workers and held that "honest labor," a term they employed to evoke ideal working conditions, was a divine charge. It was no mystery to them that their labor accounted for others' wealth. They identified slavery—and by extension, greed rather than race—as the source of the many cruelties they had endured. They thus uncompromisingly condemned the scourge of avarice in any society. They had a creative grasp of how honest labor and political activism could improve the moral landscape. That understanding would fuel immediate and insistent demands for enfranchisement after emancipation, without which they could not hope to substitute the rule of humanistic law for the fallacy of race.

These ethics derived from two chief material and social contexts. Slaves' bonded labor commanded the greater volume of their toil by far, performed for the benefit of slaveholders under threat of violence. But many had also worked in underground economies, also known as slave or niche economies. While documentation of these niche economies has existed for some time, their full influence on African American democratic visions has been undervalued. In these economies slaves often managed their own labor, typically organizing work around kin-based units. These economies had distinct rules, including pooling of profit for the good of the whole, inheritance guidelines, land-use understandings, and distribution plans. In some cases, small-scale accumulation was possible, especially for skilled men in urban settings. Often the desire to knit kin groups together more closely, or to gain entry into a kin group or community, motivated such accumulation. Slaves frowned upon amassing wealth for its own sake. The potential for community injury existed if a given individual's only goal was self-gain, and such temptation often led to communal censure.[3] Prior to the antebellum years, independent producers sometimes could save enough to purchase themselves and their kin, always a main goal of accumulation. This possibility became more remote, however, after the cotton revolution of the early nineteenth century, which greatly expanded the regime's wealth and power.[4] A million slaves were deported from the Upper to the Lower South, and slaveholders mad with cotton fever tightened their grip on slaves and free blacks alike. Rates of manumission and self-purchase plummeted as slave prices escalated and laws proscribing black freedom proliferated. Generally, only urban skilled male slaves retained any ability to amass modest amounts of money.

Even with its many limitations, here then was the niche where "honest labor" directed toward familial and community welfare potentially could be plied. In such environments, some slaves could practice reciprocal labor ethics and a moral economy largely or even completely apart from slaveholder reach and censure.[5] Using these experiences juxtaposed to the lessons gleaned from the formal slave economy itself, slaves were able to transform the dishonesty, robbery, violence, and sexual abuse they encountered into a democratic vision of a more morally ethical universe to come.

Today a growing number of states, corporations, and public institutions are recognizing that slave labor built their enterprises, and not just in the South.[6] Slaves themselves were fully aware of that reality. This understanding was common to people with the intellectual resources of Frederick Douglass and to those whose entire lives had been spent in enforced illiteracy on a plantation or farm. When northern journalist Charles Nordhoff, who toured occupied Lowcountry South Carolina in 1863, asked Phillis how her fugitive master had built a new $20,000 house the year before the war began, he met this shared belief head-on. The elderly, ill slave woman "rose in her bed . . . and with some excitement exclaimed: 'Whar he git he money? Whar he git he money? Is dat what you ask—whar he got he money? I show you, massa.'" She thrust a "gaunt, skinny, black arm, and tapping it energetically with her fore-finger, exclaimed: 'You see dat, massa? Dat's what he got he money—out o' dat black skin he got he money.'"[7]

Phillis's incredulity at Nordoff's naiveté bespoke the tacit understanding among slaves that without their work, slaveholders and other wealthy Americans would have been far less prosperous. Numerous antebellum African American narrators took credit for the affluence of others, and their outrage at these robberies had deep roots in both African American protest literature and oral traditions across the South. In early 1817, for example, while protesting the founding of the American Colonization Society in Philadelphia, three thousand petitioners argued, "Whereas our ancestors (not of choice) were the first successful cultivators of the wilds of America, we their descendants feel ourselves entitled to participate in the blessings of her luxuriant soil, which their blood and sweat manured."[8] Few drove this point home more forcefully than the indefatigable Boston tailor and abolitionist David Walker, a free black who had mingled extensively with North and South Carolina slave populations in his youth. Robbery and theft were pet themes in his stinging *Appeal to the Coloured Citizens of the World:* "America is more our country, than it is the whites'—we have enriched it with our *blood and tears.* The greatest riches in all America have arisen from" enslaved labor; "Americans have got . . . fat on our blood and groans."[9]

Fugitive Henry Bibb, who in 1842 escaped from Kentucky to Canada, where he edited an abolitionist newspaper, addressed this topic with characteristic caustic sarcasm while praising black self-reliance. "Now with all candour in answer to this proslavery logic," Bibb began, "let me ask who is it that takes care of the slave holders and their families?" Slaves cleared forests, cultivated fields, managed livestock, harvested, cooked, and placed food on slaveholder tables, he pointed out. "Who is it that digs from the cotton, sugar, and rice fields the means with which to build Southern cities, Steam boats, School houses and churches?" He gave accounts of his new neighbors who were "about trying the *dangerous experiment* of taking care of themselves,—which has so far proved to be a very successful one. . . . they are also attending a night School." Doubtless "the slave who can take care of himself and master both can certainly take care of himself alone."[10]

Blacks' cognizance of their centrality to American economic prosperity meant that they viewed slaveholders as little more than swindlers and thieves.[11] Fugitives often cited this larceny of labor as the main reason for attempting escape. "Every slave works against his heart" because a slave "knows he is labouring for the benefit of another man." So argued John Brown, who was enslaved in Virginia, North Carolina, Louisiana, Mississippi, and Georgia for the first thirty years of his life before he escaped in 1850.[12] Austin Steward, enslaved for twenty-two years (1794–1816) in Virginia and New York, argued that "no one, I care not how favorable his condition . . . desires to be a slave, to labor for nothing all his life for the benefit of others." Steward had "often heard fugitive slaves say, that it was not so much the cruel beatings and floggings that they received" that motivated them to escape "as the idea of dragging out a whole life of unrequited toil to enrich their masters."[13] Violence certainly motivated many a fugitive.[14] But, as Steward noted, the sour realities of rarely or never reaping the fruits of one's labor certainly made for much boiling blood. William and Ellen Craft chose their course of action with this and other thefts in mind. "Our condition as slaves was not by any means the worst," William explained, "but the mere idea that we were held as chattels, and deprived of all legal rights—the thought that we had to give up our hard earnings to a tyrant, to enable him to live in idleness and luxury—the thought that we could not call the bones and sinews that God gave us our own: but above all, the fact that another man had the power to tear from our cradle the new-born babe and sell it in the shambles like a brute, and then scourge us if we dared to lift a finger to save it from such a fate, haunted us for years."[15]

Douglass held forth on the theme of stolen labor numerous times, as he did in his December 1850 speech "What Is a Slave?" An enslaved person "toils that another may reap the fruit" and is "industrious that another may live in idleness." The slave labors in the hot sun under threat of the lash so that "another may ride in ease and splendor abroad." A slave's enforced ignorance makes possible the educations of others. The slave is defamed while his tormenters become "exalted." He rests "his toil-worn limbs on the cold, damp ground that another may repose on the softest pillow." He wears "coarse and tattered raiment" so that others might "be arrayed in purple and fine linen." The slave lives in a "wretched hovel" while the master occupies a "magnificent mansion." And how was this state of affairs maintained? "To this condition," Douglass bluntly explained, "he is bound down as by an arm of iron." Nothing less than a comprehensive assault on slaves' humanity, reinforced by violence and law, enabled these thefts to continue unabated.[16]

Another grave theft that slaves mourned was the damage slavery caused to families and communities, as William Craft had underlined. By the late antebellum period, slaves in the chief selling states—Maryland, Virginia, North and South Carolina, and Georgia—had endured the deportation of about a million people to the dreaded cotton and sugar regions of the

Deep South.[17] The most highly valued slaves in the trade were children and teenagers, both male and female. The trade also siphoned off the more skilled and rebellious slaves. Although the overwhelming majority of the slave population remained in the selling states and were not sold, the fear that they or their loved ones could be ensnared in the trade at a moment's notice, or be sold locally, was ever-present. These practices rent deep gashes in slaves' cultural fabric, which they went to great lengths to repair. They used an adaptive approach that recognized fictive or quasi-kinship among those who had been sold, and they expected substantial kinship obligations from extended family and the community at large. As many historians have stressed, slave culture was at its roots kinship-based, and few developments demonstrated that fact more clearly than the effects of the interstate slave trade on families.

The agony of those who experienced sale and separation was legendary, widespread, and deep. Enslaved in Georgia, Julia Brown recalled, "A man went about the country buyin' up slaves lak buyin' up cattle and the like. . . . then he'd sell 'em to the highest bidder. Oh! It was pitiful to see chil'en taken from their mothers' breast, mother sold, husbands sold from wives. One 'oman he wuz to buy had a baby, and of course the baby came befo' he bought her and he wouldn't buy the baby; said he hadn't bargained to buy the baby too, and he jest wouldn't." Sarah Byrne, the youngest of three children born in Virginia, saw her father, Sam Goodman, sold to east Tennessee while her mother and the children were sent to Augusta, Georgia. "Chile in them days so many families were broke up and some went one way der others went t'other way; and you nebber seed them no more. Virginia was a regular slave market." Cornelia Andrews, enslaved in North Carolina, "could remember dey'd sell de mammies 'way from de babies, an' dere wuzn't no cryin' 'bout it whar de marster would know 'bout it. . . . Why? Well, dey'd git beat black an' blue, dat's why." Charity Austin was first sold at the age of ten from North Carolina to Georgia, then sold to Kinston, North Carolina, once more to Danville, Virginia, and finally to a Georgia plantation. "Dey sold my sister Lucy and my brother Fred in slavery time, an' I have never seen 'em in my life," Lizzie Baker of North Carolina testified. "Mother would cry when she was tellin' me 'bout it. She never seen 'em anymore. I jes' couldn't bear to hear her tell it widout cryin'. Dey were carried to Richmond, an' sold by old marster when dey were chillun." Phebe Brownrigg, enslaved in Edenton, North Carolina, wrote her daughter, Amy Nixon, in 1835 to tell her that she had been sold. "I have for some time had hope of seeing you once more in this world, but now that hope is entirely gone forever. I expect to start next month for Alabama, on the Mississippi river. . . . You father, brothers and sisters, join me in a great deal of love to you and my dear little grand children. . . . Farewell, my dear child. I hope the Lord will bless you and your children, and enable you to raise them and be comfortable in life, happy in death, and may we all meet around our Father's throne in heaven, never no more to part. Farewell, my dear child." James Phillips penned an agonized letter to his wife, Mary, in the summer of 1852, telling her that he was "now in a trader's hands . . . and he is agoing to start South with a lot of negroes in August. I do not like this country at all, and had almost rather die than to go South. Tell all of the people that if they can do anything for me, now is the time to do it. I can be bought for $900. Do pray, try and get" one of several former owners "to send or come on to buy me, and if they will only buy me back, I will be a faithful man to them so long as I live. . . . Feel for me now or never. . . . You may depend I am almost dying to see you and my children. You must do all you can for your husband."[18]

These thefts of family members received extensive attention from fugitive and ex-slave narrators. Both Douglass and Harriet Jacobs showcased what slavery did to families in their widely read narratives, to brilliant effect. They were hardly alone. John Brown told how his Georgia mistress, Betty Moore, gave the slave children garlic and rue so that they would "grow likely for market." Moore's will divided the slaves among her children, Brown's "first serious tribulation." Brown remembered "well the grief this caused us to feel, and how the women and the men used to whisper to one another when they thought nobody was by . . . about what was coming. They would speculate . . . on the prospects they had of being separated; to whose lot they and their children were likely to fall, and whether the husbands would go with their wives. The women who had young children cried very much. My mother did, and took to kissing us a good deal oftener. This uneasiness increased as the time wore on, for though we did not know when the great trouble would fall upon us, we all knew it would come and were looking forward to it with very sorrowful hearts." In the end, the heirs placed slaves' names on pieces of paper and drew from a hat. "It was a heart-rending scene when we all got together again, there was so much crying and wailing. I really thought my mother would have died of grief at being obliged to leave her two children, her mother, and her relations behind."[19]

Cruel treatment was bad enough, but "it was inhuman to separate families as they did," Louis Hughes recalled. "Think of a mother being sold from all her children—separated for life. . . . many died heart-broken, by reason of it. Ah! I cannot forget the cruel separation from my mother. I know not what became of her, but I have always believed her dead many years ago. Hundreds were separated, as my mother and I were, and never met again."[20]

*　*　*

Fugitive slaves on the abolition circuits stressed family separations as a chief sin of slavery. But identifying the profits separations generated as the germ of slavery's origins and the chief cause of its durability likewise informed many fugitives' strategic approach to abolition. After joining the abolitionist lecture circuit, fugitive John Brown gave a withering critique of the moral suasion tactic that most white and many African American abolitionists embraced, a naïve conviction that educating slaveholders on the immorality of their ways would result in emancipation. Brown knew firsthand that slaveholders rarely reflected on the morality of their deeds—except perhaps on their deathbeds. Brown instead argued to northern audiences that only an assault on slaveholders' wealth, not their consciences, would lead to emancipation. Having endured and witnessed many of the more naked terrors of slavery, Brown was skeptical of slaveholders' abilities to register moral qualms, reflecting an independence of thought based upon his experience. Principled stands like moral suasion had a certain rhetorical cachet, but that was all. Paeans to honorable and just human relations translated poorly or not at all for people who commanded concentrations of wealth and power and who relied compulsively on violence for their very existence.

The chinking of the dollars in his pocket makes such a noise that he cannot hear you; and so long as his pocket is full you may talk, but he only keeps on never minding you. Now, if you could prevent his getting the dollars, he would begin to think there must be something very wrong in slave-holding; and as the dollars slipped away, his notion of the system's being wrong would grow bigger and bigger, till he would be so full of it he could not but abandon it.

Abolitionists thus needed "to pay a little more attention to the commercial part of the subjects," Brown opined. They should boycott slave-produced goods—if they persisted in economic collusion with slavery, planters had little reason to take antislavery seriously. "I do not see how the system is to be put down except by ... underselling it in the markets of the world," Brown argued. "I believe there is very little or no difficulty in getting free-labour Sugar and Rice. The chief difficulty is in procuring a sufficient supply of free-labour Cotton." But he was learning that parts of Africa, the West Indies, India, and Australia furnished possibilities.

Even sympathetic audiences rejected Brown's ideas as quixotic, causing him to despair "of the indifference of the anti-slavery public, who will not pay a small advance on the price of an article made of free-labour cotton; nor encourage enterprises set on foot to increase the supplies of the raw staple." Instead, most self-professed slave allies confined themselves to anguishing "over the sufferings of the poor slave, who labours under the lash, from morning till night, in the cotton, rice, or sugar-cane fields," but their compassion vanished when they saw that "the markets have improved."[21]

Slaves saw no contradiction between the fact that their stolen labor fed national prosperity and another closely linked truism: as much as slavery fattened pockets, it also undermined potential resources and thus the common good. One of slavery's most viral consequences on free as well as enslaved individuals was its sharp curb on labor productivity and its hobbling of efficiency generally. Louis Hughes had a native understanding of this problem. Born in Virginia and sold as a young boy to the cotton fields of Mississippi, Hughes penned his autobiography in order to explain the "potent but baneful influence" slavery had on the formation of the country's "social, civil and industrial structures" and its "utter incompatibility with industrial improvement and general educational progress."[22] Many slaves concurred with such arguments. Common beliefs were that slavery promoted economic stagnation, corrupted the dignity of labor, fostered the widespread habit of shirking at work among slaves, and created an abiding aversion toward labor among slaveholders and non-slaveholders alike.[23]

"Slavery has made labor dishonorable to the white man," as Henry Watson observed, and whites who did not have slave labor tended to resort to theft and gambling rather than work.[24] "A contempt for workers characterizes every one in any way connected with slavery," Francis Fedric stressed. "Nothing seems so degrading to them as to do the slightest menial office, such as making a pie, or tart, or any little article of cooking. . . . Slaves do everything."[25]

The message that labor was disgraceful, potent among whites, rang hollow in the slave community, where the distinction between honest and dishonest labor was stark. Slavery clearly tarnished the economic character of all it touched. But that did not mean that slaves sought an idle freedom, or that they failed to take pride in their abilities as laborers. In a differently principled world, everyone would have work to do, work that should be compensated fairly and done willingly for the benefit of self, kin, and community. "If each man in the world did his share of honest work, we should have no need of a millennium. The world would teem with abundance, and the temptations to evil in a thousand directions, would disappear," Douglass argued.[26]

Slaves thus honored the responsibility for tackling one's own work, rather than either coercing labor from others or neglecting work to an extent that forced others to pick up the slack. This belief that self-reliance sustained the common good was deeply embedded in black abolitionist rhetoric, particularly among fugitive slaves. Douglass, for example, in a July 1848 address that also ran in his *North Star* newspaper under the title "What Are the Colored People Doing for Themselves?" berated those who failed to confront the challenges at their own hand. This argument had brought him afoul of abolitionist William Lloyd Garrison, Douglass's erstwhile mentor and editor of the premier abolitionist journal *The Liberator*. "If there be one evil spirit among us, for the casting out of which we pray more earnestly than another," Douglass insisted, "it is that lazy, mean and cowardly spirit, that robs us of all manly self-reliance, and teaches us to depend upon others for the accomplishment of that which we should achieve with our own hands." Douglass penned these words shortly after his split with the Garrisonians, a rift caused in part by Garrison's determination that the decision-making process of the American Antislavery Society should remain in white hands, chiefly his own. "Our white friends can and are rapidly removing the barriers to our improvement, which they themselves have set up," Douglass acknowledged, "but the main work must be commenced, carried on, and concluded by ourselves." It was crucial to be ever aware "that our destiny, for good or for evil, for time and for eternity, is, by an all-wise God, committed to us," and no amount of assistance could "release us from this high and heaven-imposed responsibility.... We must rise or fall, succeed or fail, by our own merits."[27]

Harriet Jacobs echoed these tenets when she recalled that after her free grandmother, Molly Horniblow, finally was able to buy her son Philip out of slavery, "The happy mother and son sat together by the old hearthstone that night, telling how proud they were of each other, and how they would prove to the world that they could take care of themselves, as they had long taken care of others."[28] This theme of self-reliance also appeared in a widely circulated abolitionist cartoon featuring whites at ease watching blacks hard at work. "Poor things, they can't take care of themselves," remarked one of the idle observers.[29]

John S. Rock, a Boston dentist, attorney, and abolitionist orator with many fugitive acquaintances, addressed the issue of self-reliance in a January 1862 speech before the Massachusetts Anti-Slavery Society entitled "What If the Slaves Are Emancipated?" "The idea seems to prevail," Rock observed, "that the poor things would suffer if robbed of the glorious privileges they now enjoy!" Proslavery advocates actually argued that slaves "would pine away and die" if they were not "flogged, half-starved, and worked to support in ease and luxury those who have never waived an opportunity to outrage and wrong them." In slavery, "they can take care of themselves and their masters too; but if you give them their liberty, must they not suffer?" Resonating with fugitive John Brown's assessment of slaveholder morality, Rock asked whether the audience had "not observed that the location of this organ of sympathy is in the pocket of the slaveholder and the man who shares in the profits of slave labor." If masters did not have slaves they would have to "leave their gilded *salons* and take off their coats and roll up their sleeves and take their chances" as others did. But such they would not do, "for they have been so long accustomed to live by robbing and cheating the Negro that they are sworn never to work while they can live by plunder."[30]

Self-reliance also meant that the able-bodied should not seek special favors. Fugitive John Brown underscored that he did "not want charity help," pointing out that he was "a strong man yet, in spite of the privations, hardships, and sufferings I have undergone." His worst handicap was his lack of formal education, but he still possessed "experience which I believe I could turn to account were the field open. I am what is called a 'handy fellow' . . . a good carpenter, and can make just what machinery I want, give me only tools." He knew "all about the growth of cotton. . . . I am a good judge of its quality, too, and know what is the best kind of jin for the various sorts." Such talent had "not come naturally. . . . I have acquired it in a very hard school." Brown felt "that with a fair field I can earn my own living. I want to do it. I want to rise." Brown wrote his narrative partly to raise seed money for these goals. "The coloured people must do their own work," he stressed. "If they stand by till other folks do it for them, slavery may take a long lease yet." Once they understood that "they have a work to do, and set about it in earnest . . . Slavery may call in all the doctors the South can muster—including old Sam himself [the devil]—but it must die, in spite of every thing they can do to keep it alive."[31]

Few of the many robberies laid at slavery's feet brought more lasting pain than the proscriptions against literacy, whose effects were irremediable. John Quincy Adams's dearest loss to slavery was that "they took my labor to educate their children, and then laughed at me for being ignorant and poor, and had not sense enough to know that they were the cause of it."[32] Maryland fugitive and abolitionist minister James W. C. Pennington keenly rued what enforced ignorance had cost him in freedom, the "one sin that slavery committed against me" that he never forgave: Slavery "robbed me of my education; the injury is irreparable; I feel the embarrassment more seriously now than I ever did before." After Pennington escaped, it took him two years "to unshackle my mind," another three to cleanse his "language of slavery's idioms," and still another to throw off "the crouching aspect of slavery." Even at the end of this process, Pennington sorrowfully acknowledged that he could not correct the "great lack of that general information, the foundation of which is most effectually laid in that part of life which I served as a slave." Acutely conscious of opportunities lost to time, he often felt "grievously overwhelmed with a sense of my deficiency" and vehemently condemned the "*vile monster*" of slavery for having "*hindered my usefulness, by robbing me of my early education.*"[33] For Louis Hughes, too, lack of education proved uniquely galling as he began to "make an honest man of myself, and to earn an honest living" after emancipation: "it was one of the bitterest remembrances of my servitude that I had been cheated out of this inalienable right—this immeasurable blessing." In an effort to overcome this handicap and the deep despondence it evoked, the adult Hughes, like so many thousands of others, attended night school faithfully and with resolute determination.[34] Douglass first felt this sting of lack of instruction at a young age, when his owner, Hugh Auld, forbade wife, Sophia, to teach Douglass to read: "*I had been cheated,*" was his immediate response. "I saw through the attempt to keep me in ignorance . . . and I treated them as robbers and deceivers."[35]

*   *   *

The body of thought that answered the question, "What is a slave?" pivoted around themes of larceny, especially the theft of labor, but also of family, of education, and many times of sanity. The next three chapters will explore the related ethical inquiries that were intimately intertwined with this basic philosophical foundation. The causes and consequences of violence and rape that so many suffered further augmented the criminal case against slavery. Developing an understanding of the meaning of race and of slavery's impact on slaveholders was a critical intellectual pursuit that provided additional evidence of the economic genesis of slavery. These insights reinforced slaves' foundational belief in the centrality of honest labor to any ethical human society.

2

"I Found That There Were Puzzling Exceptions"

The Economic Foundations of Race during Slavery and Jim Crow

Slaves and free African Americans, both before and after emancipation, recognized that white supremacy, like slavery itself, was an issue whose origins were best understood in economic terms, and that race and racism had to be reckoned as consequences rather than causes of slavery. The same held true for many of their descendants who endured the post-Reconstruction nadir. Profiting through the theft of labor was the nucleus of enslavement. Were proslavery logic to be believed, slaves reasoned, no explanation existed for slaves to behave in anything other than docile, submissive, and imitative ways. But resistance to enslavement had a long and distinguished history in the slave quarters, from the creation of distinct cultures and independent ethical codes, to acts of everyday disobedience, and on to the organized rebellions that earlier antebellum generations had attempted.[1] By continually measuring slaveholders' gusty rhetoric against their own experience, slaves easily repudiated race and religion as primeval determinants of conduct or rank. Racism was obviously a learned rather than natural behavior, they concluded. One investigation into slave ideologies about whiteness found that slaves rarely ascribed racial characteristics to whites, but rather defined them as people with power and privilege, which were consequences of slavery rather than race.[2] Many flatly rejected a self-image of inferiority in favor of a belief in their own moral equality, if not superiority. Slaves and free African Americans were also adept at deciphering racial rhetoric, a process that reinforced democratic humanism and egalitarianism. Many slaves also understood that the economic exploitation operating not only against them but among whites as well required racial ideologies. Thus, in no small part, racism's economic causation had to be cloaked from non-slaveholders to protect the planter class from challenges from lower-class whites. From slaves' perspectives, the countless contradictions and realities about race were hidden in plain view, demolishing slaveholder logic on a daily basis. Race failed to define who was and was not enslaved, or who was or was not a slaveholder. Racial ideology's obvious purpose was to control people's views in such a way as to defuse resistance—white as well as black.

Frederick Douglass scrutinized the doctrines of proslavery ideology as a young boy, shortly after he realized that he was a slave. "I found," he recalled, "that there were puzzling exceptions" to racial dogma. "I knew of blacks who were *not* slaves; I knew of whites who were *not* slaveholders; and I knew of persons who were *nearly* white, who were slaves." He could only conclude that "Color . . . was a very unsatisfactory basis for slavery. . . . It was not *color*, but *crime*, not *God*, but *man*, that afforded the true explanation of the existence of slavery."[3] When he acquired literacy, his first love was the *Columbian Orator*, where he read speeches about the rights of man that confirmed his childhood observations: "If I ever wavered under the consideration, that the Almighty, in some way, ordained slavery . . . I wavered no longer. I had now penetrated the secret of all slavery and oppression, and had ascertained their true foundation to be in the pride, the power and the avarice of man."[4]

By the 1830s, people who could potentially pass as white figured disproportionately among the total number of fugitives.[5] Slaves often commented on the growing numbers among them who could pass for white, if not in daylight then in dark, or who were only barely "tinged." Everyone knew that slaveholders often sold their own children fathered with slave women, if they did not keep the children as their own slaves. It was common knowledge that "thousands are ushered into the world, annually, who—like myself—owe their existence to white fathers," Douglass observed, "and, most frequently, to their masters, and master's sons."[6] Kidnapped or orphaned white, European, and Native American children were known to be among the enslaved.[7] As Douglass sarcastically noted, "if the lineal descendants of Ham are only to be enslaved . . . slavery in this country will soon become an unscriptural institution." This state of affairs left slave girls and women "at the mercy of the fathers, sons or brothers of . . . master[s]. The thoughtful know the rest."[8]

"Slavery in America is not at all confined to persons of any particular complexion," William Craft explained. This he knew only too well; his wife, Ellen, was fair enough to pass for white, a fact that was central to their escape plan. Ellen not only camouflaged herself as white, but as male and a slaveholder, with William acting as her slave accompanying his master on a search for medical care. "There are a very large number of slaves as white as any one," Craft explained, "but as the evidence of a slave is not admitted in court against a free white person, it is almost impossible for a white child, after having been kidnapped and sold into or reduced to slavery, in a part of the country where it is not known (as often is the case), ever to recover its freedom. I have myself conversed with several slaves who told me that their parents were white and free; but that they were stolen away from them and sold when quite young. As they could not tell their address, and also as the parents did not know what had become of their lost and dear little ones, of course all traces of each other were gone." He then told the story of two young German emigrants, Dorothea and Salome Muller, who were sold into slavery when their father died. Salome was not freed for twenty-five years. Moreover, Craft had known "worthless white people to sell their own free children into slavery; and, as there are good-for-nothing whites as well as coloured persons everywhere, no one, perhaps, will wonder at such inhuman transactions; particularly in the Southern States of America, where I believe there is a greater want of humanity and high principle amongst the whites, than among any other civilized people in the world."[9] Lewis Clarke, a Kentucky fugitive who could pass for white, "knew a slave that was *all* white" who had been "stolen from Virginia when he was a very little boy, and he had been kept in slavery ever since."[10]

These mercurial links between race and status meant that slaves became adept at plumbing the actual content of a person's character, and exercised caution about relying reflexively on race to judge someone's integrity. Fugitives, in particular, had to be especially skeptical about facile connections between race and behavior. Race could be a useful parameter in taking the measure of character, and most slaves wisely lacked any trust whatsoever in whites, though not because they were white, but because of their collective historical reputation. Slavery had wrought that outcome, leaving race as one factor among many to be taken into account when assessing behavior. Particularly when blacks were in danger and in an unfamiliar environment, color proved an unreliable indicator of loyalty often enough to warrant prudence.[11] The problem of black informants was a case in point. Runaways exercised due diligence about the reliability of unknown African Americans, sometimes especially those who were enslaved. Both free blacks and slaves were known to inform in order to collect rewards, with which many planned to purchase themselves or kin. Some became turncoats to save their own lives. In Louisiana, Solomon Northup knew the architect of a plan for mass escape to Mexico, Lew Cheney, who turned informer when the plan was uncovered. Cheney told his captors that the group had intended to "murder every white person along the bayou." An "indiscriminate slaughter" of slaves ensued, and Cheney "was even rewarded for his treachery. He is still living, but his name is despised and execrated by all his race throughout the parishes of Rapides and Avoyelles."[12]

Abolitionist David Walker was especially vexed by black informants and acidly addressed their immorality in the *Appeal* and in his speeches. He knew that race dissected from historical context furnished shallow water in which to float sweeping arguments about human nature. "We see, to our sorrow, in the very midst of us, a gang of villains, who, for the paltry sum of fifty or a hundred dollars, will kidnap and sell into perpetual slavery, their fellow creatures!" he reminded an 1828 Boston audience. "And, too, if one of their fellow sufferers, whose miseries are a little more enhanced by the scourges of a tyrant, should abscond from his pretended owner ... to take a little recreation, and unfortunately fall in their way, he is gone! For they will sell him for a glass of whiskey! ... shall we suffer such notorious villains to rest peaceably among us?"[13] Walker seized upon an attempted escape by a gang of sixty slaves being marched from Maryland to Mississippi in 1829 to illustrate this point in his *Appeal*. Having killed two traders and left a third for dead, the fugitives took their money and fled. One of the women, however, helped the third trader onto his horse, enabling his escape. Walker drew attention to "the *ignorant* and *deceitful actions* of this coloured woman. . . . this *servile woman* helped him upon his horse. . . . what do you think of this? Was it the natural fine feelings of this woman, to save such a wretch alive? I know that the blacks ... are more humane and merciful than the most enlightened and refined European that can be found in all the earth. Let no one say that I assert this because I am prejudiced on the side of my colour, and against the whites or Europeans. . . . Natural observations have taught me these things; there is a solemn awe in the hearts of the blacks, as it respects *murdering* men: whereas the whites . . . where they have the advantage, or think that there are any prospects of getting it, they murder all before them, in order to subject men to wretchedness and degradation under them. This is the natural result of pride and avarice. But I declare, the actions of this black woman are really insupportable. . . . we must remember that *humanity, kindness* and the *fear of the Lord*, does not consist in protecting *devils*. . . . The black men acted like *blockheads*. Why did they not make sure of the wretch? He would have made sure of them, if he could."[14]

By the same token, being able to judge when a white person might reasonably be trusted was a skill long practiced in the community. In 1800, for example, a white shipmaster sheltered Virginia rebel leader Gabriel, and Gabriel likely recognized this man as one who, like many revolutionary-era tars, took his egalitarianism seriously. It was a free black intent upon the reward money who ultimately betrayed Gabriel.[15] Brotherhood of Sleeping Car Porters president A. Philip Randolph's formerly enslaved father, James Randolph, made this issue about race and character clear for his sons. "You have no right to hate anybody because of his color," he taught them. Instead, analyze character based upon actions. "There are white men and women who have as deep a sense of Christianity as I have and your mother has or any Negro. Therefore they must be given support when issues arise that have social significance, meaning that the work that they do is of benefit to all Negroes."[16]

In making her protracted escape from slavery, Harriet Jacobs decided to rely on a slave mistress who had a close relationship with Jacobs's grandmother, Molly Horniblow, and whose slave Betty, a friend of Jacobs, vouched for the mistress's dependability. The mistress hid Jacobs in her Edenton, North Carolina, home for some time, and she and Betty carefully kept Jacobs's presence securely hidden from another slave, the unreliable Jenny. The mistress colluded in sending Jacobs's master, James Norcom, off Jacobs's trail. Norcom was certain that Jacobs was in New York, whence she had contrived to have a letter sent to him. When Norcom came to the home where Jacobs was hiding out, he did so not because he suspected Jacobs was present, as she so deathly feared, but because he wanted to borrow five hundred dollars for the trip to recapture her in New York. The benefactress's sister lent Norcom the money at interest. "The doctor will merely lighten his pocket hunting after the bird he has left behind," the mistress joked with the terrified fugitive. When finally forced to abandon this refuge, Jacobs was unable to thank the mistress since the woman had left town in order to avoid implication should Jacobs be captured. "I never again saw her who had so generously befriended the poor, trembling fugitive! Though she was a slaveholder, to this day my heart blesses her! Because of her role in shielding the young woman from her licentious master."[17] Jacobs never provided her benefactress's name to ensure the woman's safety.

Jacobs's patron, like other white allies, was, of course, the exception that proved the rule. Slaveholders as a class rarely diverted from racial protocol, either privately or publicly. This they did in no small part for defensive purposes: to keep non-slaveholders, the majority population of the slave regime, confused about the actual cause of their economic marginality. Douglass, among others, recognized this tried-and-true tactic easily. Non-slaveholders were "robbed by the slave system, of the just results of" their labor as a result of "being flung into competition with a class of laborers who work without wages." The enmity non-slaveholders should have directed toward slaveholders instead was deflected onto slaves. "Slaveholders blind them to this competition," Douglass explained, "by keeping alive their prejudice against the slaves, *as men*—not against them *as slaves*. They appeal to their pride," so as to disabuse non-slaveholders of the fact that "they are already regarded as but a single remove from equality" with slaves. The racial propaganda planters aimed at non-slaveholders was "cunningly made" to send the message "that slavery is the only power that can prevent the laboring white man from falling to the level of the slave's poverty and degradation.""The slaveholders," Douglass knew, "with a craftiness peculiar to themselves, by encouraging the enmity of the poor, laboring white man against the blacks, succeed in making the said white man almost as much a slave as the black slave himself. The difference between the white slave, and the black slave, is this: the latter belongs to *one* slaveholder, and the former belongs to *all* the slaveholders, collectively."[18]

Non-slaveholders were a target audience for racial ideology, but pro-slavery logic was also designed to instill a sense of inferiority in slaves and free blacks. Some succumbed to such propaganda. Douglass "met many religious colored people . . . who are under the delusion that God requires them to submit to slavery, and to wear their chains with meekness and humility. I could entertain no such nonsense as this." For those who did, Douglass knew how the result had been achieved—not through argument or debate. "To make a contented slave, you must make a thoughtless one. It is necessary to darken his moral and mental vision, and, as far as possible, to annihilate his power of reason. He must be able to detect no inconsistencies in slavery. The man that takes his earnings, must be able to convince him that he has a perfect right to do so."[19] Douglass himself had experienced the baneful psychological effects of steady cruelty and deceit when he was leased to slave breaker Edward Covey: "I was completely wrecked, changed and bewildered; goaded almost to madness at one time, and at another reconciling myself to my wretched condition."[20] David Walker, along with fugitive Henry Highland Garnet, had an abiding belief that the cruelties of slavery damaged slave and free black psyches and promoted docility and submission. A century and a half later, Malcolm X steadfastly insisted that African Americans had internalized a sense of inferiority as a result of slavery and segregation.[21] As Douglass acknowledged, many had, even if only temporarily.

But the humanism that typified slave cultures also clearly demonstrated that planters had failed to persuade a wide swath of the enslaved of their inferiority. Some even believed in their moral superiority. Charles Ball saw no reason to be regarded as equal to whites and held that the very idea was anathema to many slaves. This was a "matter of strict justice to the whites, who will, by no means, be of an equal rank with those who shall be raised from the depths of misery, in this world." It was, after all, "every where laid down, that those who . . . have lived in ease and luxury, at the expense of their fellow men will surely . . . be punished, for having withheld from others the participation of those blessings, which they themselves enjoyed."[22]

Instances of rejections of racial ideology are not difficult to find. Austin Steward, for example, understood as a young man that a chief justification for slavery was that blacks were an inferior race, likely not even human. But based upon his religious views and the material evidence at hand, he dismissed this proslavery principle as "utterly false." The Bible informed Steward that "God hath created of one blood all the nations of the earth."

In physical stature and stamina "the colored man is quite equal to his white brother, and in many instances his superior." Both black and white had "the same desires and aspirations." Everyone needed food to live, and "they alike require to be warmed by the cheerful fire . . . alike they welcome the cool spring and the delightful shade of summer." He could reach no other conclusion but that "God created all men free and equal, and placed them upon this earth to do good and benefit each other."[23]

African Methodist Episcopal bishop Daniel A. Payne, a freeborn Charlestonian and later the president of Wilberforce University, stated in an 1839 speech that he opposed slavery "not because it enslaves the black man, but because it enslaves *man*. . . . were all the slaveholders in this land men of color, and the slaves white men, I would be as thorough and un-compromising an abolitionist as I now am." Significantly, Payne said that he based his remarks on "what I have both seen and heard from the slaves themselves."[24]

The understanding that race was a human creation born of slavery en-abled slaves to eschew racial explanations for character and station. These were among the most deeply rooted of all slave beliefs, and they were passed along scrupulously to subsequent generations. And with good reason, for at the end of the century, the descendants of the emancipation generation began to encounter racial ideologies that borrowed from the slave past but were tailored to the industrial present. In the 1890s, disenfranchisers and segregationists, with able assistance from the academy, set out to elaborate in earnest upon the naturalness of human inequality.[25] Their need for a refurbished racial ideology had an old purpose: to undermine class-based economic challenges, this time to advancing capitalism. Their arguments rested heavily on Darwinian precepts of survival of the fittest and natural selection, ideas that predated Darwin's findings by several decades.[26]

Contemporary African Americans had little difficulty understanding this racial strategy. As Mississippian George Washington Albright, a for-mer slave who became a state representative, observed, "The rich people regained control . . . with the help of the Klan. Unfortunately, they got many of the poor whites on their side. The poor white people felt that their interests lay with the Negroes—for the first time they had voting rights, and schools for the children. But the landlords kept poisoning their minds, saying 'You're voting with niggers. You're lining up with niggers.' The landlords split many of them away from their own best interests."[27] Former slave Susie King Taylor had worked as a nurse, laundress, cook, and teacher in the First South Carolina Volunteers during the Civil War, where she came to know and respect many whites as friends of slaves. She remembered Colonel C. T. Trowbridge, their commanding officer, as an ally of particular integrity: "No officer in the army was more beloved than our late lieutenant-colonel, C. T. Trowbridge." When she reflected on the shocking turn of events of the late nineteenth century, she did "not condemn all the Caucasian race because the negro is badly treated by a few of the race. No! for had it not been for the true whites, assisted by God and the prayers of our forefathers, I should not be here to-day. There are still good friends to the negro. Why, there are still thousands that have not bowed to Baal. So it is with us. . . . God is just; when he created man he made him in his image, and never intended one should misuse the other. All men are born free and equal in his sight."[28]

When South Carolina called for a constitutional convention in 1895 for the express purpose of disfranchisement, Republican delegate Thomas Ezekiel Miller identified the purpose of such legislation, which called for those who had less than three hundred dollars of property or were uneducated to lose the ballot. "The purpose for which this convention was called," Miller said to the legislature, "is to disfranchise the Negro in the rice fields and his poor, uneducated white brother, who plows the bobtail ox or mule on the sandhills." As a consequence, "a governor will be elected who will turn the machinery over to the wealthy, to the managers of corporate rights, to the goldbugs, the whisky trust, and we will have a spectacle like this: The poor, ignorant white man, the poor, educated white man, the poor, ignorant Negro, and the poor, educated Negro will be nonentities in the government, with no voice to say who shall rule, with no representation in the legislative halls, with no representation in the courts; it will be turning back the wheel of progress, and revolution should never go backward." When he insisted that blacks wanted equality, not domination, as was charged, he employed a humanistic logic.

In the image of God, made He man, all equal, in the possession of inalienable rights, but at all times it has been the property-owning class who have sought to grind down, impoverish and brutalize their own blood if that blood was in the body of the poor and the weak. It is against class legislation that I stand here and raise my voice, and in the name of the poor, struggling white man and the peaceful, toiling, loving Negro. I ask that this act of feudal barbarism against the poor and common people do not be engrafted into and become a part of the Magna Charta of free white and black South Carolinians.[29]

Like Miller, black people who entered the nadir recognized that late nineteenth-century racial rhetoric justified abuse against blacks, their allies, and the poor, all vulnerable to attack for the sake of greed.

The powerful drugs of race and racism in the nineteenth century were capable of deforming the thoughts and behaviors of whites of all backgrounds. But for slaves, understanding race as a human and therefore social construction with clear economic origins was a much easier analytic exercise. Their failure to develop a racial profile of whites—associating whites instead with political, economic, and social power—testified to their understanding that race dictated neither status nor character. Since race failed to satisfactorily explain human behavior and conditions, other factors had to be considered, and slavery easily topped the charts as the cause of race and racism. An in-depth examination of the effects of the institution on slaveholders, the subject of the next chapter, buttressed this ethical belief.

support

3

In a Cage of Obscene Birds

Slavery's Consequences for Slaveholders and the Nation

The plethora of ill effects slavery and racism had on slaveholders was a bell-wether issue slaves addressed at length and that deeply informed their ethical views. They did so in part to disprove the transparent fallacies of racial rhetoric. But they were also intent on illustrating the inevitable malignant consequences of slavery on not just slaveholders but everyone in the nation. Because they were known to employ every species of violence, torture, threat, coercion, and trickery to keep their power, slaveholders had become a people skilled at exploiting vulnerability to astoundingly imaginative lengths. Bondage had rendered slaveholders spiritually and psychologically diseased; left untreated, their souls were doomed. Slaveholders clearly had fallen far wide of the unambiguous moral imperative to engage in honest labor. What conditions enabled them to exploit the labor of others with so little compunction? Race did not explain this behavior; slavery and greed did. Many believed that slaveholders could at any moment achieve earthly and heavenly redemption if they embraced immediate emancipation and equality. Fittingly, the same was true for the nation.

As historical environmentalists, slaves understood that greed provided more satisfactory explanatory power than either race or religion regarding the origins and persistence of slavery. Such convictions necessitated a comprehensive appraisal of slavery's effects on slaveholders in particular, and on other whites as well. Cupidity on such a grand scale required three key ingredients: violence, duplicity, and the brace of law. Without them, slaveholders could not maintain control over slave labor. Slaveholders stood ready to launch sexual assaults on slave women and girls—and

and made guns illegal for them ✓

some men and boys as well—and exercised control and profited materially by attacking slave families through sale and separation.[1] They made
formal education of slaves a crime and went to great lengths to safeguard
illiteracy, at which they often failed. When they could not reach these ends
through their own power, local, state, and federal law stood ready to shore
up their position.[2] They likened slaves to animals to deny their humanity.
These behaviors, particularly once engrained over a lifetime and especially
over generations, had had crippling consequences for slaveholder character.
Even when individual slaveholders practiced a less marauding style, these
exceptions merely highlighted the overwhelming truth that the institution
of slavery and the violence it required polluted planters' souls. No matter
how many acts of so-called kindness occurred, they would never erase the
many cruelties of slavery or its intrinsic toxicity.

Stories about deteriorating transformations in behavior as the consequence of steady exposure to slavery were mainstays in slave narratives. The
literature brimmed with accounts of how slavery had turned potentially
decent folks into tense, cruel, lazy, mendacious, and unhappy monsters.
Slaves regularly characterized seasoned slaveholders as the most brutish,
uncivilized, inhumane, vicious, sadistic, and devilish people around. Frederick Douglass's observation was typical: "Slavery was the parent of anger
and hate," and slaves believed "that those go to hell who die slaveholders;
and they often fancy such persons wishing themselves back again, to wield
the lash."[3] In 1852, fugitive Henry Bibb wrote one of his six former masters,
Albert G. Sibley, "to warn you of the great danger to which you are exposed
while standing in the attitude of an incorrigible slave-holder. I mean that
you shall know that there is a just God in heaven, who cannot harmonize
human slavery with the Christian religion." Receiving no reply, Bibb addressed Sibley once more. "Again I ask how you feel, brother, with all of
this guilt resting upon your head as an acceptable class leader in the M. E.
Church south! . . . you have an awful account to render to the great Judge
of the Universe, slave holding religion is of the devil, and your only chance
for salvation lies in repentance before God."[4] "If you want to go to the next
world and meet a God of love, mercy, and justice, in peace," Jackson Whitney informed his former owner William Riley in 1859, "[you] had better
repair the breaches you have made amoung us in this world, by sending
my wife and children to me; thus preparing to meet your God in peace; for,

if God don't punish you for inflicting such distress on the poorest of His poor, then there is no use of having any God, or talking about one."[5]

Ex-slave Louis Hughes joined the multitude who stressed that slavery had a "degrading influence upon both master and slave."[6] "The poor wicked slaveholder that is now living upon the face of the earth," added another, "does not know his right hand from his left. . . . their hearts are shut up with sin and iniquity."[7] "It is said that no man is wholly bad," Sam Aleckson reflected, but his master "had from his youth exhibited an ugly disposition, and . . . elevation to power did not tend to improve his character. . . . Some say that even the devil is not as black as he is painted." But because of the sadism of his master, Sam concluded, "I could never endorse that statement."[8] "I was twenty-one years in that cage of obscene birds," Harriet Jacobs reminded her readers. "I can testify, from my own experience and observation, that slavery is a curse to the whites as well as to the blacks. . . . It makes the white fathers cruel and sensual; the sons violent and licentious; it contaminates the daughters, and makes the wives wretched." But rare was the slaveholder who displayed any awareness "of the widespread moral ruin occasioned by this wicked system. Their talk is of blighted cotton crops— not of the blight on their children's souls."[9] Austin Steward, who regarded his cruel master as hardly among the worst, observed that "so degrading is the whole practice of Slavery, that it not only crushes and brutalizes the wretched slave, but it hardens the heart, benumbs all the fine feelings of humanity, and deteriorates from the character of the slave-holders themselves,—whether man or woman." No one could otherwise explain how "a gentle, and in other respects, amiable woman" could observe "scenes of cruelty, without a shudder of utter abhorrence." But many a mistress looked on violence not only coolly "but with approbation; and what is worse, though very common, they can and do use the lash and cowhide themselves . . . and that too on those of their own sex! Far rather would I spend my life in a State's Prison, than be the slave of the best slave-holder on the earth!"[10] "I do not think people know what Slavery means," John Brown began his passage on this topic. "It is not possible they should be able to understand how wicked a thing it is, and how it affects the free, as well as the bond."[11]

Solomon Northup saw that "Slavery in its most cruel form among them [slaveholders] has a tendency to brutalize the humane and finer feelings of their nature. . . . It is not the fault of the slaveholder that he is cruel, so much as it is the fault of the system under which he lives. He cannot withstand the influence of habit and associations that surround him."[12] Some slaveholders agreed. As Thomas Jefferson famously observed, "The whole commerce between master and slave is a perpetual exercise of the most boisterous passions, the most unremitting despotism on the one part, and degrading submissions on the other."

> Our children see this, and learn to imitate it; for man is an imitative animal. This quality is the germ of all education in him. From his cradle to his grave he is learning to do what he sees others do. If a parent could find no motive either in his philanthropy or his self-love, for restraining the intemperance of passion towards his slave, it should always be a sufficient one that his child is present. But generally it is not sufficient. The parent storms, the child looks on, catches the lineaments of wrath, puts on the same airs in the circle of smaller slaves, gives loose to his worst of passions, and thus nursed, educated, and daily exercised in tyranny, cannot but be stamped by it with odious peculiarities. The man must be a prodigy who can retain his manners and morals undepraved under such circumstances.[13]

Frederick Douglass was particularly adept at documenting the baneful influences of slavery on masters and mistresses. "The slaveholder, as well as the slave," he stressed, "is the victim of the slave system. A man's character greatly takes its hue and shape from the form and color of things about him." Douglass's initial owner, Colonel Edward Lloyd, "very early impressed me with the idea that he was an unhappy man . . . he wore a troubled, and at times, a haggard aspect." "Muttering to himself" Lloyd "occasionally stormed about, as if defying an army of invisible foes. . . . walking, cursing and gesticulating, like one possessed by a demon." Douglass believed Lloyd was "a wretched man, at war with his own soul, and with all the world around him." What was the cause? "Was he dead to all sense of humanity? No. I think I now understand it. This treatment is a part of the system, rather than a part of the man."[14]

Fugitive slave James W. C. Pennington equated long exposure to slaveholding with steady moral decay. "There is no one feature of slavery to which the mind recurs with more gloomy impressions, than to its disastrous influence upon the families of the masters, physically, pecuniarily, and mentally," he underscored. "It seems to destroy families as by a powerful blight," leaving "large and opulent slave-holding families . . . like a group of shadows at the third or fourth generation." For as long as he could remember, "it was a remark among slaves, that every generation of slaveholders are more and more inferior." The brother-in-law of Pennington's master furnished a classic example of this generational accumulation of moral rot. The family's decline began with the man's second marriage, which produced a number of children. The sons, not having to work, became thoroughly dissipated. When the spendthrift father died, he left "a widow and large number of daughters, some minors, destitute, and none of his sons fitted for any employment but in the army and navy." The eldest daughter then "married a miserable and reckless gambler," sealing the family's ruin.[15] Pennington's analysis rooted this family's deterioration in the debilitating institution of slavery.

Douglass used the termination of his reading instruction as a young boy to emphasize the voracious appetite slavery had for devouring slaveholders' character. His young, newlywed, and as yet undomesticated mistress, Sophia Auld, initially displayed "a most beaming, benignant countenance" and was "kind, gentle and cheerful." Significantly, she had not been a slaveholder before her marriage and "a thing quite unusual in the south—depended almost entirely upon her own industry for a living." The naïve Mistress Auld did not expect Douglass to cringe or avert his eyes around her, and "Feddy" felt almost as if he had a mother in her. But "the fatal poison of irresponsible power, and the natural influence of slavery customs, were not long in making a suitable impression on the gentle and loving disposition of my excellent mistress." When husband Hugh forced her to treat Douglass as property, rather than a child, a "fretful bitterness" replaced Sophia Auld's erstwhile "natural and spontaneous" approach to people.

The breaking point came when Hugh Auld discovered that his wife was teaching Douglass to read. Master Auld "was amazed at [her] simplicity" and explained "for the first time . . . the true philosophy of slavery." First of all, "the thing itself was unlawful; . . . it was also unsafe, and could only lead to mischief." Literate slaves were "disconsolate and unhappy" and often resorted to escape. Douglass declared Hugh Auld's instructions to be "the first decidedly antislavery lecture to which it had been my lot to listen. . . . 'Very well,' thought I; 'knowledge unfits a child to be slave,'" and "from that moment I understood the direct pathway from slavery to freedom."

Mistress Auld complied with her husband's demands, but it took a while for her to absorb the requisite principles and behaviors. "It is easy to see, that, in entering upon the duties of a slaveholder, some little experience is needed," Douglass explained. "Nature has done almost nothing to prepare men and women to be either slaves or slaveholders." "Successful" slaveholding required "rigid training, long persisted in." To treat slaves as brutes, required Mistress Auld, who at first "knew and felt" Douglass to be human, to enter into a "mighty struggle with all the noble powers of her own soul." Her husband ultimately won the argument but "did not, himself, escape the consequences." He was "injured in his domestic peace" because the household became a far more disagreeable place. "Nature," Douglass said of his relationship with Sophia Auld, "had made us friends; slavery made us enemies."[16]

Henry Watson told a similar story to demonstrate how the steady, dispensation, of cruelty caused a slaveholder's moral gauge to malfunction. When Watson accompanied a new owner who had yet to prove violent on a slave-purchasing trip, the master "instructed me to tell all slaves who should inquire of me if he was a good master, that he was, to which I readily assented." The slaveholder maintained that he did not want any slave who was unwilling to go with him. "I gave them satisfactory proofs of his kindness" and, remarkably, the gang was allowed to travel without being shackled. But once at home trouble arose soon enough in the person of the mistress, who "beat the old cook most shockingly" and made torture "a pastime; she inspired everyone about her with her terror." She "soon exerted her wicked influence over her husband . . . and he became . . . a most cruel man, lashing and goading the slaves as she bid him."[17]

Fugitive slave authors and lecturers often confronted audiences that were unconvinced of slavery's negative consequences on slaveholders. They insisted that creatures they called "kind" or "good" slaveholders not only existed but were the norm. Narrators therefore were obliged to address the theme of "kindness" regularly. Douglass's tactic was to employ bouts of humanity among slaveholders as foils to throw violence and depredation into bold relief. He acknowledged that slaves appreciated even the most erratic and mundane acts of compassion. Young Mas' Daniel had protected

Douglass from the bullying of older boys, and mistress Lucretia Lloyd had given the pinched young boy the occasional treat of bread and butter. "For such friendship," Douglass said, "I felt deeply grateful, and bitter as are my recollections of slavery, I love to recall any instances of kindness, any sunbeams of humane treatment" that made their way "through the iron grating of my house of bondage. Such beams seem all the brighter from the general darkness into which they penetrate, and the impression they make is vividly distinct and beautiful."[18]

Many other slaves acknowledged those who dispensed the occasional "kindnesses" or who had established less venal reputations than others. They felt lucky to have escaped outright sadism. Slaves who arranged their own annual hire not surprisingly sought out people with such reputations. Harriet Jacobs noted that "the slave is sure to know who is the most humane, or cruel, master within forty miles of him. It is easy to find out . . . who clothes and feeds his slaves well," since on the traditional hiring day, 1 January, such a person would be "surrounded by a crowd, begging, 'Please, massa, hire me this year. I will work very hard, massa.'"[19]

But the larger point was that kindness and slavery cohabited capriciously and infrequently. Fugitive slave lecturer J. Sella Martin spoke for many when he told his audiences that "While there is an irresponsible power committed to the hands of the slaveholder, and while human nature remains as it is, it is impossible to talk about treating slaves kindly. You cannot do it."[20]

Everyone knew that illness, death, marriage, and debt could abruptly relegate the least abused to the worst victimized, or that a bad day could turn a "kind" owner inexplicably violent in an instant. Elizabeth Sparks's mistress, Jennie Brown, was "a good woman" even though she would "slap an' beat yer once in a while. . . . Course no white folks perfect."[21] And as J.W.C. Pennington emphasized, "kind" slaveholders in particular needed to realize that even sporadic acts of benevolence hardly ameliorated the overall condition of enslavement: "We ask for justice, truth and honour as other men do."[22] John Brown felt that it was "all very well to talk about kind masters. I do not say there are none. . . . though I never had the experience of them." But ultimately the environment they inhabited, buttressed by their wealth and the power of the state, proved far more significant than any fleeting humanitarian impulses. "If there are any" kind masters, Brown noted, "they are good in spite of the laws, which would make the best master bad, because they give him such an almighty power over his slaves, he cannot help abusing it. If he does not do so himself, those about him do; and that brings it to the same thing, as far as we are concerned."[23] "I do not say there are no humane slaveholders," Harriet Jacobs acknowledged. "Such characters do exist, notwithstanding the hardening influences around them. But they are 'like angels' visits—few and far between.'"[24]

Louis Hughes acknowledged his master "was in some respects kinder and more humane" than many. "Whatever of kindness was shown me . . . I still gratefully remember, whether it came from white master or fellow slave," he recalled in his old age. Hughes and his fellow slaves did not want for food or clothing, albeit very coarse. "But while my master showed these virtues," Hughes explained, "similar to those which a provident farmer would show in the care of his dumb brutes," he still bought and sold human beings, separated families at will and, while he did not himself whip slaves, regularly hired "an irresponsible brute . . . to perform this barbarous service." Hughes's owners "were always ready to contribute to educational and missionary funds, while denying, under the severest penalties, all education to those most needing it, and all true missionary effort."[25]

Douglass penned perhaps the most famous of all statements on "kind" slaveholders: "Beat and cuff your slave, keep him hungry and spiritless, and he will follow the chain of his master like a dog; but, feed and clothe him well,—work him moderately—surround him with physical comfort,—and dreams of freedom intrude. Give him a bad master, and he aspires to a good master; give him a good master, and he wishes to become his own master. . . . the kindness of the slavemaster only gilds the chain of slavery, and detracts nothing from its weight or power. The thought that men are made for other and better uses than slavery, thrives best under the gentle treatment of a kind master."[26]

One of the most repugnant effects of slavery on slaveholders was their scorn for labor, which engendered widespread slothfulness and dependency. Many whites, of course, castigated slaves as lazy miscreants without a thought for the morrow, consummately ignorant and inferior beings—the alleged results of race. But slaves developed a scorching critique of slaveholders and most whites as idlers without equal. Slaves' stalwart appreciation for the dignity of work and the necessity of self-reliance stood in sharp contrast to the laziness of most slaveholders. The transparency of such hypocrisy left many slaves to regard the leisured rich with profound contempt and to level their own dead aim at idleness, the prime enemy of the common good and the direct result of slavery.

So rare was it to see whites actually working that shortly after his escape from Maryland, Isaac Mason was astounded by the sight of a farmer's daughter "standing by the side of her father's workmen with a hay-fork in her hand, not idly standing by to see the work done properly, or that the men did not idle away their time, but to share in the labor of spreading and stacking the hay."[27] Body servant William Mallory was enslaved for fourteen years to Susten Allen, "a member of the White House at Washington . . . who, like many others at that time, was too lazy and indolent to wait on himself."[28] Harriet Jacobs's jealous mistress, Mary Norcom, "like many southern women, was totally deficient in energy. She had not the strength to superintend her household affairs; but her nerves were so strong, that she could sit in her easy chair and see a woman whipped, till the blood trickled from every stroke of the lash." When master James Norcom jailed the entire Jacobs family as a consequence of Harriet's escape, Aunt Fanny, the cook, was released early because Mistress Norcom "was tired of being her own housekeeper."[29]

"Our southern brethren," explained another ex-slave, "were reared up in complete idleness. They have blacks to wait upon them, to feed them, and carry them to bed when they are between 8 and 9 years old. Reared up in complete idleness, then when they are reared up, they go to gambling and cockfighting."[30] One of Charles Ball's owners, "having never been accustomed to regular work, or to the pursuit of any constant course of personal application . . . was incapable of long continued exertion. . . . He had not been trained to habits of industry, and could not bear the restraints of uniform labor."[31]

Fugitive William Wells Brown mocked slaveholders' laziness using excerpts from their speeches in which they drew upon ancient political texts to justify their need to avoid manual labor so as to become inspired public figures. These maxims about the relationship between work and "higher" civilization stemmed from thinkers like Aristotle, who believed that a labor mudsill was necessary for the development of "advanced" cultures. "The Citizens must not live the life of mechanics or shopkeepers," Aristotle made

not honorable in tending to
character or purpose / obstruct or harm

clear, "which is ignoble and inimical to goodness. Nor can those who are
to be citizens engage in farming: leisure is a necessity, both for growth in
goodness and for the pursuit of political activities."[32] Slaveholders used
such texts to argue that great civilizations, such as they alleged theirs was,
existed only when the elite was left free from everyday toil to pursue a con-
templative life. Implied in such logic was the belief that workers lacked all
ability to engage in intellectual analysis.

Virginia state representative B. W. Leigh's hyperbolic comments along
these lines struck Brown with special force. In 1829 Leigh argued in the
legislature that "'Those who depend on their daily labor for their daily sub-
sistence can never enter into political affairs, they never do, never will, never
can.'" Brown also targeted a South Carolina congressman's 1836 comments
on the "natural" order of things, which likewise utilized such sophistry:
"'All society settles down into a classification of capitalists and laborers,'"
the politician intoned. "'The former will own the latter, either collectively
through the government, or individually in a state of domestic servitude
as exists in the southern states.'" And if laborers ever did obtain political
power, he presciently noted, that country would be "'in a state of REVO-
LUTION.'" No less than slaveholders, the northern elite required "'a strong
federal government . . . to control the labor of the nation.'" Leaving aside
states' rights theory for the moment, he argued that slaveholders, by contrast, already had "'not only a right to the proceeds of our laborers, but we
own a class of laborers themselves.'"[33] Brown selected these comments to
showcase the intellectual calisthenics and moral turpitude that slaveholders
needed in order to justify their idleness.

Endemic laziness's close companion, greed, likewise drew sharp criti-
cism as one of the most baneful and inexcusable of all slavery's effects on
slaveholders. Louis Hughes believed that because slaveholders had "grown
rich" from slaves' "unrequited toil, they became possessed by the demon of
avarice and pride, and lost sight of the most vital of the Christly qualities."[34]
Drunkenness for material possessions, necessarily founded upon disregard
for collective welfare, ranked as one of the most contemptible of all human
qualities. "O Heaven!" David Walker exclaimed to a Massachusetts General Colored Association meeting in 1828, "what will not avarice and the
love of despotic sway cause men to do with their fellow creatures, when
actually in their power?"[35] Ex-slave Henry Highland Garnet identified "the

Extreme greed for wealth & material gain

a despot is a tyrannical ruler

despotism

fear

besetting sins of the Anglo-Saxon race" as "the love of gain and the love of power."[36] Jack Maddox, enslaved in rural Georgia, thought that if slave-holders went to heaven, "they'd turn the Heaven wrong side out and have the angels working to make something they could take away from them."[37]

When William Wells Brown summed up the effects of slavery on slave-holders and the nation in an address to the Female Anti-Slavery Society of Salem, Massachusetts, in November 1847, he utilized the tenet of slave ethics that recognized the nation as a whole of its victims.

> Where we find one man holding an unlimited power over another, I ask, what can we expect to find his condition? Give one man power ad infinitum over another, and he will abuse that power; no mat-ter if there be law; no matter if there be public sentiment in favor of the oppressed. The system of Slavery, that I, in part, represent here this evening, is a system that strikes at the foundation of society, that strikes at the foundation of civil and political institutions. It is a system that takes man down from that lofty position which his God designed that he should occupy; that drags him down, places him upon a level with the beasts of the field, and there keeps him, that it may rob him of his liberty.

Brown's audience shared in this degradation, simply by virtue of inhabiting the same polity as slaveholders. Slavery's influence extended to "the mor-als of the people; not only upon the morals of the Slave-holding South, or of the Slave, but upon the morals of the people of the United States of America." One could not "draw a line between the people of the North and the people of the South. So far as the people of the North are connected with slaveholding, they necessarily become contaminated by the evils that follow in the train of Slavery."[38]

Slaves often sought clues that slave owners experienced any remorse whatsoever for the glut of abuse they inflicted, and their examinations un-covered a number of truths about slavery and race and the relationship between them. In the rare instances when slaveholders' penitence surfaced, slaves studied such behavior closely. At these weak junctures, slavehold-ers confirmed fundamental facts to the slave community, among them that slavery was not divinely ordained but secularly ordered, and that the institution of slavery—not race—was responsible for the violence, theft, and deceit that saturated their worlds.

John Brown found that slaveholders' deathbed experiences produced telling evidence of the depths of their corruption. These confessions tended to come from men and women who "had rioted in cruelty to their slaves, but who, when the dark hour came, could not leave the world without asking pardon of those they had ill-used." Brown's master had anticipated death several times, and at each instance, "in his frights he sent for us all and asked us to forgive him." Slaves generally believed, Brown observed, "that all the masters die in an awful fright.... So we come to think their minds must be dreadfully uneasy about holding slaves." Deathbed agonies proved that although masters tried "to make us believe that they are superior to us in every thing, and a different order of beings, almost next to God himself," in fact "there is some one superior to them, who can make them feel pain and torment too," and so "we come at last to learn that they are only poor human creatures like ourselves." Such events proved "that there is something wrong in slave-holding. When a man cannot die happy it is a sure sign his mind is heavy about something, and our masters do not leave us in doubt what it is."[39]

From just such contexts and episodes as these, slaves deduced that they were locked in combat with people who were severely compromised ethically and psychologically, at times more so than slaves. It was impossible to believe that so much ingrained venality could not but result in psychological impairment. These examinations of slavery's effects on slaveholders and other whites reinforced other evidence that race was an unnatural category of the human condition. Slaveholders' corrupt characters devolved not from any inbred racial traits, but from the environment of slavery itself. Unrepentant slaveholders clearly were destined for an agonizing hereafter. By extension, the same held true for the American nation. But slaveholders' vulnerability to violent and dishonest behaviors, a product of their environment, had pernicious effects on slaves as well. Slaves' evaluation of the role of terror in their lives formed the basis for other basic components of their ethical world, as the next chapter demonstrates.

gradual,
harmful effect

4

"Cruelty Is Inseparable from Slavery"

Violence, Rape, and the Right of Self-Defense

How slaves interpreted the significance of the violence, torture, and terror practiced against them constituted one of the most trenchant and self-reflective—and perhaps least understood—features of their ethos. Repeated observations of the noxious effects that brutality had on those who employed it led slaves to view wanton cruelty as a profound character failing caused by slavery itself. Some believed in the righteousness of revenge against such people. Certainly the violence meted out created an environment that would seem to have begged for retaliation. But a substantial portion of the slave, and later the freed, population—probably a majority—rejected vengeance, bearing in mind memories of their own victimization and the effects violence had on slaveholders. Slaves sharply distinguished between their own use of physical and psychological resistance, which they defined as self-defense, and the willful cruelty of slaveholders. The distinction was vital, since it meant that everything from deceit to slave rebellions were principled actions taken in the spirit of justice and liberation. Slaves who resisted violent attacks by physically defending themselves—feats of great courage—acted well within slave cultures' ethical guidelines. Folding all instances of physical or armed engagement into one undifferentiated category of violence that rendered self-defense little different from slaveholder mayhem made little sense to slaves.

Slave testimony is riddled with accounts of violence and rape, oftentimes ghoulish and sadistic acts that frequently were difficult or impossible to revisit. Their frequent silences on the effects of violence on them could be simultaneously as deafening as they were revealing. Slaves would do almost anything to avoid violence, developing a range of physical to psychologically manipulative actions for self-defense. Men were better poised to employ physical self-defense, whereas girls and women had comparatively few protections against sexual exploitation, although they could and did, like men, use deception and psychological resistance to good effect.[1]

While they shunned testifying about the psychological impacts of violence, they had less hesitation in reporting acts of violence, intent that audiences grasp brutality as a keystone of enslavement. Particularly those who testified on the abolitionist circuit (and, later, those who approached Freedmen's Bureau agents or testified before congressional investigative committees during Reconstruction) gave detailed accounts of the tortures meted out against them. Victims and witnesses felt an urgent purpose in this matter, understanding that they were engaged in yet another propaganda war with slaveholders who aimed to convince northerners that slaves were treated better than northern wage workers. Slaveholders often held that in the rare instances when it occurred, violence was justified. Slaves—being lazy, savage and unaccepting of their God-given station in life—required force to be made to work. Indeed, force, or the ever-present threat of it, was necessary to make slaves work, but not because of their inferiority. It was vitally necessary to debunk slaveholders' misinformation. Slaves and fugitives had no shortage of examples from which to choose, often remarking that they shared but a handful of the possibilities at their disposal. They furnished abundant evidence that slaveholders, overseers, professional floggers, and non-slaveholders were capable of staggeringly vicious acts of physical and mental ruthlessness.[2]

After years spent in the coastal regions of North and South Carolina in the late eighteenth and early nineteenth centuries, free black David Walker knew firsthand that slaveholders "are resolved to assail us with every species of affliction that their ingenuity can invent."

> No trifling portion of them will beat us nearly to death ... they keep us sunk in ignorance ... they brand us with hot iron ... they cut us as they do horses, bulls, or hogs ... they chain and hand-cuff us, and while in that miserable and wretched condition, beat us with cow-hides and clubs—they keep us half naked and starve us sometimes nearly to death under their infernal whips. ... They put on us

fifty-sixes and chains, and make us work in that cruel situation, and in sickness, under lashes to support them and their families.—They keep us three or four hundred feet under ground working in their mines, night and day to dig up gold and silver to enrich them and their children. . . . They take us . . . and put us as drivers one over the other, and make us afflict each other as bad as they themselves afflict us—and to crown the whole of this catalogue of cruelties, they tell us that we . . . are an inferior race of beings! Incapable of self government!!. . . . That if we were free we would not work, but would live on plunder or theft!!!! That we are the meanest and laziest set of beings in the world!!!!! That they are obliged to keep us in bondage to do us good!!!!!!—That we are satisfied to rest in slavery to them and their children!!!!!![3]

"Now, what can be more aggravating, than for the Americans, after having treated us so bad, to hold us up to the world as such great throat-cutters?" Walker seethed.[4] Fewer passages about violence in the annals of antebellum African American letters better summarized the flagrant hypocrisy of slaveholders on the matter of who was savage and who was not. As Walker drove home, slaveholders embodied the very characteristics—barbarism, cruelty, torture, and thievery—that they used to describe the enslaved. These glaring inversions that glorified slaveholder character while demeaning that of slaves infuriated Walker, as they did many slaves.

Fugitive slave John Brown was one of the many who found it mandatory to explain that violence sanctioned by state power was indispensable to the maintenance of slavery. "When I think of all I have gone through, and of the millions of men, women, and children I have left behind me in slavery, every one of whom may be undergoing similar or even greater sufferings," Brown wrote, he most keenly felt the exigency of abolition. "To make them work they must have complete control over them, and the laws are framed with an eye to this object," he stressed. "In order to compel them to labour for the sole advantage of another, the whip and all sorts of coercive means are employed." Once the habit of violence without repercussion is ingrained, "a man soon gets hardened into it, and then he can go to any lengths. Cruelty is inseparable from slavery . . . for it is only by it, or through fear of it" that slaveholders can survive.[5] Douglass too identified "the fear of punishment" as a slave's "sole motive for any sort of industry."[6]

The attacks of choice that slaves universally testified to were whippings, "a gateway form of violence," noted one historian, "that led to bizarrely creative levels of sadism."[7] The least vicious lashings called for twenty to thirty-nine stripes, usually described as "well laid on." Between fifty and two hundred lashes were not uncommon, sadistic sprees that often required the lasher to take a break or call in a substitute. Attackers stripped victims male and female, young and old, tied them to trees or placed them in stocks or other restraints made especially for the purpose. Afterwards they doused victims in brine, pepper, tar, or candlewax, excruciating finales allegedly meant to prevent infection and speed healing.

Henry Bibb witnessed a beating of a young woman who had displeased the wife of his owner, Deacon Whitfield, a man of the cloth. Bibb used the example to showcase the identity of the real perpetrators of violence. Whitfield used the young woman's suffering to instruct Bibb in one of his new duties as driver. After fifty lashes, he "lectured her for a while" about obeying her mistress, whereupon the desperate woman "promised to do all in her power to please him and her mistress, if he would have mercy on her." But the deacon only continued "in the most inhuman manner until she had received two hundred stripes on her naked quivering flesh, tied up and exposed to the public gaze of all. And this," Bibb concluded bitterly, "was the example that I was to copy after."[8] Bibb himself became a victim shortly thereafter. When Whitfield recaptured Bibb following an escape attempt with his wife and children, he summoned the other slaves to witness the assault, a commonplace aspect of torture meant to instill collective horror. With Bibb stripped and tied facedown to four stakes in the ground, Whitfield instructed another man to administer the first fifty lashes. Whitfield then took over with the notorious paddle. This wooden instrument, often called a cobbing paddle, had large holes drilled though. Wetted and sanded, the paddle raised large blood blisters with each blow, which assailants then burst with a whip or knife. Captured runaways often had the soles of their feet attacked with these paddles.[9] After the assault, Whitfield brined Bibb and fitted him with a familiar device, "a heavy iron collar riveted on my neck with prongs extending above my head, on the end of which there was a small bell" unreachable by hand. Bibb wore the collar for six weeks, was left to sleep in stocks or chained to a log, had no contact with his family, and was still required to toil in the fields.[10]

Slaves distinguished bullwhips from other varieties because of their ability to inflict especially fierce torment—they were also employed against unruly cattle. John Brown provided a detailed explanation of what made the bullwhip the "master of all whips": "First . . . the butt . . . is loaded with lead, to give the whip force," then the lash is cut into strips and plaited to a fine taper, resulting in a weapon between six and ten feet long and "as limber and lithesome as a snake." This whip cut rather than bruised the victim, but experts wielded bullwhips "with such dexterity" that they could either "just raise the skin and draw blood, or cut clean through to the bone." Brown had seen such whips slice wooden boards.[11]

Louis Hughes, like most, first witnessed violence as a child. One of his comrades, falling ill, had slaughtered a pig for nourishment, for which the master, Edmund McGee, had him ravaged so badly with a bullwhip that a doctor was requested. The overseer who performed these whippings was a man "not only cruel, but barbarous." A memorable bullwhip attack occurred when Riley, principal plower on the McGee plantation and among its most skilled workers, was detained by a broken bridle, which a mule had chewed. When Riley arrived at the field, the overseer "sprang upon him with his bull whip, which was about seven feet long, lashing him with all his strength" until the end of the whip "buried itself in the fleshy part of the arm, and there came around it a festering sore." Riley suffered for days "until one night his brother took out the knot, when the poor fellow was asleep, for he could not bear anyone to touch it when he was awake." Hughes also had seen naked people tied to trees and whipped "with a rawhide, or long, limber switches, or the terrible bull whip."[12]

Hughes reported that attacks such as these were the norm on his plantation, but hardly the only form of torture employed. McGee also used "bucking" to torture a victim: "that is, fasten his feet together, draw up his knees to his chin, tie his hands together, draw them down over the knees, and put a stick under the latter and over the arms," leaving the victim wholly defenseless and usually left bleeding on the ground. Numerous slaves bore testimony to this widespread method of torture. It was also common for McGee's slaves, men, women, and children, to be formed in a "bull ring," into which a naked sufferer was thrust. Each member of the ring was armed with "a switch, rawhide, strap or whip, and . . . compelled to cut at the poor victim as he ran around the ring." With forty or fifty people in the ring, "by the time the victim had made two or three rounds his condition can readily be imagined."[13] The effect on the slave community made to participate in such violence was a consequence on which Hughes himself did not elaborate. But doubtless the horror engendered by such episodes led many slaves to be as nonthreatening as they could possibly be, a strategy that in turn could make them perfect future victims.[14] It also braced their aversion to violence.

John Glasgow, a free British subject and sailor who was kidnapped and sold into slavery, met a particularly brutal fate on the same plantation where John Brown was enslaved in Georgia. Though he had a wife and two daughters in England, Glasgow's sorrows were such that after four years of enslavement he married—"in the nominal way"—a slave on a nearby holding named Nancy. Master Thomas Stevens subjected Glasgow to "the picket" for having visited Nancy against orders. This instrument featured a whipping post that "consisted of two solid uprights, some ten feet high, with a cross-beam at the top, forming a kind of gallows." Pulleys along the top lifted the victim off the ground. After being stripped, Glasgow's wrists were tied and his "left foot was . . . drawn up and tied, toes downwards, to his right knee, so that his left knee formed an angle by means of which, when swung up, his body could conveniently be turned." Below his untethered foot was a sharpened stake. Once suspended, Glasgow's "body swung by its own weight, his hands being high over his head and his right foot level with the pointed end of the oaken 'stob.'" When rotated in this state, "the skin of the victim's back is stretched till it shines, and cuts more readily under the lash." The only respite was to place the unstrung foot on the sharpened stake: "The excessive pain caused by being flogged while suspended, and the nausea excited by twirling round, causes the victim of the 'picket' to seek temporary relief by staying himself on the 'stob.'" When Glasgow yielded to that temptation, "one of the bystanders taking hold of the bent knee, and using it as a handle, gives the unfortunate a twirl, and sends him spinning round on the hard point of the stake, which perforates the heel or the sole . . . quite to the bone."

Glasgow's torture lasted for an hour, with two- to three-minute breaks "to allow him 'to come to, and to fetch his breath.' His shrieks and groans were most agonizing . . . but as the punishment proceeded, they subsided into moans scarcely audible." All the slaves were made to attend the torture, and some were forced to participate. At the end, Glasgow's back was "fearfully lacerated, his wrists deeply cut . . . and his foot pierced through in three places." Below him a pool of blood congealed, "whilst the oaken stake was dyed red. . . . He could not stand, much less walk." Glasgow was brined and "left to die or to recover as might be." It was five months before he could stand. Brown told Glasgow's story in his narrative, which he published in England, in hopes of it finding its way to Glasgow's family and to the British and Foreign Anti-Slavery Society. "To John I owe a debt of gratitude," Brown memorialized his severely tortured friend, "for he it was who taught me to love and seek liberty."[15]

Brown endured singular forms of torture as well. His master loaned him to a local doctor, Thomas Hamilton, who used him for medical experimentation to find a remedy for sunstroke. Hamilton dug a pit in the ground that he heated to excess, then placed the naked Brown inside, covered by wet blankets. He administered various medicines, and when Brown fainted, measured the temperature in the pit, repeating the experiment to gauge which medicine enabled Brown to withstand heat the longest. Hamilton subsequently made good money selling the quack cures he developed. He also placed Brown on debilitating diets and bled and blistered him, leaving permanent marks behind, to find out "how deep my black skin went."[16]

Slaveholders were also known to practice water tortures that constituted nineteenth-century variations on waterboarding. James Williams, a driver on a cotton plantation, testified to one such event. In his area of Alabama, people kept large cisterns to catch rainwater, below which they dug storage tanks from eight to ten feet deep. "Into one of these tanks the unfortunate slave was placed," Williams explained, "confined by one of his ankles to the bottom of it, and the water was suffered to flow in from above." The victim had to bail water as quickly as it entered, but could not begin until the water had reached the waist. "Any pause or delay after this, from weakness and exhaustion, would have been fatal, as the water would have risen above his head. In this horrible dungeon, toiling for his life, he was kept for twenty-four hours without any sustenance."[17]

Charles Ball encountered water torture in Georgia after his new master "came into the field one day, and . . . told me that I had now fallen into good hands, as it was his practice not to whip his people much." It turned out that he had "discovered a mode of punishment much more mild, and, at the same time, much more effectual than flogging." That evening the master showed Ball "a pump, set in a well in which the water rose within ten feet of the surface of the ground." The pump handle rose thirteen feet above ground level, reachable only by a ladder, and dispensed a forceful stream of icy water. Ball's master was preparing to punish a female slave, and he wanted his new slave to witness the event. "The woman was stripped quite naked, and tied to a post that stood just under the stream of water." A young boy was forced to "pump water upon the head and shoulders of the victim," and within a minute, "she began to cry and scream in a most lamentable manner" and tried desperately to escape. As she weakened, "her head fell forward upon her breast," which brought the torture to a halt. In "a state of insensibility" she was taken away. Though complaining of light-headedness the next day, she was put back to work. Ball understood from victims of such torture that in a matter of seconds, "it produces the sensation that is felt when heavy blows are inflicted . . . until the skull bone and shoulder blades appear to be broken in pieces." Eventually, the victim lost her senses, had difficulty breathing, and passed out. "This punishment is in fact a temporary murder," Ball explained, since "all the pains are endured, that can be felt by a person who is deprived of life by being beaten with a bludgeon."[18]

As these examples demonstrate, slaveholders put men and women alike through the same methods of torture and attack. "It may be thought that the female slaves are perhaps, as a rule, less badly treated," responded John Brown to this common perception. But such was not the case, he stressed. "Men and women, boys and girls, receive the same kind of punishments, or I would say rather, that the same kind of tortures are inflicted upon them." Not even pregnant women were "spared from the infliction of the most dreadful scourgings, with the cow-hide, the bull-whip, and the cobbing-paddle."[19] Indeed, slaveholders fashioned special methods for their attacks on pregnant women. Accounts of men digging a hole in the ground to accommodate a pregnant stomach during a beating were common. Solomon

Bradley, enslaved in North and South Carolina, had witnessed such an attack, as had South Carolinian Robert Smalls. Marie Harvey testified that when her grandmother was threatened with such a whipping when young, her "grandpa got an ax and told them that if they did he would kill them."[20]

Teenage girls and young women, in particular, faced the added persecutions of sexual predation and assault. Slaves regarded rapes and sexual abuses to be among the most abhorrent violence slaveholders committed. They especially rued the situations of attractive girls and women. Travelers to the South, Austin Steward warned, might regularly witness "the wild, dispairing [sic] look of some frightened young slave girl, passing under the lustful gaze of some lordly libertine, who declares himself 'in search of a fancy article for his own use!'"[21] Frederick Douglass's Aunt Esther was such a young woman "who possessed that which is ever a curse to the slave-girl; namely,—personal beauty." The designing master, Colonel Edward Lloyd, forbade Esther's relationship with fellow slave Edward Roberts and resorted to torture when Esther disobeyed. One early morning before the plantation inhabitants were aroused, Lloyd stripped Esther, hung her from the ceiling, and before beginning his attack, uttered "all manner of harsh, coarse, and tantalizing epithets." As a concealed and terrified young Douglass watched—this was the first scourge he had seen—Lloyd began his assault, and "protracted the torture, as one who was delighted with the scene . . . her piercing cries seemed only to increase his fury. His answers to them are too coarse and blasphemous to be produced here." The attack "was revolting and shocking, to the last degree; and when the motives of this brutal castigation are considered, language has no power to convey a just sense of its awful criminality." Thereafter Lloyd beat Esther often, "and her life, as I knew it, was one of wretchedness."[22]

Solomon Northup, a free black of New York who was kidnapped into slavery in 1841 at the age of thirty and spent the next twelve years in Rapides and Avoyelles parishes in Louisiana, one of the roughest regimes in the country, told of the brutality that befell fellow slave Patsey. An attractive and "joyous creature, a laughing, light-hearted girl, rejoicing in the mere sense of existence," Patsey yet "wept oftener, and suffered more, than any of her companions." Owner Edwin Epps raped Patsey on numerous occasions, whipping her when she showed any opposition. The jealous mistress Epps was in the habit of hurling "a billet of wood, or a broken bottle perhaps" at Patsey's face at unforeseen moments, an act that many slave women endured.[23] "The enslaved victim of lust and hate, Patsey had no comfort of her life," Northup lamented. As a consequence of her precarious position, Patsey suffered "the most cruel whipping that ever I was doomed to witness—one I can never recall with any other emotion than that of horror." The attack occurred after Epps suspected Patsey of consorting with a white neighbor, whose black wife, Harriet, was Patsey's friend and confidante. One day Patsey visited Harriet in search of soap. "'Missus don't give me soap to wash with, as she does the rest,'" Patsey told Epps, "'and you know why. I went over to Harriet's to get a piece,'" which she pulled out of her pocket. Epps and his wife, "with an air of heartless satisfaction" and surrounded by their children, thereupon commenced "an infernal jubilee over the girl's miseries."

Epps ordered Northup to drive four stakes in the ground, strip Patsey and tie her facedown. He forced Northup to begin the assault. "Nowhere that day, on the face of the whole earth, I venture to say, was there such a demoniac exhibition witnessed as then ensued." After laying on some forty-five lashes, Northup refused to continue, and Epps then applied the whip "with ten-fold greater force than I had. The painful cries and shrieks of the tortured Patsey, mingling with the loud and angry curses of Epps, loaded the air." The ferocious beating left Patsey "literally flayed. . . . At length she ceased struggling. . . . She no longer writhed and shrank beneath the lash when it bit out small pieces of her flesh. I thought that she was dying." Northup looked on Epps "with unutterable loathing and abhorrence, and thought within myself—'Thou devil, sooner or later, somewhere in the course of eternal justice, thou shalt answer for this sin!'" Patsey was never the same. "The burden of a deep melancholy weighed heavily on her spirits" and she lost her "buoyant and elastic step" and the "mirthful sparkle in her eyes." She grew depressed and withdrawn, "toiling all day in our midst, not uttering a word." Northup knew that Patsey's life had become "one long dream of liberty. . . . To dwell where the black man may work for himself— live in his own cabin—till his own soil, was a blissful dream of Patsey's."[24]

Esther's and Patsey's experiences were far from unique. By the antebellum era sexual rapaciousness may well have been worsening significantly because of the demographic profile of slavery in its mature decades. By emancipation, the slave population had increased tenfold over total imports from Africa, or from about four hundred thousand to about four million. Most of that increase came from reproduction, which distinguished the U.S. slave population from nearly all other slave regimes in the hemisphere, where crippling work regimens and rates of natural decrease kept fueling demand for more slave imports through the Atlantic slave trade. By contrast, in the United States the Atlantic trade ended legally in 1808, although smuggling brought in an estimated additional fifty thousand people. For many years historians, as they reflected on these patterns, rejected arguments that large-scale forced breeding took place in the antebellum United States, noting that slaveholders found it more productive to allow slaves to choose their mates, a practice which many believed enhanced reproduction.

But other evidence indicates that sexual abuse grew increasingly devastating for antebellum slave girls and women after the regime had to rely on natural increase to reproduce the slave population, and after the cotton revolution of the nineteenth century sent about a million Upper South slaves, most of them young, to the booming cotton lands of the Mississippi Valley and beyond. Slaveholders exercised voracious control over slave women's reproductive potential. Some regional regimes were notoriously bad. Those enslaved in the infamous Louisiana sugar parishes often had been bought through the interstate slave trade both for their labor and to increase the slave population. Forced to rely on the Upper South as a source of slave labor for the new sugarlands of the gulf, sugar masters consciously engaged in demographic engineering of the slave population, a pattern detected from their purchasing habits. They selected slaves on a clear sex- and age-specific basis. They preferred teenagers and young adults, in very high sex ratios—roughly 85 percent of the slaves they bought were male. Slave traders who plied the Upper South slave marts understood the lucrative Louisiana market well and purchased slaves with the sugar lords' special needs in mind. They sought young, strong, and fertile bondspeople. Purchasers made thorough, often public, inventory of slave bodies and prided themselves on having a good eye for human merchandise. Similar patterns emerged in the cotton regions.

Louisiana slave women told harrowing stories of rape, abuse, forced couplings with multiple mates, and repeated pregnancies—for if they proved fertile, they became favored targets. In a situation where they were in a decided minority and where their ability to reproduce was crucial, girls and young women had practically no chance to escape the worst that slavery had to offer. They literally lived among predators, sometimes black as well as white, and endured the additional burdens of cane agriculture and a regime noted for violent severities of all sorts.[25] Historians have found many cases in which slave girls and women were physically or psychologically able to defend themselves against such depravity. But such choices came at very high prices—vicious beatings, sales, and retributions directed at family and friends being the most common. The majority could exercise little or no resistance against this curse of slavery.[26]

*　　*　　*

Slaves desperately hoped to avoid violence and exploitation and developed numerous defenses against it. These strategies encompassed a wide range of everyday resistance techniques that slaves developed over the centuries: feigning illness, lying out (a temporary escape), and using deceit, for example. One tactic, not always successful, involved performing work so well that no excuse for violence could possibly be found. When Henry Watson was sold to "a very bad-looking man" named Alexander McNeill of Vicksburg, Mississippi, and learned that he was "'to jump when . . . spoken to, run when sent upon errands'" lest he "'be flogged like h—l,'" Watson "at once concluded to please him in all things." But to no avail. On his first morning he was beaten severely for improperly arranging McNeill's clothing on a chair. The next day insufficiently polished boots provoked another attack. "Thus he went on in cruelty, and met every new effort of mine to please him with fresh blows from his cowhide." McNeill's wife had left him because of his sexual abuse of a slave, and when efforts at reconciliation failed, this "cruel man . . . became a perfect tyrant, lashing his slaves without mercy." Watson was made to apply the salt at the frequent whippings at the plantation stocks, inflicted by an overseer "whom it was impossible to please." Watson was then demoted to the cotton fields when he refused to inform on two comrades who had taken a pig. Slaves throughout the cotton South had daily individual quotas of cotton to pick, and any amount they fell short was paid for in cowhide or worse.[27] Watson, an inexperienced hand, received repeated lashings "without any just cause" while struggling to master his task.

After a year, Alexander McNeill told Watson to hire himself out, and

Watson selected a man who wanted a stage driver. "I entered the duties of my new situation with pleasure," Watson said, "not that I saw anything more pleasing in my new master" except for having escaped McNeill. Watson once more resolved to "do everything in my power to please my master, so that he would have no occasion" to return him to McNeill. His plan worked well enough that this new master trusted him with the keys to the house. He then placed Watson in one of his Vicksburg hotels as a waiter, where Watson fell to gambling because tips for waiters were the paltriest of all the establishment's workers. He consequently received sixty lashes, while a compatriot, a free man, lost his left ear, was tarred and feathered, placed in a leaky boat, and sent down the river. A few more years of witnessing "the sufferings of my brothers and sisters in bondage" left Watson so jaded that he became "indifferent to my own punishment" as well as that of others, and he stopped trying to use competent labor as a shield against violence. Finally, at the age of twenty-six, Watson managed to escape to Boston, leaving "the land of Bibles and whips" behind.[28]

John Quincy Adams likewise tried "to do the best I can," but the violence he nonetheless encountered meant his "feelings are very often hurt, and more particularly so when I am trying to do all I can to please people."[29] Virginian Henry Banks "always tried to do the work faithfully that was assigned me,—not because I felt it a duty, but because I was afraid not to do it." One day the overseer beat Banks while he was harvesting wheat because the tool he had been given was inadequate for the job. "You can make that cradle cut better if you choose to,—but you don't choose to," the overseer accused him. Banks objected that he "had tried to make it do the best I knew how." While being tied up, he frantically promised again that he would "do all I know how to do," and he made the pledge a third time when released. But the experience marked a breaking point, and Banks ran away: "I left him on account of work," he explained, by which he meant not so much the work per se, but the lack of respect for his work and the gratuitous violence that accompanied it.[30]

As Watson's and Banks's testimony demonstrated, escape was an option that many considered when violence became intolerable. Young single men were at a decided advantage among potential fugitives; upwards of 80 percent of fugitives in the late antebellum era fit this profile. Lighter-skinned, literate, intelligent, and skilled people also had better chances of success, as did individuals rather than groups. Many runaway advertisements included information on the scars, deformities, and branding marks that fugitives bore, strong suggestions that repetitive violence had been the final provocation for their escape.[31]

Outright rebellion was another possible response to such treatment, but by the antebellum era, slaves keenly felt the overwhelming futility of this method of resistance. The sheer power of the antebellum regime severely mitigated against revolt. Not even in earlier and more propitious times did slaves enter into rebellions with spontaneous haste. Throughout the Americas rebellions erupted not sporadically but with considerable forethought, strategizing, and a sharp eye for the main chance.[32] By the eve of the Civil War southern slaveholders had long since perfected the use of torture, terror, and sexual abuse to control the slave population, buttressed by the powers of state and federal governments. The Constitution guaranteed the support of the federal military to any state battling slave rebellions, and the federal government had made good on this promise in every instance of revolt.[33] The Old South was the wealthiest and certainly the most extensively policed slave society in the hemisphere. In Virginia, the state with the single largest slave population and where the last major revolt occurred, fully 10 percent of the free white male population garrisoned the Old Dominion against slave revolt as early as the 1830s. Thus during slavery's mature years, obstacles to revolt proved nearly insurmountable, and they hampered individual acts of resistance and self-defense as well. As Henry Bibb recalled of his enslaved days, "The only weapon of self defence that I could use successfully, was that of deception."[34] Military-style resistance became akin to committing suicide and could only bring large numbers of innocent people into lethal danger.[35]

Despite their fierce hold on power, slaveholders exhibited a near constant fear—some historians have called it paranoia—of vengeful violence from slaves, in the belief that if they themselves had been the victims of slavery and violence, the impulse to lash out in revenge would be irresistible. But many slaves were as suspicious of the cost of revenge as they were certain of the outcome of rebellion. Many believed that willful, violent reprisal blighted the avenger's soul, in addition to exposing family and friends to almost certain retaliation. But perhaps most significantly of all, revenge resembled the violent behaviors they had long despised and feared in slaveholders. Having seen firsthand the effects of hatred and terror on slaveholders and other whites, many chose not to invite the same consequences upon themselves.

Consider the ethical dilemma that Josiah Henson, the fugitive whose life story became the inspiration for Harriet Beecher Stowe's *Uncle Tom's Cabin*, faced when he was about to be sold to the Deep South. Henson and his master's young son, along with three other white men, had been ordered to travel from Kentucky to New Orleans by flatboat on the Mississippi, ostensibly to attend market. Henson had always been productive and proud of his work. He was in the process of buying his freedom, and owed a balance of one hundred dollars. But his owner added an extra zero to the amount on the document, thus leaving Henson to find one thousand dollars before he would be free.

Aware that his master was having financial difficulties, Henson suspected the real purpose of the trip was to sell him. Pacing the deck one night as watchman, Henson had "many a painful and passionate thought. After all that I had done . . . such a return as this for my services . . . and the intense selfishness with which they were ready to sacrifice me . . . turned my blood to gall and wormwood, and changed me from a lively, and I will say, a pleasant-tempered fellow, into a savage, morose, dangerous slave. . . . I felt myself becoming more ferocious every day . . . I became more and more agitated with an almost uncontrollable fury." He had met others who had been sold to New Orleans, "and their haggard and wasted appearance told a piteous story of excessive labor and insufficient food. I said to myself, 'If this is to be my lot, I cannot survive it long. I am not so young as these men, and if it has brought them to such a condition, it will soon kill me. . . . Why should I not prevent this wrong? . . . They have no suspicion of me, and they are at this moment under my control, and in my power. There are many ways in which I can despatch them and escape, and I feel that I should be justified in availing myself of the first good opportunity.'" These thoughts were not transitory, but "fashioned themselves into shapes which grew larger, and seemed firmer, every time they presented themselves; and at length my mind was made up to convert the phantom shadow into a positive reality. I resolved to kill my . . . companions, take what money there was in the boat, then to scuttle the craft, and escape to the north. It was a poor plan, may-be, and would very likely have failed; but it was as well contrived, under the circumstances, as the plans of murderers usually are; and blinded by passion, and stung to madness as I was, I could not see any difficulty about it."

Henson spied his chance when the party was almost to New Orleans. He was once again alone on deck at night, the three men and his master's son asleep below. He entered their cabin with an axe.

Looking by the aid of the dim light . . . my eye fell upon Master Amos . . . my hand slid along the axe-handle, I raised it to strike the fatal blow,—when suddenly the thought came to me, "What! commit murder! and you a Christian?" I had not called it murder before. It was self-defence,—it was preventing others from murdering me,—it was justifiable, it was even praiseworthy. But now, all at once, the truth burst upon me that it was a crime. I was going to kill a young man, who had done nothing to injure me, but obey commands which he could not resist; I was about to lose the fruit of all my efforts at self-improvement, the character I had acquired, and the peace of mind which had never deserted me. All this came upon me instantly, and with a distinctness which made me almost think I heard it whispered in my ear; and I believe I even turned my head to listen. I shrunk back, laid down the axe, crept up on deck again, and thanked God, as I have done every day since, that I had not committed murder. My feelings were still agitated, but they were changed. I was filled with shame and remorse for the design I had entertained, and with the fear that my companions would detect it in my face, or that a careless word would betray my guilty thoughts. I remained on deck all night, instead of rousing one of the men to relieve me, and nothing brought composure to my mind, but the solemn resolution I then made to resign myself to the will of God, and take with thankfulness, if I could, but with submission, at all events, whatever he might decide should be my lot. I reflected that if my life were reduced to a brief term, I should have less to suffer, and that it was better to die with a Christian's hope, and a quiet conscience, than to live with the incessant recollection of a crime that would destroy the value of life, and under the weight of a secret that would crush out the satisfaction that might be expected from freedom and every other blessing.[36]

To interpret Henson's remarks about submission to God as being indicative of docility would be to ignore the ethical dilemma he was forced to confront. He was considering an act not of self-defense but of violence against people he regarded as innocent. As it happened, the master's young son contracted a severe case of river fever in New Orleans. Fearing death, the son took Henson back with him on the slow upriver trip to Kentucky. Although the slaveholding family was grateful that Henson had saved their son, Henson knew that another betrayal would not be long in coming. He resolved not to pay another penny for his freedom. Within months he made a harrowing escape to Canada with his wife, Nancy, and their four children. Henson subsequently preached, became an active abolitionist, and lived unencumbered by guilt, although he never forgot how close he had come to endangering his soul and the well-being of his family.

*   *   *

Not surprisingly, many slaves found it impossible to forgive slaveholders for the violence and treachery they had inflicted. When the sexually predacious James Norcom died, his victim Harriet Jacobs could not summon the same exoneration for him that her pious grandmother Molly Horniblow did. When Jacobs "remembered how he had defrauded my grandmother of the hard earnings she had loaned" and "how he had persecuted her children," such crimes, she decided, "even the grave does not bury. The man was odious to me while he lived, and his memory is odious now."[37] Anna Harris refused to admit white people into her home because her sister Kate was sold in 1860 and she never heard from her again. "Folks say white folks is all right dese days," Harris noted in the 1930s. "Maybe dey is, maybe dey isn't. But I can't stand to see 'em. Not on my place." While relating the misery her mother suffered during slavery, which included repeated beatings for refusing the overseer's sexual advances, Minnie Folkes declared, "Lord, Lord, I hate white people and de flood waters gwine drown some mo.'"[38]

Frederick Douglass, who urged forgiveness of slaveholders on more than one occasion, nonetheless knew that planters courted resistance because they were "the every hour violator of the just and inalienable rights of man." Any slaveholder should know that he was "silently whetting the knife of vengeance for his own throat. He never lisps a syllable in commendation of the fathers of this republic, nor denounces any attempted oppression of himself, without . . . asserting the rights of rebellion for his own slaves."[39] Here, though, Douglass advocated not retributive violence but a principled resort to self-defense.

Other slaves were disposed to absolve slaveholders' deeds, but drew the line at forgetting them. The lessons they had learned had been too hard-won. "I have forgiven him for all he done to me when a slave," one said, "but I believe I cannot forget."[40] "While it is sweet to forgive and forget, there are some things that should never be forgotten," Sam Aleckson believed. "As Frederick Douglass has said, 'How can we tell the distance we have come except we note the point from which we started?'"[41] Jeff Hamilton recounted the abuses inflicted by his cruel owner, Texan Sam Houston, "not because I bear him any hate on account of his mistreatment of my mother and her children. Even if I cannot forget it, I have forgiven him all that long ago."[42] To demonstrate his superior character, in 1844 fugitive newspaper editor Henry Bibb issued a sarcastic public invitation to his former owner, William Gatewood, to visit him at his new home in Detroit. "I will use you better than you did me while you held me as a slave," he assured Gatewood. "Think not that I have any malice against you, for the cruel treatment which you inflicted on me while I was in your power," Bibb emphasized. "As it was the custom of your country, to treat your fellow men as you did me and my little family, I can freely forgive you." Bibb was even "willing to forget" the past if Gatewood acknowledged and repented of his crimes.[43] James L. Smith, enslaved in eastern Virginia, believed that "colored people, unlike all other nations on the face of the earth, are ready to fulfill that passage of Scripture: 'Therefore, if thine enemy hunger, feed him; if he thirst, give him drink; for in so doing thou shalt heap coals of fire on his head.'"[44] Edward Hicks was certain that if emancipation occurred and planters offered to hire ex-slaves at fair rates, "they would jump at the chance; they wouldn't cut throats."[45] Even David Walker charged slaveholders, "Treat us like men, and there is no danger but we will all live in peace and happiness together."[46]

Thus, while slaves did not widely support revenge, the right of self-defense, whether in the form of physical or psychological confrontation, was firmly established in slave cosmology. The "doctrine that submission is the best cure for outrage and wrong," Douglass insisted, "does not hold good on the slave plantation. *He is whipped oftenest, who is whipped easiest.*" Anyone with "the courage to stand up for himself" would emerge "in the end, a freeman, even though he sustain the formal relation of a slave." Douglass used his unforgettable encounter with slave breaker Edward Covey to drive this point home. Having endured several brutal attacks from Covey, and with another in the offing, he walked seven miles to his owner to "beseech him to get me another master." Instead, he was instructed to return and take the flogging that his master expected he deserved. A desolate Douglass complied, but not without swearing "to defend and protect myself to the best of my abilities." When the anticipated confrontation occurred, Douglass "remembered my pledge to *stand up in my own defense. . . . I was resolved to fight*" but "strictly on the *defensive*, preventing him from injuring me, rather than trying to injure him." When Covey was unable to prevail over Douglass he called in a cousin for reinforcement. Douglass was then "compelled to give blows, as well as to parry them" with the cousin, but remained "*defensive* toward Covey." The fight with the cousin ended after Douglass "dealt a blow . . . which fairly sickened" him. For two more hours Douglass stood Covey off and wore down his energies, until Covey gave up, saying he "would not have whipped you half so much as I have had you not resisted." But "the fact was, *he had not whipped me at all*." Douglass claimed victory "because my aim had not been to injure him, but to prevent his injuring me." Covey never threatened Douglass again and Douglass declared the battle "the turning point in my '*life as a slave*.'" He was no longer "*afraid to die*. This spirit made me a freeman in *fact*, while I remained a slave in *form*. When a slave cannot be flogged he is more than half free" and has "a domain as broad as his own manly heart to defend." He closed his moral tale with a verse from Lord Byron: "Hereditary bondmen, know ye not/ Who would be free, themselves must strike the blow?"[47] David Walker, who often despaired of any significant numbers of slaves embracing self-defense, urged them never to fail in this divine injunction: "believe this, that it is no more harm for you to kill a man, who is trying to kill you, than it is for you to take a drink of water when thirsty; in fact, the man who will stand still and let another murder him, is worse than an infidel, and, if he has common sense, ought not to be pitied."[48]

* * *

Many people today argue that victims of repeated violence and abuse are often destined to inflict similar abuse against others. No doubt such outcomes occur. But victims can also learn a great deal about ethical behavior from the negative examples set by their attackers. Such was the case with the majority of enslaved victims of torture and violence. While not all were able to deploy physical self-defense, the principle itself was ingrained as an ethical imperative manifestly distinct from slaveholder violence. The ignorance of most contemporary whites that violence was linked with white slaveholders, rather than black slaves, is a testament to the power of pro-slavery ideology. The message that blacks are almost innately violent has had remarkable durability into the twenty-first century. The misrepresentation of Black Power advocates and their portrayal as the violent mirror opposites of peaceful direct action practitioners, the mass incarceration rates of African American men, the stop-and-frisk police tactics and stand your ground laws, and the increasing frequency of African American victimization by police—these examples and more demonstrate the resilience of the stereotype of black violence. We still need to distinguish those who are economically, physically, and psychologically violent from those who practice self-defense. Freedpeople's ethical expeditions after emancipation demonstrated that they too understood how vital it was to battle these fabrications, as the next chapter will show.

5

Democracy Meets the Industrial Revolution

Reconstruction Achievements and
the Counterrevolution against Them

> It was not, then, race and culture calling out of the South in 1876; it was property and privilege, shrieking to its kind, and privilege and property heard and recognized the voice of its own.
>
> —W.E.B. Du Bois, *Black Reconstruction in America*

> Sorrowing at the situation, pained at the necessity which yet drives our brethren from pillar to post, or binds them to the wicked caprices of their old masters, yet we appreciate the open hearts that welcome them to new homes, and the willing hands that minister to their dire necessities. We have yet much to ask of others; we have much more to accomplish for ourselves. What has been wrought in the past cannot be overcome at once. Gradually the work of demoralization does its work, and not much swifter must be the work of regeneration. We cannot save ourselves without aid and sympathy from others; without the protection of just laws and righteous judgment; others cannot save us without our aid—without the consecration of all our best faculties to the work before us. Let us, then, work mutually in unfolding the mysteries of that Providence which is not only bringing us up out of bondage, but which is to redeem the whole race of mankind from the gloom of darkness and the thralldom of sin. With these thoughts I leave, asking you to give your hearts to wisdom, restraining yourselves from selfishness, and living for the good of others. There has been enough of pain, and sorrow, and despair. The whole current of life must be changed, and men be taught no longer to hedge the way of others, but to scatter sunbeams, solar sunbeams; the sunbeams of life in their path.
>
> —James L. Smith, *Autobiography of James L. Smith*

Slaves' ethical cosmos, the result of their interpretations of their labor experiences, prepared them to seize emancipation as an opportunity to share their democratic humanism with the postwar world. They mixed optimism about freedom's potential with a realistic view of the rocky road ahead. They believed they possessed a unique vision that could redeem the country from a host of inequities, not the least being racism and its causes. Their work was cut out for them, in no small measure because it coincided with the rise of another revolution—the industrial one. Marx's observation that people "make their own history," although not "under circumstances chosen by themselves, but under circumstances directly encountered, given and transmitted from the past" was perhaps truer for African Americans in the age of emancipation than for any other group.[1] More than any other factor, the advance of monopoly capitalism was responsible for a counter-revolution against freedpeople and the poor that became unstoppable by the end of the century.

The meaning of free labor underwent a dramatic redefinition after the Civil War. The wholesale shift to capitalism that unfolded in emancipation's wake solidified an economic understanding of freedom as synonymous with wage labor. This change reinforced the beliefs of many whites that the replacement of slavery with wage work in the form of sharecropping had brought about incontrovertible "freedom" based on contractual agree- [*notisputable*] ments. As this process accelerated, unbridled greed and reckless individual accumulation among industrial elites became common and more than a little reminiscent of slavery. Far from endorsing democracy, industrial elites dreaded it. To contain the democratic impetus behind Reconstruction-era [*the force that makes something happen*] black activism, they imposed limitations on workers of all backgrounds, sharply curbing access to economic and political power through generous use of violence and anti-labor laws and with the blessing of the federal government.

Such was the uneven nature of the contest in which freedpeople engaged. Nonetheless during the first decade of freedom they scored an impressive number of hard-won democratic victories, so much so that counterrevolutionaries decided that more robust measures were needed to defeat them. Beginning in earnest in the 1880s and especially in the 1890s, white elites pulled out the big guns of disfranchisement, segregation, and vigilante terror in a scorched-earth effort to control black democrats and their allies. Thus, when the Civil War removed slaveholders as obstructions to capitalist progress, the outcome did not contribute to greater democracy, but to substantially less. Ultimately, reactionaries succeeded in reversing the gains of Reconstruction democrats. But they failed to destroy the slave-based ethos that guided the drive for greater equality. The emancipation generation protected and bequeathed that vision to future generations, who then joined the lessons of segregation to those of slavery and Reconstruction and elaborated on the links between labor and morality in the industrial age.

* * *

In 1865, freedpeople plumbed their collective experience for direction as they confronted the revolutionary task of reconstruction, hoping to instate democratic institutions and laws as broadly as possible. During Presidential Reconstruction, between 1865 and 1867, an array of daunting obstacles confronted them. Many former Confederate states passed black codes, pernicious laws with a central object: to keep black labor dependent on whites. Freedpeople in most states could not buy or rent land. Anyone who refused to work under oppressive conditions was declared a vagrant subject to fines, imprisonment, and forced labor. Migration to towns and cities was forbidden or severely circumscribed; many areas enacted pass systems to restrict freedom of movement. Ownership of firearms was often illegal. Freedpeople's taxes were higher than those of landowners. Any skilled person who wished to establish a business first had to pay an exorbitant fee. No one could vote, not even black troops who had secured the victory at Appomattox. Black men were not permitted to sit on juries, nor could they testify against a white person, a holdover of slavery that enabled whites to defraud blacks at will. Republican policy required freedpeople to enter into annual contracts with landholders, many of whom were dishonest, violent, and intent upon keeping as many of the prerogatives of slavery as possible.

President Andrew Johnson summarily pardoned ex-Confederates and reinstated their political authority. Former rebels reappeared in the halls of Congress, and in state and local governments as well. Johnson overturned plans to redistribute condemned and abandoned plantation lands, occupied during the war, to as many freedpeople as might be accommodated. He acquiesced to planter insistence that black troops be removed from the South. Johnson was willing to let the Freedmen's Bureau continue to exist for its one-year authorization, but did nothing to stop ex-Confederate persecution of bureau officials. Instead he authorized militias to attack them and the freedpeople they were assigned to protect.[2]

At the end of 1865, most freedpeople who had entered contracts for the months following emancipation saw little if any payoff for their labor and had experienced a range of abuses reminiscent of slavery. Apprenticeship programs bound out orphans or children who did not live in nuclear households for years to unscrupulous planters who routinely underreported their ages in order to hold them to longer terms of labor. Fraud, violence, murder, and harsh working conditions fostered widespread resistance. When they began to contract for work in January 1866, freedpeople demanded change. Many refused, for example, to work under overseers, and insisted that contracts be made with kin groups responsible for a given section of the plantation, rather than being made collectively with all workers. They insisted on the right to live on these allotted sections in family units, rather than in the old slave quarters. They wanted higher wages, paid monthly rather than extended only in December. They demanded freedom of movement, and greater leisure time. Women and children were not to be called upon for household or temporary labor unless specific agreements had been made. The hated apprenticeship program had to end. The black codes had to go. When these demands went unanswered, freedpeople used the weapon of labor: they refused to work. Several dramatic labor strikes occurred. Freedpeople met frequently to discuss how best to advance their ideas of freedom. They made collective decisions about contract terms in their areas. And they called loudly for the extension of the franchise, without which they would be unable to protect themselves or advance their democratic visions.[3]

Radical Republicans in Congress, angered by what they deemed policies at odds with the installation of wage labor, troubled by escalating reports of southern white violence, and disturbed by intransigent ex-rebels in Congress, concluded in 1866 that Johnson's plans for Reconstruction were failing. One leading opponent, Massachusetts senator Henry Wilson, announced in December 1865 at the opening of the Thirty-Ninth Congress that "armed men are traversing portions of the rebel States to-day enforcing these black laws upon men whom we have made free, and to whom we stand pledged before man and God to maintain their freedom. A few months ago these freedmen were joyous, hopeful, confident. To-day they are distrustful, silent, and sad, and this condition has grown out of the wrongs and cruelties and oppressions that have been perpetrated upon them."[4]

Congress subsequently ordered the establishment of the Joint Committee on Reconstruction to review Johnson's policies and investigate conditions in the former Confederacy. In January 1866, Congress renewed the Freedmen's Bureau bill and introduced the first civil rights bill in American history. The bill enumerated fundamental civil rights—the rights to contract, to sue and be sued, and to hold property without respect to race—but failed to extend suffrage. When Johnson vetoed both bills, Congress countered with the Fourteenth Amendment, a measure intended to bypass presidential authority by investing protection for freedpeople in the Constitution, which would require a public referendum. The amendment defined citizenship by requiring states to enforce equality before the law. It reduced representation in the House of Representatives proportionately to the number of disenfranchised male citizens, and barred from state and federal office those who had sworn allegiance to the Constitution but then became Confederates. Finally, in early 1867, Congress addressed an issue that seemed inevitable to many: universal manhood suffrage. Over another presidential veto, they passed the Reconstruction Acts, which divided the South into five military districts under control of the army and stipulated the requirements whereby former Confederate states could reenter the Union. They had to enroll a loyal electorate that included freedmen for fall elections that would send delegates to state constitutional conventions. These bodies then had to produce new constitutions required to include the Fourteenth Amendment and manhood suffrage.[5]

Thus began Radical, or Congressional, Reconstruction, a ten-year period during which freedpeople flexed their political muscles to promote measures that fostered the rights of labor, checked greed and economic corruption, improved public services, and expanded civil rights. We can readily see these ethical goals being put into play on the political stages of the Reconstruction South. Not surprisingly, freedmen registered to vote in droves. Between 70 and 90 percent of the black electorate showed up at the polls, and similar rates of participation continued throughout most of Reconstruction.[6] They joined Union Leagues in great numbers, where they studied the mechanics of government; learned about the issues of the day; and debated courses of action at the local, state, and national levels.[7] They held their own state conventions to clarify their positions. Observers of their many public meetings frequently remarked on freedpeople's healthy presence in the galleries of legislative and judicial halls. Although men alone exercised the ballot, public assemblies were thoroughgoing democratic affairs in which the entire community participated and where the vote was considered a collective possession. Women and children were active partakers in political debates, and women regularly sanctioned companions who refused to represent the general will.[8] The majority aligned with the leftmost faction of the Republican Party, the Radicals. Festivals and parades that enthusiastically celebrated emancipation, which had begun before the Confederate surrender, continued. Often their purpose was to honor the pride blacks had in themselves as workers; many communities designated days on which to honor their heritage as producers and skilled laborers.[9]

The early black electorate tended to return those people they found especially accomplished to the halls of power. Generally, black politicians possessed some identifiable skill or recognized achievement that would help them govern effectively. Literate, if not necessarily formally educated, representatives were preferred, but many semiliterate people joined them. Numerous teachers entered postwar politics, as did those possessing oratorical and rhetorical talents. Men with artisanal skills, like carpentry, shoemaking, or barbering, figured prominently, along with ministers and Union Army veterans. Sizeable numbers of people who had been free before emancipation entered into the political ranks in each southern state.[10]

Freedpeople commonly regarded the potential fruits of emancipation as fully national in scope, much as slavery's influence had been. If slavery had tainted the entire nation, then freedom was destined to bring about sweeping structural reformations that reflected an appreciation of the dignity of labor. Both words and deeds demonstrated that this vision of the future depended on a clear view of the past. Douglass began addressing this theme in a speech that he gave weekly in the aftermath of the Emancipation Proclamation, forecasting the end of an era "which required Northern merchants to sell their souls as a condition precedent to selling their goods."[11]

What we now want is a country—a free country—a country not saddened by the footprints of a single slave—and nowhere cursed by the presence of a slaveholder. . . . Not because we love the Negro, but the nation; not because we prefer to do this, because we must or give up the contest and give up the country. We want a country, and are fighting for a country, where social intercourse and commercial relations shall neither be embarrassed nor embittered by the imperious exactions of an insolent slaveholding oligarchy. . . . the manifest destiny of this war to unify and reorganize the institutions of the country . . . is the secret of the strength, the fortitude, the persistent energy—in a word, *the sacred significance*—of this war.[12]

Former fugitive slave Henry Highland Garnet also employed these redemptive themes in the first speech by an African American to Congress on 12 February 1865. Garnet exalted emancipation as an event destined to open "a path of prosperity" that would bring "justice to the poorest and weakest" in the nation. The emancipation generation stood poised to bequeath to the world "a model Republic, founded on the principles of justice and humanity and Christianity, in which the burdens of war and the blessings of peace are equally borne and enjoyed by all."[13]

Many another echoed this conviction. B. K. Sampson, addressing a white audience on Thanksgiving Day in 1867 in Fairfield, Ohio, asked if they wished "to see the righteousness of God prevail." He urged them to align "in His great name to His cause" and to subdue "all these passions of prejudice and injustice." Cultivate instead, he urged, "a sentiment of purest philanthropy; a sentiment so radical in its nature" that it would foster among other whites "the spirit of equality and right. Then will the government of God and all men of all races become one grand mutuality of intellectual and moral design."[14]

When abolitionist Martin Delany addressed a group of slaves on St. Helena Island, South Carolina, on 23 July 1865, he too made this redemptive mission plain. "Only you," he underscored, "were the means for your masters to lead the ideal and inglorious life. . . . As before the whole depended upon you, now the *whole country* will depend upon you" for a moral regeneration made possible, indeed necessary, after the end of two and a half centuries of slavery.[15]

Frances Ellen Watkins Harper, a free northern woman who was active in the abolitionist movement and worked to advance freedpeople's education in the postwar years, delivered a similar message of general salvation in a speech before the Equal Rights Association in May 1866. Trying to patch the rift in the feminist movement over the likelihood that women would be excluded from the franchise, Harper grounded her appeal in the humanistic ethos that defined freedpeople's philosophical universe. "We are all bound up together in one great bundle of humanity," she told her audience, "and society cannot trample on the weakest and feeblest of its members without receiving the curse in its own soul." She argued that slavery had proven this truth repeatedly, because in keeping slaves fettered, "the moral strength" and "spiritual energies" of whites had become "crippled."[16] Recuperation from this illness demanded reformation among whites, which would enable freedom to reach its full measure. Like B. K. Sampson had attempted in Ohio, Harper emphasized a racially redemptive inclusiveness in an effort to encourage whites to incorporate the moral economy of the freed population for the good of the nation. It was an integrationist vision only in the sense that she hoped to assimilate whites into a biracial democratic movement.

This emphasis on redemption meant that most postwar African Americans rejected retribution against former masters, but they did demand equal justice and an even playing field going forward. Garnet argued this point in his February 1865 congressional address. Freedpeople would "only ask, that when our poor, frail barks are launched on life's ocean, *Bound on a voyage of awful length / And dangers little known,* that, in common with others, we may be furnished with rudder, helm and sails and charts and compass." With the proper protections, "if it shall please God to send us propitious winds or fearful gales, we shall survive or perish as our energies or neglect shall determine." The freed would seek "no special favors, but we plead for justice." They despised "unmanly dependence" but insisted on "the right to live and labor and enjoy the fruits of our toil." Notwithstanding the sufferings of enslavement, they sought not revenge but pitied "our land and [wept] with those who weep."[17]

At the black convention of Virginia held in 1865, delegates hoped "to live upon the most friendly and agreeable terms with all men; we feel no ill-will or prejudice towards our former oppressors; are willing and desire to forgive and forget the past, and so shape our future conduct as shall promote our happiness and the interest of the community in which we live."[18] Henry McNeal Turner, born of free parents in South Carolina and ordained in the African Methodist Episcopal (AME) Church, moved to

Georgia after emancipation, where he entered politics. Addressing the Georgia legislature in September 1868 after duly elected black members, including himself, were refused seats, Turner denounced vengeance while recounting African American contributions to the nation. African Americans had "accomplished much," pioneering civilization itself. "We have built up your country; we have worked in your fields and garnered your harvests for two hundred and fifty years!" What would be proper recompense? "Do we ask you for compensation for the sweat our fathers bore for you—for the tears you have caused, and the hearts you have broken, and the lives you have curtailed, and the blood you have spilled? Do we ask retaliation? We ask it not. We are willing to let the dead past bury its dead; but we ask you, now for our *rights*."[19] Former slave James D. Lynch, a postwar AME missionary and secretary of state for Mississippi, told audiences that the charge for the race was to court a reunion in which "North and South, white and black shake hands—join hearts—shout for joy" and embrace "a love of justice and mercy like that which is Divine, and a hope as high as the objects of promise, go on in the pursuit of further development."[20] Turner urged freedpeople to show whites that "we can be a people, respectable, virtuous, honest, and industrious, and soon their prejudice will melt away, and . . . we will all be brothers."[21]

Rejection of retaliation did not mean that reparations were not in order. Immediately after the Confederate surrender, the radical *New Orleans Tribune* was one of the first African American newspapers to call for the forfeiture of former rebel properties. In the same breath, the *Tribune* also supported former Confederate repatriation on grounds that would have been familiar to many beyond Louisiana: "We are not enemies of amnesty" precisely because "we do not ask to visit the iniquity of the fathers upon the children unto the third and fourth generation of them that have Union and freedom." As a "strong and generous" people, freedpeople knew how important it was "to disdain retaliation." Revenge was simply wasted time, since "the assassins of Fort Pillow" would "expiate their crime by a long and miserable existence. . . . we do not ask for the lives of the bloodthirsty foes." Support of amnesty was "something magnanimous, and worthy of our great and generous Republic." But amnesty and reparations could coexist: "at the same time that we spare the lives of our vanquished foes, let their property be forfeited."[22]

Although support for redemptive inclusiveness, equal justice, land redistribution, and respect for labor typified postwar black demands, planters were blind to the message, seemingly deliberately so. Instead they were riven with dread over the possibility of vengeance. They fanned this fear of black retaliatory violence among whites North and South, much as they previously had done with proslavery ideology.

Some organizations chose to investigate these phobias. In early 1863, just after the issuance of the Emancipation Proclamation, Boston's Emancipation League asked officers in charge of contraband camps in the occupied regions of the Confederacy to assess the potential for retributive violence from freedpeople in their jurisdictions. "I never heard the negroes here express a desire to be revenged upon their masters," Richard Soule Jr. reported from St. Helena Parish, South Carolina. "But they make no secret of their wish never to see their masters again." From Washington, D.C., D. B. Nichols replied emphatically: "I answer, *no!* they pray for the success of the Union army, and that their masters may lay down their arms, but there is no mention made of a spirit of revenge." Samuel Sawyer, chaplain of the 47th Regiment, Indiana Volunteers, reporting from Helena, Arkansas, found "None whatever. They make no threats. They seem to wish well to their masters, but fear that it will not be well with them in the next world, however they fare here." "I came to this Department without any knowledge of the negro character, prepared to meet a race of savages not only thirsting for 'the horrors of a servile insurrection,' but quite ready to tear me limb from limb unless I could succeed in making myself agreeable to them," reported Captain E. W. Hooper, aide-de-camp to General Rufus Saxton in Beaufort, South Carolina. "I have since found them as a very general rule gentle and ready to obey reasonable orders—almost too gentle in many cases to stand up for their own rights. I have very seldom seen any disposition to revenge upon their masters."[23]

Widespread fears of insurrection surfaced in the fall of 1865, when planters expected that in the aftermath of the collapse of planned land redistributions, freedpeople would rise up at Christmas. Their concerns stemmed in part from the numerous meetings freedpeople held. Many freedpeople also had armed themselves in anticipation of and in response to planter violence. Alarmed by these acts of self-defense, ex-slaveholders peppered Union officials with suspicions of planned insurrection.

The Freedmen's Bureau and other northern inspectors investigated these charges across the former Confederacy and concluded that no evidence existed for the panicked allegations. Captain Andrew Geddes, assistant superintendent of the Freedmen's Bureau for Tuskegee, Alabama, made a typical report in October 1865. Geddes could not "calm [the] delusive and heated imaginations" of the "committee of citizens" who had brought their fears of impending vengeance to him. Geddes, however, dismissed such a possibility out of hand. On the contrary, freedpeople in Pike County, whence the committee came and which did not have a bureau presence, "have certainly been treated very badly . . . and no wonder of [sic] they should feel resentful. . . . the white people have done with the negro what they pleased,—*cut, hung,* and whipped and abused them unmercifully." He warned his superiors to guard against complaints from Pike County whites, since they were "very apt to *magnify* even the slightest error of the negro."[24]

As Geddes's report suggested, black violence during Reconstruction paled compared to the terror whites meted out. Freedmen's Bureau agents' reports on "outrages" overflowed with accounts of severe violence perpetrated against freedpeople. As a consequence, numerous black communities formed self-defense clubs and militia units to defend themselves against attacks, which occurred nearly without cease during Reconstruction.[25] Republican activist Edward C. Billings traveled from New Orleans back to his hometown of Hatfield, Massachusetts, in 1873 to report on the recent bloody Colfax massacre in Louisiana's Red River Valley, a Democratic attack on black (not white) Republicans that left more than one hundred African Americans dead on Easter Sunday. In the course of his remarks on the failures of federal policy to protect freedpeople, he stressed that the African American people in Louisiana "avoid violence almost to a fault. Hardly ever do they provoke an attack. Whenever you read of a skirmish between the former slaves and the former masters, in ninety-nine cases out of a hundred, you may know that the masters compelled it."[26] Such was the case in the Colfax massacre, when African Americans under attack acted in self-defense against a mob composed of conservative Republicans and Democrats bent on ousting them from power.[27]

Such violence was not based simply on the fact that black people had entered into the body politic. It was what they had done with their political power that provoked terrorism. Black politicians generally followed common agendas, though they did not always agree on policy. Overwhelmingly they worked as one to promote public education and civil rights legislation. They built the South's public school systems, although they faced uphill battles in stipulating that schools be unsegregated.[28] They supported public responsibility for the poor and infirm; worked to institute orphanages, insane asylums, and penitentiaries; and tried to establish relief for the poor. They scoured the law of such relics as whippings; property ownership as a prerequisite for voting, holding office, and serving on juries; and incarceration for debt. They scaled back the list of crimes qualifying as capital offenses. Gerrymandered districts were redrawn along fairer lines. South Carolina passed its first divorce bill, and most states legalized some limited property rights for married women. Black politicians called for equal access to public accommodations—ratified into law in the 1875 Civil Rights Act—and tried, unsuccessfully, to decriminalize interracial marriage. They rejected calls for ex-Confederate disfranchisement, fearful of the precedent it would set as well as the consequences it would unleash. They recognized the importance of installing blacks in a wide variety of local political posts; the job of sheriff, for example, was regarded as a position of great consequence because of its potential to protect freedpeople from violence and fraud.[29]

But legal and political rights alone could not bring full equality. Economic opportunity was critical to full freedom, and measures to promote it were widely supported. Reconstruction-era African Americans regularly denounced fraud and greed, familiar scourges that gained traction in the context of the industrial revolution. They instituted fairer tax codes and, while supporting such modern enterprises as railroads and industry, passed measures to ensure that business contributed responsibly to public interests. They invalidated usury statutes and capped interest rates. They battled against funding the Confederate debt, having particular success in Virginia.[30] And while many continued to support reparations, typically the redistribution of condemned plantation lands, most preferred laws that guarded workers' rights and protected equal economic opportunity in general. As radical politicians, they left an impressive democratic stamp on the emerging political and economic landscape, contributing to the adoption of a set of constitutions in 1868 generally regarded as remarkable in their liberality—even revolutionary to many. The progressive and humanistic values that these documents and other local statutes embodied unambiguously reflected the ethical influence of the freed population and their allies.[31]

As a result of their achievements, African Americans felt just as responsible for postwar civic revitalizations as they previously had for antebellum wealth and prosperity. Near the end of the century, when disfranchisement was under way, South Carolina Republican Thomas E. Miller proudly reflected on the record he and his fellow black politicians had compiled. African American voters and their representatives had "displayed greater conservative force, appreciation for good laws, knowledge for the worth of financial legislation, regard for the rights of . . . fellow citizens in relation to property and aptitude for honest financial state legislation than has ever been shown by any other people." After only eight years in power, "We had built school houses, established charitable institutions, built and maintained the penitentiary system . . . rebuilt the bridges and reestablished the ferries. In short we had reconstructed the state and placed it on the road to prosperity."[32] The first African American elected to Congress, Joseph Rainey from Charleston, South Carolina, similarly defended black legislators' accomplishments on the congressional floor in March 1871. "Our convention which met in 1868, and in which the Negroes were in a large majority, did not pass any proscriptive or disfranchising acts, but adopted a liberal constitution, securing alike equal rights to all citizens, white and black, male and female, as far as possible. . . . we did not discriminate, although we had a majority. . . . You cannot point to . . . a single act . . . by which the majority . . . have undertaken to crush the white men because the latter are in a minority."[33]

"No wonder the plantation owners hated that convention [of 1868], and the legislatures that followed it," said Mississippian George Washington Albright, a former slave who became a state senator. "No wonder the rich folks hate the memory of those legislatures to this very day! The convention made a new constitution, the first in the history of the state under which poor people, white and Negro, had any rights. . . . there was to be no property qualifications for holding office or for voting." The new constitution "stopped all the discrimination against the Negroes to travel, in hotel accommodations, in the right to give testimony in court, in the right to vote and serve on juries. The poor whites who sat in the convention favored these measures as much as did the Negro delegates." Radical Republicans in Mississippi also took early action to eliminate the state debt. "There was a lot of talk among the plantation owners about our 'extravagance,'" Albright recalled, "and people even today try to discredit our rule . . . by saying that we spent money right and left, wasting the state's resources. As a matter of fact, the tax rate in Mississippi was less than nine mills on the dollar, and one-fifth of the total we collected was for schools." The legislature retired the debt "at 25 percent each year until every dollar of debt the state owed was wiped out. Out of that money we built roads and schools and hospitals, trained teachers, kept the state running." The state government also built free schools in every county, and "had Negroes in many responsible positions," including those of lieutenant governor, secretary of state, superintendent of public instruction, and commissioner of immigration. When violent whites threatened them, Albright "helped to organize the Negro volunteer militia, which was needed to keep the common people on top and fight off the organized attacks of the landlords and former slave owners. We drilled frequently—and how the rich folks hated to see us, armed and ready to defend ourselves and our elected government! The militia helped fight off the Klan which was organized by the old slaveowners to try to make us slaves again in all but name."[34]

When "A Republican" from New York claimed that poor economic management in South Carolina had led to the party's demise, journalist T. Thomas Fortune took on this "typical Yankee" who "would weigh in the same scales dollars and cents and human rights." What destroyed the party in South Carolina, he insisted, was the perfidy of the Grant administration and the Republican Congress, which failed to send troops into Hamburgh when African Americans were under attack in 1876. And as for the "Republican's" charge that black politicians had stolen funds from the state, Fortune spat, "Where under the sun can you find a more unscrupulous thief than the white man? Does he not live by robbery? What is Wall street but a den of genteel sharpers? The white merchants, speculators and farmers of the country—do not they live by gouging their neighbors?"[35]

Aside from promoting democracy and self-defense, the emancipation generation also left a record of their determination to practice self-reliance, work for an honest living, and strive for economic independence as much as possible—mandates from the antebellum years. After freedom, Archie Millner's father took his family off the farm where they had been enslaved, "fixed up a shack on de edge of de woods," and refused to return to work for his former master even though he was begged to do so. "But pa never would go back. . . . he felt better workin' fo' hisse'f. 'Member he used to send me wid a sack of corn all de way to Henderson Mill . . . 'bout eight miles—to git it ground rather dan use" his former master's mill. "Henderson took one-eighth fo' toll, but pa said it made him feel like a free man to pay fo' things jus' like anyone else."[36] Other freedpeople chose to enter into collective land purchases and operated such holdings communally. The best-known example took place at Davis Bend, Mississippi, where former slaves of Confederate president Jefferson Davis assumed control in 1862, when Union troops appeared. But others could be found across the South, particularly in lowland South Carolina, which contained a black majority and where the Union established an early wartime occupation, driving out the planter class.[37]

In another context, Isaac Myers, an early black labor leader, organized the Chesapeake Marine Railway and Dry Dock Company in 1867 after white workers opposed to working with black mechanics and longshoremen struck. More than one hundred African Americans consequently lost their jobs on Baltimore's docks. Myers persuaded them to jointly purchase $10,000 of company stock, which he used to launch a thriving business with an interracial workforce. His success compelled the white caulkers' union to admit blacks as members. Two years later Myers told the National Labor Convention (NLC) that "white laboring men of the country have nothing to fear from the colored laboring man," and the way he ran his business proved just that. The aim of black workers was "to see labor elevated and made respectable" and to profit at a level that reflected the worth of their labor. Members of the NLC could wholly "rely on the support of the colored laborers of this country in bringing about this result." As he insisted, "American citizenship with the black man is a complete failure" if African Americans remained proscribed in the labor force. "If citizenship means anything at all," Myers told the convention, "it means the freedom of labor, as broad and as universal as the freedom of the ballot." Black workers "mean in all sincerity a hearty cooperation with all working men. . . . We carry no prejudices," he insisted. "We are willing to forget the wrongs of yesterday and let the dead past bury its dead."[38]

Thus, the slave ethic that extolled "honest labor" suffused the words and deeds of many former bondspeople. Freedman John Quincy Adams felt "almost as happy as the president with a compensation of twenty-five thousand dollars a year, knowing that when my work is done the pay is mine." He rejoiced in the potential of seeing a world that "'let every one live by the sweat of his brow.'... [b]ut [did] not 'let every one live off of the sweat of another's brow without paying for it.'" With the idealism common during early emancipation, Adams believed that living off the labor of others would come to be regarded as a violation of "the laws of God and the just laws of the land."[39]

At the California Convention of Colored Citizens, held in October 1865, delegates serving on the Committee on Industrial Pursuits gave a similar paean to an honest work ethic. "It is an ordination of God," they insisted, "that man shall earn his bread by the sweat of his brow; toil and suffering, care and sorrow, are in this life our allotted inheritance.... we must possess a knowledge of mechanism, become owners and tillers of the soil, abandon the cities, drop menial employments and become producers as well as consumers. We ... conceive it to be the imperative duty of parents and guardians to give their sons trades and teach them the dignity of labor. He who will not work shall not eat, is the stern declaration of the *Sacred Writ*." The committee members denounced "vocations which not only infringe upon the civil law but come in conflict with the higher law of Heaven," insisting "that the entrance into industrial pursuits alone will secure ... health, wealth, contentment and respect." The committee recommended that blacks buy land, collectively if possible, encourage traders and mechanics among them, and seek employment in such remunerative enterprises as laying the Pacific Railroad.[40]

Despite freedpeople's efforts to achieve economic independence through honest labor, most whites believed that black freedom would become synonymous with idleness—although what they really feared was that blacks would work for themselves rather than for whites. Republican Party members, northern philanthropists, military authorities, and Freedmen's Bureau officials took these concerns seriously, in part because they nervously shared them. The Bureau solicited many a report in search of answers about freedpeople's approach to working for wages. The resulting documents reported that some—young single men in particular, and especially "demoralized" communities or plantations—resisted wage labor. But overwhelmingly Bureau officials reported that, especially among families—who organized their labor along lines reminiscent of antebellum-era niche economies—"experiments" in wage labor worked far better than slavery ever had, and yielded superior results when workers received fair treatment and just compensation.[41]

Brigadier General E. A. Paine's report from occupied Gallatin, Tennessee, in late January 1864 was typical. When nearly a third of the 167 slaves from the nearby Fairview estate sought refuge from violence and exploitation at Paine's post, he sent them back, saying he could offer as much protection there as he could in Gallatin. Subsequently, "violent, vindictive Rebels" who were "determined that they would never again recognize the U.S. Government" severely persecuted the returnees. Consequently, blacks at Fairview, Paine reported, "had become more and more insubordinate" and refused to work. After repeated pleas by Fairview's owners for Paine to "act the Overseer or Negro Whipper for them," Paine went to Fairview and instead promised fair wages. Afterwards, even though the season started late because of the work stoppages, "more was produced on the Estate— than had been for any one year, for ten years before—Besides enough to pay all of the laborers and Overseer, there is at least $1200 clear for the Estate." But after the harvest and sale, Fairview's owners refused to pay the laborers. The lesson Paine wished to underscore was that freedpeople worked badly, if at all, when treated violently or when cheated, but worked well when paid and when their agricultural or mechanical expertise was respected, as many freedpeople themselves had argued.[42]

At an October 1865 meeting in Vicksburg, Mississippi, freedpeople issued a sarcastic statement about fears they would not work. Whites were "constantly carping about the idleness and vagrancy, the lying and stealing habits of the colored people, and. . . . Conventions and Legislatures are greatly exercised about our morals and industry." This group invited their detractors to "look over the records of the courts and jails, of churches and moral societies, to compare the list of laborers in various branches of industry in the South, to which the colored man is admitted, and see how much the favored race excel us in the good habits of society."[43]

In light of such reports as these and in search of more information about freedpeople's views of the future, the Freedmen's Bureau and the military asked freedpeople to itemize their definition of freedom. John Quincy Adams recalled that he and his acquaintances heard this question all the time: "Now we are free. What do we want?" Adams spelled out a vision basic to many: "We want education, we want protection, we want plenty of work; we want good pay for it, but not any more or less than any one else; we want good trades, such as good mechanics' trades, we just want a good chance to get them, and then you will see the down-trodden race rise up."[44] In postemancipation communities across the South, freedpeople placed a premium on land—particularly land where they had lived and buried their dead—as inseparable from the independent social and communal lives they viewed as the very definition of freedom. Land and the community it reinforced also provided relative safety against endemic violence. Most believed land was just compensation for generations of enslavement.

An iconic explanation of the difference between labor in slavery and in freedom came from retired Baptist minister and former slave Garrison Frazier. Frazier was the spokesman for a group of twenty ministers and other community leaders who discussed freedom with Secretary of War Edwin M. Stanton and General William T. Sherman in Savannah, Georgia, in January 1865. Slavery, Frazier told the two,

> is, receiving by *irresistible power* the work of another man, and not by his *consent*. . . . freedom . . . is taking us from under the yoke of bondage, and placing us where we could reap the fruit of our own labor, take care of ourselves and assist the Government in maintaining our freedom. . . . The way we can best take care of ourselves is to have land, and turn it and till it by our own labor—that is, by the labor of the women and children and old men; and we can soon maintain ourselves and have something to spare.[45]

Days later, Sherman issued Special Field Order 15, which until the end of the war distributed confiscated and condemned rebel lands among freedpeople in a thirty-mile-wide strip of coastal land in Georgia and South

Carolina. "No white person whatever," the order stipulated, "unless military officers and soldiers detailed for duty, will be permitted to reside; and the sole and exclusive management of affairs will be left to the freed people themselves, subject only to the United States military authority, and the acts of Congress."[46] The ultimate disposition of the lands legally belonged to Congress and the president, and no legal fee-simple titles were distributed. Resettled freedpeople believed that these land redistributions should become permanent, their just due for generations of stolen labor and payment for helping to save the Union. It was this plan for redistribution that Andrew Johnson revoked, in one of the first acts of his presidency. Numerous other betrayals were to follow.

*   *   *

The humanistic, democratic bent of postwar black activists, their allies, and the community at large was unambiguous, and during Radical Reconstruction, some people found the leeway to put their ideas and plans into motion. As they did so, they became increasingly threatening to the economic elite. As the engine of industrial production geared up, the enemies of democracy gathered political and economic force. The counterrevolution that resulted relied on time-honored tactics of terror, intimidation, and violence, and new tactics of disfranchisement and segregation, all intended to derail interracial class-based cooperation and democracy. The Republican Party may have been tired, as the traditional answer to the question of "Why did Reconstruction end?" posits, but that explanation merely begs another question: tired of what? The answer was that white Republicans could not tolerate revolutionary democracy because it undermined economic momentum for the wealthy. The end of Reconstruction was thus not a matter of general malaise but a dynamic and purposeful reaction against one of the nation's most democratic movements.

Counterrevolutionaries spared few efforts to render freedpeople's humanistic ethos a shambles, and they knew exactly what would leave them most vulnerable. When in the 1880s and 1890s counterrevolutionaries began the betrayal of emancipation in earnest, they first took aim at political protections, like the Civil Rights Act of 1875, which the Supreme Court invalidated in 1883, and the ballot. Without such safeguards, African Americans would be hobbled in their continued pursuit of their goals, and unable to resist the subsequent onslaughts of segregation and the terror that enforced it. The thoroughgoing viciousness of these attacks reflected how great a dent democratic activists had made in just a few years. To roll back democratic gains, it was necessary to rewrite history and rescript African American achievements as corrupt malfeasance, directly assaulting the slave-generated ideologies that had informed Radical Republican public policy. As had been the case with proslavery rhetoric, the target audience for these counterrevolutionary arguments was largely poor and working-class whites, but emancipation required counterrevolutionaries to have an audience even larger and more diverse than the one slaveholders had addressed in the antebellum years.

Southern elites had a long history of attacking democratic, interracial class alliances. But none had gotten so out of hand as the one that emerged during Reconstruction. Not surprisingly, then, these late nineteenth- and early twentieth-century assaults became distinguished for barbarity and cruelty. This counterrevolution also had durable, damaging consequences for the nation, requiring as it did a mauling of African American character, intelligence, family, community, and morality; and, as one historian termed it, a festival of violence, particularly lynching, against the black population.[47]

Contemporaries, though shocked at the terror they increasingly faced, immediately understood such counterrevolutionary tactics; they had either seen or heard about them before. Douglass observed in 1892 that violence and sham arguments about black immorality proved "that the Negro is not standing still. He is not dead, but alive and active. . . . A ship rotting at anchor meets with no resistance, but when she sets sail . . . she has to buffet opposing billows." Enemies of democratic achievements saw that blacks were "making progress" which "they naturally wish to stop."[48]

Decades later, Walter White, an anti-lynching activist who was executive secretary of the National Association for the Advancement of Colored People from 1931 to 1955, interpreted lynching as "much more an expression of Southern fear of Negro progress than of Negro crime." That was precisely what Ida B. Wells-Barnett had discovered in her research on lynching, published in 1892. She resolutely collected statistics, many of them gleaned from white newspapers, which demonstrated conclusively that economically independent and politically active African Americans, their allies, and those who stepped out of "place" were the favored targets of lynchings.[49]

As their forebears had done when they strategized about how to resist slavery, the generation entering the nadir debated their own best courses of action. The realities of raw violence, terror, humiliation, demonization, disfranchisement, and segregation forced many to weigh sheer survival against economic independence and continued activism, which was precisely what counterrevolutionaries aimed for. By century's end, when the captains of industry and their minions had safe headwind, southern African Americans had three basic choices: accept poverty as the price of survival, migrate, or join the opposition. The majority landed in the first category.

Prior to the Great Migration of the World War I years, only trickles of middle-class people could escape the increasingly lethal South. Even during the war years, the 400,000 who left the South represented a small and desperate minority—less than 5 percent of the total black population. The rest were left to defend themselves against a sadistic spree of burnings, hangings, barbaric tortures, and unfettered capitalism. Landowners defrauded black labor with impunity; blacks had difficulty renting or buying arable land; most unions denied them entry; and educational resources became limited largely to Tuskegee-like industrial training institutions. Debt peonage and the convict lease system ensnared thousands.[50] People became fixed in a Machiavellian world of poverty and terror. Publicly committed grisly murders drew crowds who mutilated the victims' bodies for souvenirs, some of which wound up gracing the desks of governors and other public officials.

In and around Washington, D.C., a group of African American playwrights began producing lynching dramas to demonstrate the effects that mob violence had on surviving family members and communities. These works, along with a plethora of publications like the National Association of Colored People's *The Crisis*, aimed to publicize the internal community conversation on what lynching was about: an effort to erase families and communities, the centerpieces of African American ethical values and views. Usually set in the household, these works also emphasized the dignity and accomplishments of African Americans, reinforcing the truth of their full citizenship.[51]

As the carnage continued, the industrial elite cultivated and garnered a level of support from the so-called accommodationist wing of the African American community, a vocal and sometimes conservative minority associated chiefly with Booker T. Washington. These endorsers of "uplift," while not uniformly Washingtonian in outlook, had managed to enter the middle class either economically or culturally. One of their strategies to combat the counterrevolution was to instill bourgeois values into a black working class they deemed culturally deficient, a feature they felt gave counterrevolutionaries evidence to prove the inferiority of all blacks. Piety, temperance, thrift, and patriarchal gender relations were hallmarks of the uplifting mission. They stressed the need for a reformed work ethic, scorning what they saw as a lackadaisical approach to labor among the black working class, which they misidentified as derivative of "slave habits." They denounced the forms of worship of the rural working class as embarrassing to a free people— they were too public, too physically charismatic, and too democratic. They criticized the singing styles for relying on lining-out hymns and improvisational and collective participation.[52]

While espousing this "politics of respectability," many maintained social distance from workers in an effort to prove to whites that some blacks, like themselves, could in fact achieve "civilization." They thus recognized a "Negro problem" that demanded their attention. The stakes for uplifters were high, because they acted in the name of self-preservation—individuals of their class were often victims of violence and lynching. Only by leaving the legacies of slavery behind would the working class improve whites' views of all blacks. Otherwise—or so uplifters reasoned—restitution of political and civil rights and economic progress would never occur. In 1898, Presbyterian minister Francis J. Grimké decried this response to the counterrevolution. "The saddest aspect" of the political and economic reversals blacks were experiencing, he said, "is that there are members of our race . . . the intelligent, the educated—who are found condoning such offenses, justifying or excusing such a condition of things on the ground that in view of the great disparity in the condition of the two races, anything different from that could not reasonably be expected. Any Negro who takes that position is a traitor to his race, and shows that he is deficient in manhood, in true self-respect. . . . But, thank God, the cowardly, ignoble sentiment to which

I have just alluded, while it may find lodgment in the breast of a few weak-kneed, time-serving Negroes, is not the sentiment of this black race. No, and never will be."[53]

Uplifters and the working class might appear to have been polar opposites in the antiquated rendering of the Du Bois/Washington split. But uplifters, no less than the working class, were engaged in philosophical debates that had a common antebellum foundation. They were branches of the same tree that was rooted in slave ethics. Both identified labor as central to human existence, but class divisions caused uplifters and the working class to interpret that reality differently within the context of disfranchisement, segregation, and counterrevolution. The interdependence of individual and community labor, linked to a broad-based and inclusive civic activism, had been the trademark of early emancipation-era politics and derived directly from slave ethics. That imperative continued to define the strategies of both uplifters and workers.

Some uplifters may not have fully comprehended how firmly counterrevolutionaries had enforced poverty on the black working class, literally making economic marginality a requirement for survival. This inability to fully appreciate the potentially dangerous connections between economic independence, or even modest accumulation, and becoming a prime target for violence was odd for a group whose class status left them especially vulnerable to terror. But it was a calculus that the working class understood only too well. As one historian of uplifters underscored, "The problem with *racial* uplift ideology is . . . one of unconscious internalized racism" that "led African American elites to mistake the effects of oppression for causes" and caused them to castigate poor "blacks for supposed weaknesses branded into the race's moral fiber by slavery."[54] But the conflict involved here was not of the deadly variety that defined interracial life. Rather, this intraracial debate actually helped foster a wide-ranging exploration into the problems and nature of leadership that would come into flower as the civil rights movement unfolded.

* * *

The insistence that any consequential strides toward freedom had to be based upon resistance to the economic exploitation of anyone was a fundamental tenet of slave cosmology and the emancipation generation. Those who had been enslaved and then embarked upon the early years of freedom located the roots of racism in economic exploitation. Their struggles focused upon, but were not were not narrowly concerned with, their own plight. They aimed for a far broader humanitarian movement with inclusive and universal goals. Dangerous enough to warrant terror and counterrevolution, this legacy nonetheless survived and was passed along, informing those engaged in the long fight against Jim Crow. In the next chapter, we will meet some of those who transmitted that message forward.

Ethical Transmissions

Consultations with the Emancipation Generation

Evidence of the transmission of the emancipation generation's central messages—that labor was the very basis of the human condition, that its exploitation represented a serious ethical violation, and that race and racism had clear economic roots—is strong. But the process by which subsequent generations received it was varied, uneven, and contingent upon the changing historical circumstances in which they lived. The lesson became most diluted, and civil rights efforts consequently less effective, when people chose to stress white immorality or the psychology of racism at the expense of racism's economic foundations. Although never uniform in a philosophical or tactical sense, notable periods when such imbalances occurred include the early twentieth century, when uplift strategy peaked; the Red Scare years, when endorsement of the economic roots of racism brought state sanction; and to some extent the early 1960s, when the immorality-of-whites focus again achieved ascendance in some quarters. By contrast, during the Great Depression and the early 1940s, the emphasis on economic exploitation as the root of segregation was more pronounced, and the same was true of the late 1960s, particularly in urban and non-southern settings. Whenever the ethical connection between labor and morality was strongest, activists tended to have more success in the fight against Jim Crow. They also proved stronger when they incorporated vigorous grassroots efforts.

Numerous examples exist of the influence, whether strong and direct or muted, of slave-based ethics in the late nineteenth and twentieth centuries. They can be identified in memoirs and tactical decisions in the battle against Jim Crow. I do not attempt here to provide comprehensive coverage of these multiple and complex ties to the ethical slave past, but rather I assemble some examples of how that past resonated among descendants and influenced their activism. People in all walks of life displayed appreciation for the legacy of the emancipation generation, sometimes consciously, sometimes less so.

Asa Philip Randolph illustrated how one twentieth-century black labor leader consciously employed the intertwined economic and moral ethics of the emancipation generation to battle disfranchisement and segregation. Born in 1889 in Crescent City, Florida, Randolph pursued an activist career spanning the decades between the onset of segregation and the modern civil rights movement in the 1960s. Best known for his leadership of the Brotherhood of Sleeping Car Porters (BSCP), he also coedited a newspaper, the *Messenger*, and organized the 1941 March on Washington Movement that forced Franklin D. Roosevelt to address racial discrimination in military industries and to establish the Fair Employment Practices Committee. Randolph's life's work centered around labor organizing and the fight for full citizenship and equality, which he viewed as a manifestly moral and economic contest that demanded the exercise of political challenge.

Randolph's family history defined his understanding of the intellectual debt twentieth-century African Americans owed to their enslaved ancestors. Randolph's father, James Randolph, was a former slave and an AME minister whose ethical views matured during Radical Reconstruction. He instilled in his two sons an unwavering belief in equality, laid great stress on education and spirituality, and taught them black history. James Randolph was, as Asa put it, "a highly racially conscious" man who made sure his children were as well. The elder Randolph once told his son that "there isn't a single Negro . . . who has any immunity from persecution by whites" and that this fact constituted "the major problem of our life." Chafing under the expanding proscriptions of segregation in Florida, Asa Randolph moved to New York City in 1911 when he was twenty-two; studied economics, history, sociology, and theater; and, in 1916, joined the Socialist Party.

As a labor organizer, Asa Randolph believed that the fabricated moral inferiority of working-class blacks was the chief impediment to their achieving economic equality in the labor force. In his view, this problem constituted the main unsettled heritage of emancipation. As had been true for the emancipation generation, civil rights were hollow for Randolph unless they included economic opportunity for all Americans.[1] He often voiced his belief that any trade union advances, or advances in the civil rights movement in general, that resulted from his work would not benefit only blacks but involved the fate of the entire nation.

In 1963, speaking about the significance of the second March on Washington, he stressed that the "civil rights revolution is not confined to the Negro, nor is it confined to civil rights." No one could have a secure future "in a society in which six million black and white people are unemployed and millions live in poverty." The goal of the movement was nothing short of "a free democratic society" for all Americans. "It falls to us," he said of his race, "to demand full employment and to put automation at the service of human needs, not at the service of profits."[2] He insisted that the 1963 march include demands for a higher minimum wage, a federal fair employment practices bill, and a public works program for the unemployed. Two years later he suggested a $180 billion federal "Freedom Budget" that would be used to end unemployment, boost incomes, provide full medical care for all citizens, and improve public education.

Randolph acknowledged that his social democratic vision was historically and morally indebted to the emancipation generation. In the April 1926 edition of the *Messenger* Randolph editorialized that as the descendants of slaves, "We, who have come after these noble souls, who suffered and sacrificed and wept and prayed and died that their children might be delivered" were "bound in duty, in reverence and devotion, to re-dedicate our hearts and minds to the unfinished task of emancipation." He credited these beliefs to his father, who told him that

> this is what I'm trying to do for you, in order that you will not only be trying to make a dollar for yourself or become rich, but will create conditions that will help the people farther down who don't have your opportunities or . . . gifts. . . . This is the thing that we as a group must do, and you're not going to live merely by getting something here and there from people clandestinely. You've got to do things . . . that will help other people as well as yourself.

The work of the BSCP, Randolph insisted, was not restricted solely to the porters themselves: "the destiny of the entire race [was] involved," as were the sacrifices and memories of "Denmark Vesey, Nat Turner, Sojourner Truth, Harriet Tubman and that vast throng of unknown and unsung heroes whose hearts beat true to the hymn of liberty." They owed a particular debt to Frederick Douglass, "that matchless champion of human justice." An intrinsic goal of black activism and the drive for economic parity was to ensure that the emancipation generation "shall not have died in vain."[3]

An ethical connection between the slave past and the segregationist present also defined the lives of Benjamin J. Davis Jr. and Paul Robeson. Both had family and friends who either had been enslaved or their immediate ancestors had been. Davis was the attorney who defended Alabama Communist labor organizer Angelo Herndon on charges of insurrection in the 1930s, a nationally publicized case that catapulted Davis into a political career as a Harlem councilman. Robeson abandoned a career in law—a field with inherent profound racial discrimination—in favor of a life spent famously in theater, sports, and film. Robeson too sympathized with the Communist Party and was brought up before the House Un-American Activities Committee in the 1940s.

Davis reflected on his connections with the emancipation generation in his memoir. A graduate of Morehouse College, Amherst College, and Harvard University, Davis had come of age in the early twentieth century as a member of the black middle class in Dawson, Georgia, a place that "still reeked with the stench of the slave market." Former slaves constituted more than half of the town's black population, and they had vivid memories of bondage. Desperate poverty dogged the majority of these hardworking men and women, who lived segregated on one side of the Seaboard tracks in shacks that were "like the slave hovels of 1860." As the son of a newspaper editor Davis escaped these dire straits, but he still "lived in the Negro-American world," attending black schools and churches, playing with black children, and patronizing black businesses in the ghetto where everyone lived. He heard numerous accounts of slavery from his grandmother, whose physical debilities, the result of abuse she suffered while enslaved, could not be assuaged by any of the many physicians the family paid to attend her.

As a young boy, Davis and everyone he knew were estranged from whites:

The only contact I had with them was hateful. I regarded them as . . . somewhat inferior, wicked, and authoritarian. I observed them as policemen—bosses with no other mission in life but to oppress, arrest and mistreat Negroes. Such was my experience. . . . Such was the experience of every Negro kid, and it drew us together in a strong common bond—one that binds all Negroes together, irrespective of social position, age, sex, color, creed, political affiliation or economic status. Any fool could figure out that the Negroes were not responsible for this attitude, nor for the conditions that gave rise to it. . . . *the thing that sets all Negroes apart . . . is plainly the oppression of the Negroes as a people.*[4]

Davis made these observations long after his experience in Herndon's cause célèbre and after he became a Communist himself, which led to his imprisonment from 1949 to 1954 for violation of the Smith Act of 1940, which criminalized sedition, the "crime" of which Davis was convicted. It was during this five-year incarceration that he penned his memoir. Despite his firm commitment to the class struggle movement, Davis readily recognized the existence of a "worldview" of oppression that united black people of vastly different backgrounds, even across class boundaries, and he located its origins in the times of slavery.

Paul Robeson identified his principles as a gift from people he knew who had been enslaved, none more so than his father, William Robeson. Paul possessed a particularly acute appreciation for the foundational influence of slave—and African—cultures on modern African American ones.[5] As a boy, Robeson delivered a speech at a reunion of the Bustill family, his maternal line. By the time he he wrote his autobiography in 1958, he had forgotten what he said in the speech, but he connected the title, "Loyalty to Convictions," to "the text of my father's life—loyalty to one's convictions. Unbending. Despite anything. From my youngest days I was imbued with that concept. This bedrock idea of integrity was taught by Reverend Robeson to his children not so much by preachment (for by nature Pop was restrained of speech, often silent at home, and among us Robesons the deepest feelings are largely unexpressed in words) but, rather, by the daily example of his life and work."[6] In his Rutgers University commencement speech, Robeson again revealed the influence of his father:

We of the less favored race realize that our future lies in our hands. On ourselves alone will depend the preservation of our liberties and the transmission of them in their integrity to those who will come after us. . . . We know that neither institutions nor friends can make a race stand unless it has strength in its own foundation; that races like individuals must stand or fall by their own merit, that to fully succeed they must practice the virtues of self-reliance, self-respect, industry, perseverance, and economy.[7]

Robeson's father began life enslaved in Martin County, North Carolina, in 1845 and escaped in 1860. By the end of the century he was a Presbyterian pastor in Princeton, New Jersey, where Robeson was reared. Robeson remembered Princeton as "spiritually located in Dixie" partly because of its large southern matriculant population, but especially because of its concentrated white wealth and corresponding black poverty. "Like the South to which its heart belonged, Princeton's controlling mind was in Wall Street. Bourbon and Banker were one in Princeton, and there the decaying smell of the plantation Big House was blended with the crisper smell of the Countinghouse. The theology was Calvin: the religion—cash."[8] Here Robeson tapped that major theme in African American labor ethics rooted in slavery: the crime of greed that had wreaked such havoc among generations of African Americans. "Hard-working people, and poor, most of them, in worldly goods," Robeson said of the community, "but how rich in compassion! How filled with the goodness of humanity and the spiritual steel forged by centuries of oppression!"[9]

Robeson's father possessed an unshakable belief in equality he acquired in slavery. Forced to appeal regularly to wealthy Princetonian whites in search of funds for his community, William Robeson never abandoned his dignity. He approached, among others, political scientist Woodrow Wilson, then the president of Princeton, who praised the 1915 Lost Cause film *Birth of a Nation* as "history written with lightning"; subsequently, as president of the United States, Wilson distinguished himself as the architect of federal-level segregation. "He who comes hat-in-hand is expected to bow and bend, and so I marvel that there was no hint of servility in my father's make-up," Robeson reflected. "Just as in youth he had refused to remain a slave, so in all the years of his manhood he disdained to be an Uncle Tom.

From him we learned, and never doubted it, that the Negro was in every way the equal of the white man. And we fiercely resolved to prove it."[10]

But not even the strong example of his father spared Paul Robeson from events and experiences that dated more directly to the counterrevolution against emancipation and the onset of Jim Crow. "From an early age," he reported, "I had come to accept and follow a certain protective tactic of Negro life in America" that he did not fully shed for years. This strategy required that "even while demonstrating that he is really an equal (and, strangely, the proof must be *superior* performance!) the Negro must never appear to be challenging white superiority"—if, that is, he chose to keep body and soul together. "Climb up if you can—but don't act 'uppity.' Always show that you are *grateful*. (Even if what you have gained has been wrested from unwilling powers, be sure to be grateful lest 'they' take it all away.)" Most importantly, "*do nothing to give them cause to fear you*, for then the oppressing hand, which might at times ease up a little, will surely become a fist to knock you down again!"[11] Thus, "When it was said (and it was said many times) that Paul Robeson had shown himself to be ungrateful to the good white folks of America who had given him wealth and fame, and that he had had nothing to complain about, the statement was bound to rub Negroes the wrong way." All blacks knew "that nothing is ever 'given' to us, and *they know that human dignity cannot be measured in dollars and cents.*"[12]

The themes embedded in these two memoirs were those of men who had not been enslaved, were not poor, and took class analysis seriously. Davis and Robeson nonetheless felt a deep camaraderie with the African American poor and identified with them on the basis of slavery and, more viscerally, segregation. Their reminiscences thus blended deeply dyed beliefs in equality, justice, and hard work—beliefs emanating from slavery—seasoned with angry bitterness at what the counterrevolution had wrought. Their lives demonstrated how consciously the lessons of the emancipation generation lived within them.

Others chose to stress related components of slave cosmology as they wrestled with Jim Crow. Just as Frederick Douglass demonstrated how it had taken time to instill slaveholding habits in masters and mistresses, so too did Robert Russa Moton believe that it would require time, and rather an abundance of it, to disabuse people of racist behaviors. Moton, successor to Booker T. Washington at Tuskegee University, believed the toll slavery took on the character of former slaveholders continued to resonate with their descendants in the 1920s. Moton learned about bondage from his formerly enslaved father, mother, and grandmother, and concluded "that somehow—in spite of the hardships and oppression which they suffered . . . the Negro, when all is summed up dispassionately, has come through the ordeal with much to his credit, and with a great many advantages over his condition when he entered the relationship. The white man, on the other hand, has reaped certain disadvantages from which the whole country still suffers and from which it will probably take several generations to recover completely."[13]

One of the strongest emancipation-era tenets to survive in subsequent generations was the insistence on the right to self-defense as distinct from violence, a term that continued to describe white behavior, in many respects as never before. The durability of this widespread and elemental embrace of self-defense cannot be overemphasized. It was a focal point of black ideology that survived the nadir easily.

In 1892, editor and anti-lynching activist Ida B. Wells bought a gun after three of her friends, economically independent grocers, were lynched in Memphis, Tennessee, at the behest of rival white grocers and local law enforcement. Her own life was endangered because she wrote an editorial in the Memphis *Free Speech* exposing the lynchers and the economic causes of the violence. Fleeing to Chicago for her life, Wells perused the phenomenon of lynching, gathering statistics and details of individual attacks, which she published later that year in *Southern Horrors: Lynch Law in All Its Phases*. "Of the many inhuman outrages of this present year," Wells observed, "the only case where the proposed lynching did not occur, was where the men armed themselves . . . and prevented it. The only times an Afro-American who was assaulted got away has been when he had a gun and used it in self-defense. The lesson this teaches . . . is that a Winchester rifle should have a place of honor in every black home, and it should be used for that protection which the law refuses to give. When the white man *who is always the aggressor* knows he runs as great a risk of biting the dust every time his Afro-American victim does, he would have a greater respect for Afro-American life."[14]

People took such advice seriously. When W.E.B. Du Bois found himself, his wife, and his daughter in the middle of the 1906 Atlanta riot that left dozens of blacks dead, he too "bought a Winchester double-barreled shotgun and two dozen rounds of shells filled with buckshot. If a white mob had stepped on the campus where I lived I would without hesitation have sprayed their guts over the grass."[15] Ned Cobb, the freeborn son of a slave, spent much of his life trying to achieve economic independence as a sharecropper, renter, and landowner. Cobb knew the importance of being armed at all times in Alabama in the late nineteenth and early twentieth centuries. He owned three breech-loaders, one given to him by his mother-in-law, a bequest of her late husband. Cobb also had a .32 Smith and Wesson pistol that was confiscated in the aftermath of a shootout against the Sharecroppers Union. Somehow one of his relatives managed to find and hide the gun, and years later, after Cobb's release from prison, his wife returned it. "I been havin that gun more than fifty long years," Cobb told his interviewer.[16]

Robert Williams, active in the civil rights movement in North Carolina in the 1950s and early '60s, was well known for his espousal of what he called armed self-reliance. Williams, like most, was an eclectic activist who employed a wide array of tactics, including both direct action and launching a local National Association for the Advancement of Colored People (NAACP) branch that drew members from the working class in Monroe, his hometown. Williams was close to his ex-slave grandmother, Ellen Isabel Williams. Her deceased husband Sikes Williams, also formerly enslaved, had been a Republican Party activist who experienced the brutal 1898 Wilmington Massacre that ended biracial democratic politics in the city. Before Ellen Williams died, she gave her grandson her husband's rifle, which he had used in self-defense against terrorists of an earlier day. The rifle remained above Williams's desk until his death.[17]

Civil rights workers found the use of self-defense ubiquitous in Mississippi in the early 1960s. Student Nonviolent Coordinating Committee (SNCC) activist Bob Moses observed, "Self-defense is so deeply engrained in rural southern America that we as a small group can't affect it. It's not contradictory for a farmer to say he's nonviolent and also to pledge to shoot a marauder's head off."[18] Moses initially may have thought that he was witness to a contradiction, but in fact he was seeing the distinction between violence and self-defense in action.

We can identify a more unconscious, perhaps less appreciative, response to emancipation-era labor ethics in the reminiscences of Ned Cobb, who structured his autobiography largely around his proud history as an industrious worker. Cobb believed that work was compulsory, honorable, and divinely ordained. He had a tense and often explosive relationship with his ex-slave father, Hayes Cobb. Most of the acrimony between them was the result of what Ned Cobb regarded as his father's indolence. Cobb condemned Hayes Cobb's choice of seasonal and itinerant labor as slavery's poison. Hayes Cobb's stints in public works, digging ditches, and clearing swamplands and forests had brought him "good money." The son sympathized with his father's repeated victimization at the hands of powerful whites who robbed him of everything he had, attacks that consistently occurred when Hayes Cobb had managed to amass property. Ned Cobb understood that his father believed, with good reason, "that it weren't no use in climbin too fast; weren't no use in climbin slow, neither, if they was goin to take everything you worked for when you got too high." He fully appreciated his father's fear of white violence and had no hesitation about the use of self-defense. But Hayes Cobb also took long sojourns from work, hired his young son out and kept his wages, and beat his son and his wife—actions Ned Cobb traced directly to slavery. Cobb believed that his father, though free, "in his acts . . . was a slave. Didn't look ahead to profit hisself in nothing that he done. . . . Anything a man do in a slum way and don't care way, I just lap it right back on slavery time days. It's that old back yonder 'ism.'"[19]

Ned Cobb was proud of the fact that he "never tried to beat nobody out of nothing since I been in this world" in contrast to the "whole class of people" who "beat the other class of people out of what they has." Although he did not recognize it, his critique of such behavior built on the philosophy of slave ancestors: "O, it's plain: if every man thoroughly got his rights, there wouldn't be so many rich people in the world—I spied that a long time ago." He had "looked deep in that angle" and concluded that greed derived directly from the exploitation of the "poor little farmers and other laboring men. O, it's desperately wrong." Cobb professed no desire for riches because "money can be detrimental to your soul," and eschewed life as "a big man, ownin this, that, and the other." But neither did he settle for dependency. Cobb's desire "to boss my own affairs" resonated with the slave and freed communities' stress on self-reliance. Cobb wanted to "help myself, regardless to what I accumulated and regardless to what I lost. I wanted to have more privileges, back myself up without havin to beg my way."[20]

After an attack on the Alabama Sharecroppers Union, a communist-affiliated organization of which he was a member, Cobb was imprisoned for labor activism in the 1930s. After his release, he resumed work with such zeal that an acquaintance accused him of worshipping property. Intensely insulted, Cobb misinterpreted the charge as a degrading legacy of slavery that discouraged ambition, rather than as a tenet that bondspeople themselves had constructed, a wariness of overly acquisitive, individualistic behavior. And yet Cobb's views too were consistent with slave ethics in that they reflected a strong sense of self-reliance and pride in one's ability to work. Cobb respected Booker T. Washington's economic formulas, which stressed work and property accumulation as keys to a better future. But he condemned the Wizard of Tuskegee for the very offense of which his acquaintance accused him: valuing personal gain above all else, particularly when it came at the expense of others. Those who refused to work, even under exploitative conditions—as Cobb believed had been the case for his father—were irresponsible. Those who neglected labor in favor of bodily security likewise were guilty of weakness. It was hard to know which was worse: those who grew fat on the labor of others, or incorrigible idlers. But Cobb nonetheless believed, as did hosts of others before and after him, that ill-gotten wealth and greed were ethical crimes, damaging to the soul and the commonweal. Although he would not have credited slave ethics on these points, Cobb's moral philosophy was firmly situated in the recognition that labor was a central feature of the human condition.

These themes of greed and its reminders of slavery appeared often in twentieth-century African American letters, many of them critiques of unfettered capitalism grounded in the lessons of enslavement.[21] Zora Neale Hurston was one writer who examined materialism's impact on people's humanity and quality of life. Hurston's 1937 novel *Their Eyes Were Watching God*, set in post-emancipation Florida, detailed the ruin that an undisciplined chase after property and status brought on protagonist Janie's first two husbands, Logan Killicks and Jody Stark, and her ex-slave grandmother, Nanny. The satisfaction Janie found in her third marriage to Tea Cake Woods derived largely from the fact that Woods's itinerant labor and relative indifference to material possessions fostered an exhilaration for life that far outdid the landowning Killicks, the ambitious Mayor Stark, or the desperately overworked and sexually abused Nanny. Nanny arranged Janie's union with Killicks in the belief that Killicks's sixty acres would spare Janie the exploitation Nanny had known. But when Killicks, and subsequently Stark, rendered Janie hostage to property if not property herself, Janie turned her hatred of equating possessions with happiness on Nanny, who she felt had a narrow vision of life and work wrought by enslavement.

> She was borned in slavery times when folks, dat is black folks, didn't sit down anytime dey felt lak it. So sittin' on porches lak de white madam looked lak uh mighty fine thing tuh her. Dat's whut she wanted for me—don't keer whut it cost. Git up on uh high chair and sit dere. She didn't have time tuh think whut tuh do after you got up on de stool uh do nothin.' De object wuz tuh git dere. So Ah got up on de high stool lak she told me, but . . . Ah done nearly languished tuh death up dere. Ah felt like de world wuz cryin' extry and Ah ain't read de common news yet.[22]

Hurston, a child of the Great Migration born in segregated Florida, used Janie's story in part as an evaluation of the relationships among ethics, acquisitiveness, and power—and by extension, slavery and its legacy for freedom. Enslavement had on the one hand generated a strong incentive to work and accumulate in the name of economic independence. But dangers to the soul lurked in that imperative if it was taken too far. Those who placed excessive emphasis on wealth and power had missed a central message from slave ancestors or—as Nanny, Killicks, and Stark had done—gone overboard in a single-minded search for property and status.

We can also see the emancipation-era stress on the law as a tool of liberation becoming greatly elaborated in the early and mid-twentieth century. Probably nowhere did this ethical branch of the tree of freedom reach greater development than in the NAACP, founded in 1909. Motivated by the legal and judicial reversals or the failures to enforce laws that had protected freedpeople—the Fourteenth and Fifteenth Amendments, the Civil Rights Act of 1875, and the 1896 Supreme Court decision in *Plessy v. Ferguson* that gave sanction to disfranchisement and segregation, for example—NAACP founders created a legal division in the organization that would come to be its hallmark. Best known for advancing the 1954 *Brown v. Topeka Board of Education* case through the Supreme Court, NAACP lawyers won numerous other important legal challenges to Jim Crow between the 1910s and 1954. Charles Hamilton Houston, the architect of *Brown* and an early member of the NAACP, educated a cadre of lawyers at Howard University, insisting that they envision the law as a tool of public interest capable of shifting ethical values: "a lawyer's either a social engineer or . . . a parasite on society," he often said.[23] In striking contrast, traditional segregation-era jurisprudence among whites held that law lacked any power whatsoever to deal with human prejudice and indeed was not meant to function in that way. Consequently, the racism of individuals or private parties fell beyond the reach of the bench. In a 1911 speech entitled "The Courts and the Negro," writer Charles Chesnutt paraphrased this legal logic as it had appeared in the 1896 *Plessy v. Ferguson* case. The Fourteenth Amendment, the court declared,

> could not have been intended to abolish distinctions based upon color or to enforce social, as distinguished from political, equality, or a commingling of the two races upon terms unsatisfactory to either. If the two races are to meet on terms of social equality, it must be the result of natural affinities, a mutual appreciation of each other's merits and a voluntary consent of individuals. When the government, therefore, has secured for each of its citizens equal rights before the law and equal opportunities for improvement and progress, it has accomplished the end for which it was organized, and performed all the functions respecting social advantages with which it is endowed. Legislation is powerless to eradicate racial instincts or to abolish distinctions based upon physical differences. If the civil and political rights of both races be equal, one cannot be inferior to the other civilly or politically. If one race be inferior to the other socially, the Constitution of the United States cannot put them upon the same place.[24]

The irony of this argument was not lost on Chesnutt nor on many other African Americans: even as the court maintained that law could not influence human behavior, its decision accomplished just such ends by establishing the judicial imprimatur for the counterrevolution against emancipation.

The Great Depression, with its particularly destructive consequences for African Americans, encouraged a refocusing on the economic roots of race and a renewed investigation into how Reconstruction ancestors had confronted economic inequality. The Southern Negro Youth Congress (SNYC), active between 1936 and the late 1940s, and its adult affiliate, the National Negro Congress (NNC), took pains to remind audiences of the significance of their emancipation-era ethical roots, placing great stress on economic exploitation as the root of racism. NNC and SNYC members consciously shared philosophical and activist ground with their Reconstruction ancestors, whose contributions to American democracy they routinely celebrated. They challenged the dominant Lost Cause interpretation of the Civil War, emancipation, and Reconstruction, emphasized the political power of African American cultural and artistic awareness, engaged in electoral politics, and stressed race as a social and therefore political construction.[25]

The SNYC-sponsored Leadership Training Conference, held in South Carolina in 1946, taught public speaking, interacting with the press, and organizing. A pivotal conference, the Columbia Youth Legislature, followed in October. More than eight hundred southern delegates defined activism in an international context and heard W.E.B. Du Bois, Adam Clayton Powell Jr., and Paul Robeson applaud and guide their work. Stressing the legacy of Radical Reconstruction, particularly its interracial efforts and focus on labor, they hung portraits of emancipation-era blacks elected to federal office on the walls of the auditorium. Howard Fast—the author of the 1944 novel *Freedom Road*, which told the story of a black Union army veteran's political efforts and identified terrorism as the cause of Reconstruction's demise—told delegates that the counterrevolution against democracy and economic justice could be overturned by economically and grassroots-oriented activists like those in the SNYC.[26]

Ella Baker was similarly well versed in Reconstruction history and its economic legacies. Baker began her activist career in New York during the Depression, when she joined consumer movements, directed publicity for the NNC, and taught in the WPA. She became one of the most pivotal grassroots organizers of the twentieth century. A member of the NAACP and the Union League, she later helped organize Martin Luther King Jr.'s Southern Christian Leadership Conference (SCLC) in 1957 and, more significantly, the SNCC in 1960, easily the most democratic grassroots organization of all in the early part of the decade. Baker's recognition and appreciation of her enslaved grandparents and her mother, born in freedom, as the inspiration for her own grassroots activism is well known. Like her emancipation-era ancestors, Baker understood activism as a confrontation with economic injustice whose roots were in slavery. She also believed that only through a successful battle with economic exploitation could the nation as a whole experience the equality it so often touted.

Baker was born in 1903 in Norfolk, Virginia, and spent much of her childhood in Littleton, North Carolina, where her grandmother Josephine Elizabeth Ross told her about the abuses she endured in slavery and how she had defied them. The young Ella thus was imbued early on with a powerful sense of the necessity of self-defense and militant resistance. Baker's grandfather, Mitchell Ross, bought fifty acres of land in North Carolina in 1888, in partnership with several relatives. The acquisition of land enabled the Rosses to live a materially comfortable life, and Mitchell Ross later gave some of his land for the construction of a school for black children. Ross was a preacher who participated in Reconstruction politics, as fierce a defender of equality as he was an outspoken opponent of injustice and ardent supporter of the local black community, embracing self-help, mutual assistance, and self-defense. The young Baker was steeped, as her biographer stressed, in a "cooperative ethos" that embraced "groups of individuals banding together around shared interests and promoting a sense of reciprocal obligation, not of individualism and competition." Baker described this community as functioning along socialist principles, although no one at the time used that word.[27]

While Baker never expressed doubts about blacks' ability to successfully challenge Jim Crow America, others had given up hope for an egalitarian democracy in American institutional life. Their reservations can be traced to the southern emigration movement that emerged between the 1880s—the end of Reconstruction and the onset of the counterrevolution—and the Great Migration of the World War I decade. Indeed, the Great Migration in no small measure was grounded in the argument that a decent life was impossible for African Americans in the former Confederacy, where disfranchisement, segregation, and terror had taken a firm hold. Many who embraced emigration lacked the means to accomplish that end, and prior to the early twentieth century, many migrated within the South, often from rural to urban areas, in search of some measure of safety and escape from deteriorating conditions on farms and plantations. After World War I opened up the possibility to leave the South, about 400,000 promptly chose that option, and migration continued until after World War II.[28]

The first large wave of southern migrants in the 1910s contained substantial numbers of people who supported Jamaican emigrant Marcus Garvey's Universal Negro Improvement Association (UNIA).[29] Garvey was an avid entrepreneur who recommended hard work, capitalism, and Washingtonian materialism to his working-class and poor followers. "There is no force like success," he told readers of his newspaper *The Negro World*, "and that is why the individual makes all efforts to surround himself throughout life with the evidence of it." Yet individual accomplishment was necessary not solely for the good of the individual, but because success collectively accrued to the good of the race.[30] Garvey opened groceries and restaurants and encouraged the establishment of businesses that catered to the black community. He established the African Communities League to facilitate such business startups, and later, the Negro Factories Corporation to oversee the UNIA's burgeoning business interests. Garvey's most famous endeavor was the Black Star Line steamship company, one of whose professed aims was to take emigrants to Africa, but which achieved its greatest success in fostering African American business acumen and self-confidence.[31]

Racial pride was a key ingredient of Garveyism, and Garvey consciously nurtured this culturally nationalistic component of his movement through his famously elaborate Harlem parades; the development of the red, black, and green UNIA flag; and his own imperial posturing. He typically appeared in military garb carrying a sword and wearing an elaborately plumed hat. Garvey believed that slavery and segregation had produced generations who had become inured to racial submission. He thus stressed African American cultural unity and solidarity not only in the United States but throughout the pan-African world.[32]

The most famous figure, though hardly the only one, to emerge from this philosophical and historical context was Malcolm X. As a Nation of Islam minister in the 1950s and early 1960s, and then chiefly as a political activist, Malcolm X, much as David Walker had done in the early nineteenth century and Garvey had in the early twentieth, chided African Americans for succumbing to oppression and a belief in their own inferiority and inability to resist. In the mid-1950s, on Garveyist bookstore owner Lewis Micheaux's street platform in Harlem, Malcolm repeatedly challenged his audience to consider these issues. He encountered audiences already primed by Micheaux and a host of other northern nationalist groups. Micheaux had told them, "I've taught nationalism and that means that I want to go out of this white man's country because integration will never happen. You'll never, as long as you live, integrate into the white man's system."[33] Malcolm charismatically amplified such northern and urban segregation-era themes.

> Who taught you to hate the color of your skin? Who taught you to hate the texture of your hair? Who taught you to hate the shape of your nose and the shape of your lips? Who taught you to hate yourself from the top of your head to the soles of your feet? Who taught you to hate your own kind? Who taught you to hate the race that you belong to so much so that you don't want to be around each other? You know. Before you come asking Mr. Muhammad does he teach hate, you should ask yourself who taught you to hate being what God made you.[34]

Malcolm also insisted that African Americans be forthright about their experiences in Jim Crow America.

> And I, for one, as a Muslim believe that the white man is intelligent enough. If he were made to realize how black people really feel and how fed up we are without that old compromising sweet talk—why you're the one who make it hard for yourself. The white man believes you when you go to him with that old sweet talk, 'cause you've been sweet-talking him ever since he brought you here. Stop sweet-talking him. *Tell him how you feel. Tell him how—what kind of hell you've been catching* and let him know that if . . . he's not ready to clean his house up, he shouldn't have a house. It should catch on fire and burn down.[35]

Malcolm X's parents, Earl and Louise Little, were both fervent UNIA supporters. Born in 1890 at the outset of the counterrevolution, Earl Little escaped Georgia's fierce racial violence by migrating first to Philadelphia, then to New York and Montreal. In Canada he met Louise Norton at Garvey events; after the couple wed, they moved to Philadelphia, a hotbed of

Garveyism, in 1918. In 1920, the UNIA sent the Littles as Garveyite ambassadors to Omaha, Nebraska, where a vibrant and public Ku Klux Klan made black life as precarious as it had been in the South. After Garvey's conviction for mail fraud in 1923, the couple and their six children—Malcolm being the youngest at the time—lived briefly in Milwaukee, Wisconsin, and Chicago, Illinois, before settling in Lansing, Michigan, where Malcolm was reared with seven brothers and sisters. Malcolm and his siblings remembered their father during these years as fiercely independent, authoritarian, and politically resolute.[36]

Earl Little likely came to know about Garveyism while in Georgia; Louise Little was Grenadan and as a Caribbean native had known of Garvey's work for some time. The two married largely on the basis of their shared political views. In Lansing, Louise became editor of the local *Negro World*, while Earl farmed and often took Garvey's message into local churches. In 1931, forty-one-year-old Earl Little was murdered, probably for his political activities but also because he was an economically independent farmer—that is, he fit the profile of the typical lynching victim.[37]

As a young hustler in Boston and New York, Malcolm grew disconnected from his strong Garveyist upbringing. But after his conversion to the Nation of Islam, he returned to the political roots of his childhood and his parents. Racial pride and racial solidarity became his chief and most recognizable political themes. His pan-Africanism was also a prominent attribute, particularly after his break with the Nation in 1963. Malcolm viewed African Americans as a group possessed of distinct cultural, psychological, social, and political views, whose solidarity was rooted in their collective history of slavery and segregation. Although chiefly remembered as a separatist nationalist, Malcolm's final self-reinvention before his assassination in 1965 turned him into an advocate for enfranchisement and the exercise of political muscle, a believer in the possibility of racial justice in the United States, and "a radical humanist whose most telling quality was gentleness."[38] He never failed to stress the duty of African Americans to defend themselves against all attacks on their right to self-determination, and he was a strong advocate of redistribution of wealth through reparations. Rather than being an aberration in African American thought and ethics, Malcolm X's intellectual and political journey traced the familiar footsteps of his ancestors and his contemporaries.

Asa Philip Randolph, Ida B. Wells-Barnett, W.E.B. Du Bois, Robert Russa Moton, Marcus Garvey, Benjamin J. Davis Jr., Paul Robeson, Ned Cobb, Robert Williams, Bob Moses, Zora Neale Hurston, Charles Hamilton Houston, members of the NNC and the SNYC, Ella Baker, and Malcolm X represented the rich diversity of African American historical backgrounds and beliefs. Yet they should not be regarded as oppositional, as the strained comparison between Malcolm X and Martin Luther King Jr. often encourages. This examination of just a few of the many people active in trying to bring the revolution of Reconstruction to fruition should illuminate how their beliefs overlapped on the central point of the emancipation generation: the centrality of labor to human existence and a stress on the economic roots of race and racism. In the twenty-first century, yet other groups continue to press for economic justice using the experiences and wisdoms of those who preceded them. Their struggle for redress and reparations will be the subject of the final chapter.

7

Ethical Legacies for the Twenty-First Century

Apologies, Regrets, Therapy, and Reparations

Any successful conclusion to the recent uptick in demands for reparations for slavery and segregation depends on an accurate understanding of what those abuses were about. Historian John Hope Franklin often insisted, "If the house is to be set in order, one cannot begin with the present. He must begin with the past."[1] How might we best use the long history of reparations efforts to bolster recent reparations demands and establish greater economic equality by acting on the blueprints that the emancipation generation and their descendants laid down? This book has in part been an effort to link together some of these pasts, and to explore the worldview out of which they grew, specifically highlighting an ethos rooted in slave labor that put a premium on not just political but economic democracy. The broad democratic vision of the emancipation generation has yet to reach fruition, but it continues to hold salience for the current reparations debates at both national and global levels.

In many respects, contemporary debates swirl around the very problems that animated black thought and action in the emancipation era. Today, heated arguments revolve around the form proper redress should take, debates the emancipation generation would find familiar. Some call for individual payments based on the value of lost labor and stunted wealth accumulation. A therapeutic model underscores the need for a keener historical consciousness about the many profound legacies slavery left for the present, largely in the truth and reconciliation tradition. Others support policies designed to launch a wholesale, class-based attack on economic and political inequality, perhaps funded from a national trust or superfund.[2] This last and most visionary approach for a thorough democratic housecleaning emanates from principles the emancipation generation articulated. They knew that setting matters right for freedpeople could not occur without a national redemption, which required establishing economic as well as political equality. They made substantial inroads on political equity, at least for a time, but economic justice has loomed as a far more difficult quest against formidable opponents.

*　*　*

The history of reparations stretches back at least to the revolutionary era. In Boston, Massachusetts, in 1783, Belinda, a freedwoman around the age of eighty, sued her former owner, loyalist Isaac Royall, for compensation for a near-lifetime of slavery. Belinda's petition to the state legislature justified the suit on the basis of labor spent to swell Royall's pockets. When the revolution forced Royall to flee to England, Belinda sued his estate for an annual allowance for herself and her invalid daughter. The suit argued that Belinda had been "denied one morsel of that immense wealth, a part whereof hath been accumulated by her own industry and the whole augmented by her servitude." Hers was not the first such effort. Beginning at least in 1770, petitions for reparations appeared regularly before Massachusetts legislators, often successfully, though enforcement proved lax. The legislators granted Belinda's petition, for example, but the estate made only one of the annual pension payments the Commonwealth mandated.[3]

Slaves themselves were the original reparationists, in that they defined appropriating slaveholder property as not robbery, but "taking," morally justified behavior based upon the theft of their labor. Frederick Law Olmsted documented this point in the 1850s as he traveled through Virginia. It was "a fixed point of the negro system of ethics," he reported, "that the result of labour belongs of right to the labourer, and on this ground, even the religious feel justified in using 'massa's' property for their own temporal benefit. This they term 'taking' . . . though 'stealing,' or taking from another than their master, and particularly from one another" was disreputable.[4] Some elevated such restitution to a fine art. In July 1841, the Madison Henderson Gang—Madison Henderson, James Seward, Amos Warrick, and Charles Brown—were hanged in St. Louis, Missouri, for the murder of two bank clerks in the course of a failed robbery. Henderson was a fugitive, and Warrick a free man who had been kidnapped into slavery. Seward and Brown were freeborn but militant egalitarians who bristled under racial injustices. Seward, a well-educated acquaintance of abolitionist Gerrit Smith, felt he was perfectly justified to "cheat the world as much as possible" and to "support myself in an easy life." The four had reputations for gener-osity in black communities, spending freely on pleasure and recreation. The gang targeted "bankers, shopkeepers, plantation owners, and merchants" and were experienced river workers on the Mississippi between St. Louis and New Orleans. They aided fugitives, traded illegally, and killed when they had to. They were proud of their intelligence and cleverness. While the flamboyant Henderson Gang might seem unusual, their historian argues that they were representative of a widespread African American river cul-ture that regularly preyed on elites. After their execution, city officials had the men's heads mounted on poles, testimony to the widespread nature of the phenomenon.[5]

More formal calls for redress abounded during the nineteenth century. David Walker argued in 1829 that African Americans should demand that whites "raise us from the condition of brutes to that of respectable men, and . . . make a national acknowledgment to us for the wrongs they have inflicted on us."[6] Free black Hosea Easton argued in *Treatise on the Intel-lectual Character and Civil and Political Condition of the Colored People* (1837) that the state should issue reparations to northern blacks who had gone through gradual emancipation. "The emancipated must be placed back where slavery found them," Easton argued, "and restore to them all that slavery has taken away. Merely to cease beating the colored people, and leave them in their gore, and call it emancipation, is nonsense. Nothing short of an entire reversal of the slave system in theory and practice—in general and in particular—will ever accomplish the work of redeeming the colored people of this country from their present condition." Likening slav-ery to thievery, Easton stressed "the work of emancipation is not complete when it only cuts off some of the most prominent limbs of slavery, such as destroying the despotic power of the master, and the laying by of the cow-hide." Emancipation without compensation left behind people who were "half dead, without proscribing any healing remedy for the bruises and wounds received by their maltreatment."[7]

Antebellum and emancipation-era reparationists had some white allies.

Timothy Dwight, Yale University's president, addressed the contentious matter of collective historical responsibility. "It is in vain to alledge [sic]," he argued in 1810, "that *our ancestors* brought them hither, and not we. . . . We inherit our ample patrimony with all its incumbrances [sic]; and are bound to pay the debts of our ancestors. *This* debt, particularly, we are bound to discharge: and when the righteous Judge of the Universe comes to reckon with his servants, he will rigidly exact the payment at our hands. To give them liberty, and stop here, is to entail upon them a curse."[8]

Solomon Northup, a free New Yorker kidnapped in 1841 and sold to southern Louisiana, where he spent twelve years enslaved before he escaped, subsequently became involved in the first attempt to obtain reparations from the federal government. Arguing that both he and his family had suffered economically during his enslavement, Northup, with the support of abolitionists Frederick Douglass and New York congressman Gerrit Smith, petitioned Congress directly for recompense. A more widespread campaign subsequently developed. Although Congress tabled all of these petitions, Northup's efforts inspired later attempts, some of them by whites, to institute federal government redress for enslavement.[9]

Numerous examples exist of people who compensated manumitted slaves with land, money, and supplies, and some religious and abolitionist groups supported material redress for the emancipated. During the Civil War and Reconstruction, Representatives Thaddeus Stevens of Pennsylvania and Charles Sumner of Massachusetts were vocal proponents of land redistribution. Stevens warned the House of Representatives about the long-term social fallout should House Resolution (HR) 29, the 1867 Slave Reparation Bill, fail to pass. He argued that economic independence through landholding would benefit not only freedpeople, but whites as well because redistribution would reinvigorate the southern economy. When Russian serfs were emancipated, the czar of Russia, Stevens noted, "did not for a moment entertain the foolish idea of depriving his empire of their labor or of robbing them of their rights. He ordered their former owners to make some compensation for their unrequited toil by conveying to them the very houses in which they lived and a portion of the land which they had tilled." Stevens also cited the biblical injunction that required Egyptians to compensate Jews after Moses led them to freedom. "There was no blasphemer then to question God's ... decree of confiscation. ... If we refuse to extend to this downtrodden and oppressed race the rights which Heaven decreed them, and the remuneration which they have earned through long years of hopeless oppression, how can we hope to escape still further punishment if God is just and omnipotent?"[10] Even Union general William T. Sherman, no friend of former slaves, established a plan to set aside lands from Georgia to Florida for black settlement, although no detailed plan for ultimate ownership appeared in Sherman's recommendations. Some consider the educational efforts of the Freedmen's Bureau, easily its most positive, if temporary, endeavor, to have been a form of reparations.[11]

After Reconstruction and on into the twentieth century, a wide array of others, including Ida B. Wells, Bishop Henry M. Turner, W.E.B. Du Bois, T. Thomas Fortune, Monroe Trotter, and Marcus Garvey carried the torch forward. Fortune, for example, argued in 1886 that "the crime of holding property in man" meant that whites were "responsible to the African people of this country for the principal and compound interest thereupon of the wages of each such slave, or his descendant, for at least the time covered by the adoption of the Federal Constitution (1787) and the manumission of the slave (1865); and that, until such principal and interest are paid to the last penny the American white man should cease to reproach us because of our poverty, ignorance, or mendacity. What we are the white man made us. He should not disclaim his workmanship."[12]

In 1898, Callie House, a former slave from Tennessee and a laundress, became the leader of the National Ex-Slave Mutual Relief, Bounty, and Pension Society, which had been founded in 1896. The society sought compensation chiefly for desperately poor ex-slaves, and House endured federal harassment for years prior to being convicted of mail fraud. She was imprisoned for a year in Missouri.[13] Between 1901 and 1907, the National Industrial Council, organized by Stanley P. Mitchell of Dallas, Texas, worked to establish a congressional ex-slave pension fund. Mitchell met with President Theodore Roosevelt and, like House, was threatened with mail fraud.[14] In the 1930s, Paul Robeson, Mary McLeod Bethune, and lawyer William Patterson announced their support for reparations. In the 1950s and '60s, A. Philip Randolph, Queen Mother Audley Moore, Malcolm X, Martin Luther King Jr., Huey Newton, and Stokely Carmichael made their cases for reparations. In 1969, former SNCC executive director James Forman interrupted services at New York's Riverside Church to issue his Black Manifesto, a $500 million reparations plan to be financed by white Christian and Jewish congregations. Forman organized the National Black Economic Development Conference to coordinate this effort. His demands focused on educational and labor strategies, as well as a southern land bank and a plan for cooperative businesses in the United States and Africa. "We seek," Forman underscored, "legitimate and modest reparations for our role in developing the industrial base of the western world through our slave labor."[15] Three years later, 8,000 people attended the National Black Political Convention held in Gary, Indiana, a municipality that had recently elected Richard Hatcher as the first black mayor of a large city. The convention called for the establishment of nationwide health centers, national health insurance, the elimination of capital punishment, an urban homestead act, guaranteed minimum wages and annual incomes, a black United Fund, and enforcement of anti-trust legislation.[16]

Today, the leading organization in the reparations movement is the National Coalition of Blacks for Reparations in America (N'COBRA), founded by Imari Obadele in 1988. Utilizing a pan-Africanist approach, N'COBRA supports a variety of means of redress.

> Reparations can be in as many forms as necessary to equitably (fairly) address the many forms of injury caused by chattel slavery and its continuing vestiges. The material forms of reparations include cash payments, land, economic development, and repatriation resources particularly to those who are descendants of enslaved Africans. Other forms of reparations for Black people of African descent include funds for scholarships and community development; creation of multi-media depictions of the history of Black people of African descent and textbooks for educational institutions that tell the story from the African descendants' perspective; development of historical monuments and museums; the return of artifacts and art to appropriate people or institutions; exoneration of political prisoners; and, the elimination of laws and practices that maintain dual systems in the major areas of life including the punishment system, health, education and the financial/economic system. The forms of reparations

received should improve the lives of African descendants in the United States for future generations to come; foster economic, social and political parity; and allow for full rights of self-determination.

N'COBRA also embraces the tenets of the therapeutic model, arguing that acknowledgment of abuses would leave "the nation as a whole . . . stronger. Truth and atonement are essential ingredients for a just and peaceful society. Although some may assert that reparations will increase racial divisiveness, this does not have to be the result. Indeed, it should decrease racial divisiveness because it is an acknowledgment that allows us to go forward rather than remain stuck in the pain of the present that is caused by the unresolved pain of the past."[17]

Harvard law professor Charles J. Ogletree has acted as longtime counsel for N'COBRA. Ogletree also participated in the suit brought against the city of Tulsa, Oklahoma, in 2003, which sought reparations for the 1921 riot that left some three hundred people dead, forty blocks of property destroyed, and more than eight thousand people homeless. Although some contemporary whites as well as the municipality acknowledged the need for reparations to the victims of the Tulsa riot, and in 2001 the Oklahoma Committee to Investigate the Tulsa Riot of 1921 concurred, the state legislature declined to support the recommendations, citing a lack of constitutional power. When the case was brought before federal courts, the statute of limitations was invoked to avoid paying the forty-some surviving victims.[18] This use of the statute of limitations defense, legally called "remoteness" in common law, has hindered numerous reparations efforts.[19]

Reparations efforts have also made their way to, though not through, Congress. In 1989, Democratic representative John Conyers of Michigan introduced HR 40, a proposal to establish a congressional investigative commission to study reparations proposals. Conyers chose "40" in reference to the "forty acres" promised but never distributed to freedpeople in the aftermath of the Civil War. Conyers has reintroduced the bill each year since 1989, but HR 40 has never made it to a floor vote. HR 40 itself does not call for reparations, but rather seeks "to further a national dialogue on the plight of African Americans in the context of slavery, Jim Crow, and other legally sanctioned discriminations." The formation of a commission would "acknowledge the fundamental injustice, cruelty, brutality, and inhumanity of slavery in the United States" and determine if remedies were appropriate. Conyers modeled HR 40 on the restitution process outlined in the Civil Liberties Act of 1988, which made payments to Japanese Americans incarcerated during World War II.[20]

Should Congress elect to address reparations, committee members would find no shortage of investigations into the racial wealth gap, in both the longer term—reaching back to slavery and segregation—and contemporary times. Calculations of the amount of money lost to slave labor, segregation, and discrimination range widely, based on varied methods of calculation, but the sums involved and the ongoing wealth gap calculations are always eye-opening. They range in the trillions of dollars, from a low of $5 to $24 trillion up to $100 trillion. The methods of payment, to whom, and for what—lost labor only, or also other factors like physical and psychological health—have also been calculated and debated in myriad ways. Most concede that these levels of restitution, particularly to individuals, are unlikely.[21]

In 2005, a team of health policy professionals made an explicit effort to support Conyers's congressional investigative initiative by analyzing health and wealth disparities by race and over time. Their analysis of the intergenerational impact of slavery, segregation, and discrimination concluded that "time alone does not change" the demonstrable gaps in black-white wealth statistics, much of which are based on inherited health differentials worsened by discriminatory policies. While the removal of obstacles to racial wealth parity might mitigate or, less often, eliminate barriers to equality, this study found that they cannot correct for historical damages. These injuries are measured in terms of human capital, especially in terms of health, a creator of wealth. African Americans have shorter life expectancies and higher death rates than whites. They suffer more from diabetes, coronary disease, breast cancer, hypertension, and addiction. Slavery and segregation have played key roles in these disparities that persist over generations. Better education alone, they argue, cannot reverse these longstanding differences. The authors therefore argue for policies that bring an end to skewed access to health care, provide insurance coverage tailored to the specific problems African Americans face, and attack residential segregation, which many scholars recognize as the central factor in ongoing discrimination.

These authors are also supportive of wealth transfers, particularly when directed toward the eradication of these ongoing causes of inequality.[22]

A number of researchers have analyzed the statistical extent of present-day racial inequality. The National Urban League (NUL) and the Pew Research Center are two of the steadiest trackers of these trends. The NUL publishes annual reports, entitled *The State of Black America*, that address these disparities based on a variety of variables. In 2015, the NUL reported that the median income of African Americans was 60 percent that of whites ($34,815 vs. $57,684); that African Americans were more than twice as likely to live in poverty (27.6 percent vs. 11.1 percent); that unemployment rates were more than twice as high for African Americans as whites (11.3 percent vs. 5.3 percent); and that the median wealth for African Americans was $6,314 compared to $110,500 for whites—which means that African Americans hold six cents of wealth for every dollar of wealth that whites control. The Pew Research Center reported that the racial wealth gap in 2014 was the largest since 1989, and that the median wealth of whites was thirteen times higher than that of African Americans; for comparative purposes, they noted that this ratio had been only eight times higher in 2009.[23]

In a widely heralded 2014 article, Ta-Nehisi Coates, journalist for *The Atlantic*, covered the history of reparations, focusing on the contract buying system for residential housing for African Americans in Lawndale, a Chicago suburb, between the 1930s and 1960s. Through contract buying, residents did not actually own or acquire equity in their homes until the home was paid for. Sold at inflated prices with increasingly steep monthly installments and growing fees, the homes soon became unaffordable, and the residents were evicted and lost their entire investment. Coates argues that such practices should be considered in any reparations investigation, such as Conyers's congressional proposal. Responses to the article have ranged from supportive to condemnatory, the latter category focusing on such themes as how reparations would undermine the work ethic and the difficulty in designating the "proper" recipients of a reparations plan. In contrast, others have argued that Coates's investigations will reinvigorate the reparations movement in the United States.[24]

While the Civil Liberties Act of 1988, the basis of Conyers's initiative, is the U.S. movement's most compelling precedent, reparations proponents point to numerous others that exist both nationally and internationally. A few have resulted in restitution, though most have taken the form of apologies or, more often, acknowledgments or statements of regret. In 1993 Congress apologized for the invasion of Hawaii. In November 2006, British prime minister Tony Blair fell shy of a full apology and instead expressed "deep sorrow" for his nation's involvement in the slave trade.[25]

Limited examples of monetary reparations exist in the United States. Florida established a $1.5 million fund in 1994 to compensate survivors and descendants of the 1923 Rosewood massacre. Nine people who could prove either that they had resided in Rosewood at the time of the massacre or that their ancestors lost property eventually received settlements. The state also established the Rosewood Family Scholarship Fund for descendants of victims, and in 2004 designated the town a Florida Heritage Landmark. A few years later, Timothy Pigford and some four hundred other black farmers filed two class action lawsuits against the Department of Agriculture for having either denied or delayed loans to black farmers. In 2010, *Pigford v. Glickman II* recognized these claims and President Barack Obama signed a bill authorizing compensation. About $1.25 billion has been paid to some 18,000 farmers, although investigations of the application process have revealed substantial fraud, chiefly on the part of law firms pressing additional claims.[26] North Carolina plans to compensate 1,500 living victims of a state sterilization program that was in place between 1929 and 1977. This eugenics policy chiefly targeted black, poor, and disabled women. The state has established a $10 million fund for this purpose, payable to those who apply. As of 2015, $4.4 million has been paid out.[27]

In the international arena Germany, along with a number of private businesses, paid $65.2 billion to survivors of the Holocaust, and Germany has also compensated the state of Israel. Argentina and South Africa launched investigations into the victims of military dictatorship and apartheid, respectively.[28] In 2003 the South African government paid $85 million in reparations—far short of the requested $360 million—to 19,000 apartheid victims who testified before the Truth and Reconciliation Commission, amounting to $3,900 per person.[29] In 1997, the U.S. House of Representatives condemned sexual enslavement of Chinese and Korean "comfort women" by the Japanese in World War II and recommended that the Japanese government pay $40,000 to each victim.[30] And the British have recently joined the reparations movement. In June 2013 Britain apologized for torturing Kenyans fighting in the 1950s Mau Mau uprising against British colonial rule, agreeing to pay $30 million to more than 5,000 victims.[31]

Ambitious and ongoing efforts at the international level have added considerable but hard-won momentum to the reparations movement. In late August and early September 2001, activists struggled to get reparations issues on the agenda for the United Nations–sponsored World Conference against Racism, Racial Discrimination, Xenophobia, and Related Intolerance (WCAR) in Durban, South Africa. By the end of the conference, the governments of Senegal and Nigeria had joined with the United States and European Union members to thwart the call for reparatory justice, with United Nations secretary general Kofi Annan's tacit blessing. The United States dispatched Secretary of State Colin Powell and National Security Advisor Condoleezza Rice to safeguard the nation from reparations demands. But these opponents were unable to squelch either the legal or historical basis for reparations or the determination of reparations activists. Their efforts continue today in lawsuits currently being pursued in Britain, France, and the Netherlands by the Caribbean Community and Common Market (CARICOM), a coalition of fourteen Caribbean nations and a group that had been in the forefront of the WCAR reparations efforts. Should these suits fail, CARICOM has pledged to take its case to the International Court of Justice.

At issue in the failed attempts at WCAR was a debate over whether slavery and slave trading had been crimes against humanity at the time they were committed. Reparations opponents maintained that since national governments had no legal sanctions against slavery and the trade—indeed, had them enshrined in law—they could not be retrospectively considered crimes. The final document that resulted from the conference stated that slavery and the trade "were appalling tragedies" and acknowledged that they were "*crimes* against humanity and *should* always have been so." Dismayed CARICOM members opposed the use of "should" in the final document, and used their dissent as the fulcrum on which to keep future reparations efforts alive. It is within that context that CARICOM, backed by the exhaustive and detailed work presented by historian Hilary McD. Beckles in *Britain's Black Debt: Reparations for Caribbean Slavery and Native Genocide* (2013), has launched its efforts through the European courts. Beckles was a pivotal member of the Durban conference, and he has been a key figure in pressing CARICOM's renewed work forward.[32]

Repeated efforts to sue the U.S. government for reparations have failed because of the principle of sovereign immunity, which allows such suits only with the government's permission. Activists therefore pursued alternate strategies. In the late 1990s, when the modern reparations movement gained momentum, they began to target corporations, seeking to force the establishment of compensatory funds. The results fell far short of demands. Lawyer Deadria Farmer-Paellmann of the Restitution Study Group brought suit against various corporations in 2002 with the intent of proving how extensively they profited from slavery and Jim Crow. She targeted a host of companies, among them FleetBoston Financial, transportation company CSX, and Aetna Insurance Company, seeking an estimated $1.4 trillion, the amount estimated to have been stolen in labor costs from four million slaves, not including interest.[33] This ambitious effort failed. But in 2005, JP Morgan Chase Bank, one of the defendants in the 2002 suit, established a $5 million scholarship fund for blacks in Louisiana after admitting that it profited from slavery. Under a 2003 Chicago ordinance that forced businesses to disclose their historic ties to slavery, JP Morgan Chase acknowledged that between 1831 and 1865, two of its predecessor banks in Louisiana accepted around 13,000 slaves as collateral and owned 1,250 of them through defaults. Many critics of the settlement denounced the amount placed in the fund as an insulting pittance, and Farmer-Paellmann argued that corporations should have no authority over how reparations dollars are spent.[34]

Most public and private officials have responded to reparations demands by embracing the therapeutic model. By the late 1990s a veritable cottage industry of apologies, near apologies, and "statements of regret" about slavery, Jim Crow, and lynching had sprouted, with state and federal legislatures, colleges and universities, corporations, church groups, a U.S. president, and a British prime minister all chiming in. Many of these statements acknowledge the foundational contributions slave labor made to the national economy, certainly something that the emancipation generation and their descendants would applaud. But the phenomenon of "statements of regret" emerged because authentic apologies, with their connotations of guilt, are more vulnerable to reparations suits.

President Bill Clinton led the pack with his May 1997 apology for the Tuskegee Project between 1932 and 1972, in which 399 poor black men in Alabama infected with late-stage syphilis had treatment withheld in order to study the effects of the disease. In 1998, Clinton issued another apology—some say a semi-apology—for the Atlantic slave trade. In 2004 the University of Alabama apologized for slavery. In 2006 the Virginia legislature issued a statement of regret about slavery which acknowledged that slave labor had built much of substance in the Old Dominion. This document appeared just as the state was about to commemorate the four hundredth anniversary of the establishment of Jamestown, where the first people of African descent were sold to British colonists in 1619. The University of Virginia, established by Thomas Jefferson, soon followed with another statement of regret. U.S. Representative Steve Cohen of Tennessee proposed a congressional apology for slavery in February 2007. The North Carolina Senate passed its statement of regret in April 2007, as did the Alabama and Maryland legislatures, which preferred to express "profound regret." New Jersey followed suit in 2008. New York, Missouri, and Georgia considered making statements but did not do so.[35]

Around this time, the North Carolina General Assembly commissioned a report on the 1898 Wilmington Riot. That 464-page report became the basis of House Bill 751, passed on 15 March 2007, one month before the state's statement of regret was issued. HB 751 was a remarkable—and accurate—acknowledgment of the riot that overturned biracial political power in that city and left twenty-two African Americans dead. Hundreds of black residents were subsequently forced to leave, losing their property and turning Wilmington into a majority white city. The bill read in part:

> Political leaders and other members of a white elite were directly responsible for and participants in the violence of November 17, 1898; engineering and executing a statewide white supremacy campaign in order to win the 1900 elections that was vicious, polarizing, and defamatory toward African-Americans and that encouraged racial violence. . . . the effects of . . . the Wilmington Riots lasted far beyond 1898, paving the way for legislation that disfranchised African-Americans and poor white citizens, for lynching and violence against African-American citizens, and for Jim Crow segregation . . . [the

state] is saddened by the full extent of leaders' involvement in the Wilmington Riot of 1898. . . . The General Assembly . . . on behalf of the people of North Carolina, acknowledges that the violence of 1898 . . . was a conspiracy of a white elite that used intimidation and force to replace a duly elected local government, that people lost livelihoods and were banished from their homes without due process of law, and that government at all levels failed to protect its citizens.[36]

Such statements and investigations have not been limited to the political arena. On 10 July 2008, the American Medical Association (AMA) apologized to African American physicians for "past wrongs" dating back to the 1870s, when the AMA refused to admit black delegates to its conferences, prompting the formation of the segregated National Medical Association in 1895. The AMA also cited the establishment of separate and usually inferior hospitals for blacks, the closing of all but two African American medical schools in 1910, and the bans against treating African American patients in white hospitals as additional wrongs. Not until 1968 did the AMA amend its constitution to bar racism in the medical profession.[37]

U.S. colleges and universities have been active in scrutinizing their ties to slavery, the slave trade, and segregation. Investigations have occurred at Yale, Harvard, and Princeton Universities, and a growing list of other institutions are currently undertaking such efforts: the College of William and Mary; Duke University; Amherst College; and the Universities of North Carolina, South Carolina, Virginia, Alabama, and Maryland to date. In 2006, President Ruth J. Simmons spearheaded efforts to detail Brown University's connections to the Atlantic slave trade through the Brown brothers, who made fortunes in the trade in the eighteenth century and then gave generously to the founding of the university. The consequent report, *Slavery and Justice*, acknowledged the controversies over economic redress and focused instead on a therapeutic process. The university would preside over community discussions designed to foster a more equitable future by promoting "truth telling" about "traumatic histories." Brown has since established the Ruth J. Simmons Postdoctoral Fellowship in Slavery and Justice, which calls for applicants to investigate "questions concerning the historical formations of slavery in global or comparative terms; issues concerning contemporary forms of indentured servitude; or philosophical, historical, and theoretical questions concerning slavery, justice, and freedom." In February 2011, Emory University organized a conference on slavery and the university, and will publish its findings in a forthcoming volume.[38]

In 2013, historian Craig Steven Wilder published *Ebony and Ivy: Race, Slavery, and the Troubled History of America's Universities*, a wide-ranging and exhaustive analysis of the role of slavery in the founding of the U.S. academy from its earliest colonial days to the antebellum period. Not surprisingly, such major southern institutions as existed in that era, like the College of William and Mary and University of Virginia, had multiple direct ties to the wealth that slavery generated. But so too did all the important northern ones, whose leaders actively courted wealthy slaveholders and slave traders for donations and either held slaves themselves or were personally invested in the slave economy. In the nineteenth century, the faculty at these institutions produced numerous "scientific" arguments about racial hierarchies and the social dangers that black and Indian peoples represented. "The academy," Wilder underscored, "never stood apart from American slavery—in fact, it stood beside church and state as the third pillar of a civilization built on bondage."[39]

The current crop of apologies and statements of regret at least recognize that slave labor built the nation—a comfortable enough admission that does not demand accountability. And indeed, many reparations proponents insist that apologies accompany any potential restitution. But in the absence of compensation, these statements ring defensive and hollow because they fail to address the economic legacies of slavery and segregation in concrete terms. As former slaves well knew, specific policies addressing political and economic injustices are essential to achieving a lasting social harmony. They also well understood that moral standards and behavior can be changed through law and the power of the state. What occurred when these protections were either never put in place or were unenforced remain bluntly plain historical lessons.

In April 2007, a local independent newspaper in Chapel Hill and Durham, North Carolina, interviewed John Hope Franklin on his reactions to the recent spate of apologies, as well as the North Carolina General

Assembly's report on the Wilmington Massacre. "It's going to become epidemic now," Franklin observed.

> People are running around apologizing for slavery. What about that awful period since slavery—Reconstruction, Jim Crow and all the rest? And what about the enormous wealth that was built up by black labor? If I was sitting on a billion dollars that someone had made when I sat on them, I probably would not be slow to apologize, if that's all it takes. I think that's little to pay for the gazillions that black people built up—the wealth of this country—with their labor, and now you're going to say I'm sorry I beat the hell out of you for all these years? That's not enough. . . . How large is the black population now living in abject poverty in this country? How large is the population of blacks who have poor health? Sometimes they inherited the poor health right from their forebears who were beaten and treated like they were animals all over this country. It's simply not enough. And I'm impatient with the piety that goes along with it. They're so syrupy in their apologies. What does it cost? Nothing.[40]

Franklin deemed the North Carolina report on Wilmington "commendable," particularly if it might lead to more instruction about the event in the public schools. But he remained pessimistic about monetary reparations. "The American government, whatever its needs are to equalize opportunity and to provide justice for all," he reflected, "is probably not responsible for making up the defects of slaveholders and shareholders in Virginia or Maryland or North Carolina. . . . I really expect though, that the government would not tolerate any continued discrimination and any continued defects in the relationship between one group of citizens and another. That if it is not in the position to make amends for everything that has happened, it can certainly see that it doesn't continue to happen. And I would settle for the government doing that." Franklin continued:

> When I was chairman of [Bill Clinton's] president's advisory board on race, I found very few groups that wanted to acknowledge that they had made mistakes in the past, and that it would be well to reconsider them and apologize for them—very seldom did I find any group that was willing to do that. I'm not at all certain that we can

find any groups that want to give up any property or any resources that they've gained through the years as a result of the way in which they acquired these properties and so forth. They simply don't want to think about it or to do anything about it.

Polls reflect Franklin's assessment. White Americans oppose reparations by margins of two-thirds and greater, whereas blacks support reparations by the same percentage. The most demagogic opponents particularly rant against the individual payment approach. They lack all sense of collective historical responsibility, preferring instead to argue that they had no personal role in slavery or Jim Crow.[41]

But some reparations proponents frame the issues more comprehensively and systemically, emphasizing community-oriented, sometimes class-based, rehabilitation programs. Some refer to these as forward-looking, rather than backward-looking, plans. Improvements in public education are always high on the list and have the support of President Barack Obama. Many have proposed to equalize public education by eliminating property taxes as the basis for funding and by providing free higher education for all citizens—as is currently done in Brazil, Germany, Finland, France, Norway, Slovenia, and Sweden. Jobs programs, stronger and better affirmative action programs, universal payer health care with provisions for conditions common among African Americans, reforms in drug offender sentencing, extensive penal reforms, and effective education of the electorate—these, they argue, would effectively combat the corruption of democracy caused by greed and generations of wealth redistribution from blacks and other exploited people to the elites. Many believe that expanding economic opportunity and democracy by establishing political protections for the most vulnerable would be vastly more effective than individual reparations payments, which would doubtless be meager, inadequate, and fleeting, benefiting chiefly the companies where such small sums would likely be spent.[42]

Lawyer Charles J. Ogletree's views are reflective of this approach:

The reparations movement should not, I believe, focus on payments to individuals. The damage has been done to a group—African-American slaves and their descendants—but it has not been done equally within the group. The reparations movement must aim at undoing the damage where that damage has been most severe and where the history of race in America has left its most telling evidence. The legacy of slavery and racial discrimination in America is seen in well-documented racial disparities in access to education, health care, housing, insurance, employment and other social goods. The reparations movement must therefore focus on the poorest of the poor—it must finance social recovery for the bottom-stuck, providing an opportunity to address comprehensively the problems of those who have not substantially benefited from integration or affirmative action. The root of "reparations" is "to repair." This litigation strategy could give us an opportunity to fully address the legacy of slavery in a spirit of repair.[43]

Were such a broadminded vision implemented, it would reflect much of what freedpeople called for in the name of reparations and greater democracy during the emancipation era and subsequent decades. Many indeed rejoiced in the promise of land redistribution, which was subsequently revoked. In the aftermath of that bitter disappointment they called at least for political protections—exercise of the ballot so as to influence laws governing economic opportunity.[44] While the emancipation generation exercised political power, they attacked greed and fraud and acted upon economic inequality and privation as best they could. They widened educational access and called for improved health care, job growth, and wage equity. They gave us a draft model for a better future that aimed to limit confrontation and establish mutual respect, the stated aims of modern reparations activists.[45] They understood that opponents directed their attacks at African American families and communities in order to compromise if not destroy their ethical pasts and presents, assaults that had formidable public policy implications. We of the twenty-first century should heed the ethical legacies of freedpeople and their descendants, people who experienced slavery and segregation and passed on wisdom which still speaks to policies that continue to debilitate the individual and common good and thereby imperil national integrity. Such an initiative would be a fitting commemoration of the 150th anniversary of emancipation.

Notes

Preface and Acknowledgments

1. Raha Jorjani, "Could Black People in the U.S. Qualify as Refugees?" *Washington Post*, 14 August 2015.

2. On the penal system, see Bryan Stevenson, *Just Mercy: A Story of Justice and Redemption* (New York: Spiegel and Grau, 2014). Stevenson is founder and executive director of the Equal Justice Initiative in Montgomery, Alabama, and a professor in the New York University School of Law. He is responsible for having historical slave markers placed in Montgomery.

3. Eric Foner, *Reconstruction: America's Unfinished Revolution, 1863–1877* (New York: Harper & Row, 1988).

Introduction. The Social and Intellectual Gifts of Black Folk: Foundations and Legacies of a Humanistic Democratic Ethos

1. Frederick Douglass, "What Is a Slave?" in *African-American Social and Political Thought, 1850–1920*, ed. Howard Brotz (New Brunswick, NJ: Transaction, 1996), 217; emphasis added.

2. W.E.B. Du Bois first used the term "counterrevolution" to describe this phenomenon. He defined the elite reaction against Reconstruction as a "counter-revolution of property." His prefatory summary to his chapter analyzing the counterrevolution reads as follows: "How, after the war, triumphant industry in the North coupled with privilege and monopoly led an orgy of theft that engulfed the nation and was the natural child of war; and how revolt against this anarchy became reaction against democracy, North and South, and delivered the land in the hands of an organized monarchy of finance while it over threw the attempt at a dictatorship of labor in the South." W.E.B. Du Bois, *Black Reconstruction in America: An Essay Toward a History of the Part Which Black Folk Played in the Attempt to Reconstruct Democracy in America, 1860–1880* (New York: Meridian Books, [1935] 1964), 580. For information on violence against freedwomen, see Thavolia Glymph, *Out of*

the House of Bondage: The Transformation of the Plantation Household (Cambridge: Cambridge University Press, 2008), chaps. 5–8; and Hannah Rosen, *Terror in the Heart of Freedom: Citizenship, Sexual Violence, and the Meaning of Race in the Postemancipation South* (Chapel Hill: University of North Carolina Press, 2008), chap. 6.

3. "The nadir" is widely employed to describe the disfranchisement and segregation years as the worst since emancipation. It originated with historian Rayford Logan's *The Negro in American Life and Thought: The Nadir, 1877–1901* (London: Dial Press, 1954). In this seminal work Logan emphasized economic exploitation; violence; and the perfidy of Presidents Hayes, Cleveland, Harrison, and McKinley; the Supreme Court; and the northern press on civil rights issues as the chief perpetrators of the counterrevolution. Logan's work shifted historiography on these topics.

4. A recent proponent of this argument is Douglas R. Egerton, *The Wars of Reconstruction: The Brief, Violent History of America's Most Progressive Era* (New York: Bloomsbury Press, 2014).

5. For an examination of how these communal efforts manifested in economic terms after emancipation and through the twentieth century, see Jessica Gordon Nembhard, *Collective Courage: A History of African American Cooperative Economic Thought and Practice* (University Park: Pennsylvania State University Press, 2014).

6. Eric Foner, *Free Soil, Free Labor, Free Men: The Ideology of the Republican Party before the Civil War*, 2nd ed. (New York: Oxford University Press, 1995), chap. 1; Daniel T. Rodgers, *The Work Ethic in Industrial America, 1850–1920* (Chicago: University of Chicago Press, 1978).

7. As one student of politics stressed, "slavery was not mere background or prologue; it was formative and foundational." Steven Hahn, *A Nation under Our Feet: Black Political Struggles in the Rural South, from Slavery to the Great Migration* (Cambridge, MA: Belknap Press, 2003), 6; David Roediger, *Wages of Whiteness: Race and the Making of the American Working Class*, 2nd ed. (London: Verso, 2007).

8. Warren Whatley, "The Transatlantic Slave Trade and the Evolution of Political Authority in West Africa," MPRA Archives no. 44932 (April 2012): 1–4, 20, http://projects.iq.harvard.edu/files/pegroup/files/whatley_2012.pdf; Michael A. Gomez, *Exchanging Our Country Marks: The Transformation of African Identities in the Colonial and Antebellum South* (Chapel Hill: University of North Carolina Press, 1998), esp. chap. 6, "I Seen Folks Disappeah," 114–53.

9. Sylvia R. Frey, "The Visible Church: Historiography of African American Religion since Raboteau," *Slavery and Abolition* 29, no. 1 (March 2008): 83–110; Mechal Sobel, "The West African Sacred Cosmos," in *Trabelin' On: The Slave Journey to an Afro-Baptist Faith* (Westport, CT: Greenwood Press, 1979): 3–21; Sylvia R. Frey and Betty Wood, *Come Shouting to Zion: African American Protestantism*

in the American South and British Caribbean to 1830 (Chapel Hill: University of North Carolina Press, 1998): xi–xiii, 1–62; Thomas L. Webber, *Deep Like the Rivers: Education in the Slave Quarter Community, 1831–1865* (New York: Norton, 1978), 118–30.

The debate on African cultural retentions in African American societies has a long and contentious history, beginning among slaves and free African Americans themselves but having a scholarly touchstone in the works of Melville J. Herskovits, *The Myth of the Negro Past* (Boston: Beacon Press, 1941); and E. Franklin Frazier, *The Negro Family in the United States* (Chicago: University of Chicago Press, 1939). Herskovits, an anthropologist who conducted research in the Caribbean and South America, argued that such retentions could be readily identified, but he had little to say about the phenomenon in North America. Frazier denied the existence of any African retentions other than music and foodways, placing heavier emphasis on the American foundations of African American cultures. Since the publication of these two books, considerable ink has been spilled on the topic. For the most recent interpretations and syntheses, see Robert Farris Thompson, *Flash of the Spirit: African and Afro-American Art and Philosophy* (New York: Vintage Books, 1981); Joseph E. Holloway, ed., *Africanisms in American Culture* (Bloomington: Indiana University Press, 1990); Paul Gilroy, *The Black Atlantic: Modernity and Double Consciousness* (Cambridge, MA: Harvard University Press, 1993); Lucius T. Outlaw Jr., "'Afrocentricity': Critical Considerations," in *A Companion to African-American Philosophy*, ed. Tommy L. Lott and John P. Pittman (Malden, MA: Blackwell, 2003), 155–67; and Tommy L. Lott, "African Retentions," op. cit., 168–89. Much of the literature remains focused on such cultural features as music, dance, costume, and religion, though some has begun to address political and economic issues. Bernard R. Boxill, *Blacks and Social Justice* (Totowa, NJ: Rowman & Allanheld, 1984) does not engage the retentions debate, but does identify several philosophical components of African American political thought between the onset of segregation and the modern civil rights movement, as do the essayists in John P. Pittman, ed., *African-American Perspectives and Philosophical Traditions* (New York: Routledge, 1997). Norm R. Allen Jr., "Humanism in Political Action," in *By These Hands: A Documentary History of African American Humanism*, ed. Anthony B. Pinn (New York: New York University Press, 2001), 147–69, provides a useful overview of this component of the ethic in the lives of some twentieth-century figures. See also Jermaine O. Archer, "Bitter Herbs and a Lock of Hair: Recollections of Africa in Slave Narratives of the Garrisonian Era," in *Diasporic Africa: A Reader*, ed. Michael A. Gomez (New York: New York University Press, 2006), 84–100.

10. Kathryn Gin, "'The Heavenization of Earth': African American Visions and Uses of the Afterlife, 1863–1901," *Slavery and Abolition* 31 (June 2010): 207–31; Webber, *Deep Like the Rivers*, 63–70, 87; Albert J. Raboteau, *A Fire in the Bones:*

Reflections on African-American Religious History (Boston: Beacon Press, 1995), 28–36.

11. John Quincy Adams, *Narrative of the Life of John Quincy Adams, When in Slavery, and Now as a Freeman* (Harrisburg, PA, 1872): 16–17, 21–22, available from *Documenting the American South*, University Library, University of North Carolina–Chapel Hill, http://docsouth.unc.edu/neh/adams/adams.html.

12. Richard Newman, *Freedom's Prophet: Bishop Richard Allen, the AME Church, and the Black Founding Fathers* (New York: New York University Press, 2008), 1–26, 266–68, 291–99.

13. Edward J. Blum, "'O God of a Godless Land': Northern African American Challenges to White Christian Nationhood, 1865–1906," in *Vale of Tears: New Essays on Religion and Reconstruction*, ed. Edward J. Blum and W. Scott Poole (Macon, GA: Mercer University Press, 2005), 93–111.

14. As Edward E. Baptist has noted,

Unlike . . . counterparts in most of the New World, the African-American culture that emerged from the crucible of nineteenth-century forced migration within the United States had no alternative but to think of itself as a political unity. . . . enslaved African Americans had to develop a sense of unity or crumble. And they did develop that unity, bending a narrative of history that bound them together around a clear-eyed assessment of their situation as victims of a vast crime. They had to recognize that without solidarity they would live only at the whim of a set of structures and practices designed to exploit them in every possible way.

Baptist, *The Half Has Never Been Told: Slavery and the Making of American Capitalism* (New York: Basic Books, 2014), 416.

15. Kevin Gaines, *Uplifting the Race: Black Leadership, Culture and Politics in the Twentieth Century* (Chapel Hill: University of North Carolina Press, 1996); August Meier, *Negro Thought in America, 1880–1915: Racial Ideologies in the Age of Booker T. Washington* (Ann Arbor: University of Michigan Press, 1963), 46–47, 149–57, 187.

16. David W. Blight, *Race and Reunion: The Civil War in American Memory* (Cambridge, MA: Belknap Press, 2001); Mitch Kachun, *Festivals of Freedom: Memory and Meaning in African American Emancipation Celebrations, 1808–1915* (Amherst: University of Massachusetts Press, 2003), chap. 4 and passim; Thavolia Glymph, "'Liberty Dearly Bought': The Making of Civil War Memory in Afro-American Communities in the South," in *Time Longer Than Rope: A Century of African American Activism, 1850–1950*, ed. Charles M. Payne and Adam Green (New York: New York University Press, 2003), 111–39.

17. My approach to slave intellectual and social history is distinct from that of earlier studies analyzing slave personalities. In 1959, Stanley M. Elkins's *Slavery: A*

Problem in American Institutional and Cultural Life (Chicago: University of Chicago Press, 1959) set off a prolonged firestorm of debates about his central premise: that slavery, which he defined as a "closed" system, depended on the development and internalization of a "Sambo" stereotype in the enslaved. This social-psychological approach to the issue of slave personality emphasized that North American slaves were docile, loyal, lazy, humble, dependent, infantile people given to thievery and incapable of launching meaningful resistance to slavery. Slaveholders' successful creation of this personality type, which required slaves to accept a self-image of dependency and inferiority, enabled the regime to function smoothly. By comparison, Elkins held that Sambos did not exist in Latin American slave populations because of the ameliorative influence of Catholicism; moreover, more rebellions occurred in Latin American regimes as a consequence of this difference. In the 1960s, a growing number of scholars began to reject the proposition that slaves should be seen solely as victims and instead began to emphasize their accomplishments under the regime, including the formation of an oppositional culture that for many represented a form of resistance more potent than rebellion. In recent years, Elkins's thesis rarely receives serious scholarly attention, but see Daryl M. Scott, *Social Policy and the Image of the Damaged Black Psyche, 1880–1996* (Chapel Hill: University of North Carolina Press, 1997); and Richard H. King, "Domination and Fabrication: Re-thinking Stanley Elkins's *Slavery*," *Slavery and Abolition* 22, no. 2 (August 2001): 1–28. For contemporary debates on the Elkins thesis, see Eugene D. Genovese, "Rebelliousness and Docility in Negro Slavery: A Critique of the Elkins Thesis," *Civil War History* 13, no. 4 (December 1967): 293–314; Kenneth M. Stampp, "Rebels and the Search for the Negro's Personality in Slavery," *Journal of Southern History* 37, no. 3 (August 1970): 367–92; Anne J. Lane, ed., *Stanley Elkins and His Critics* (Urbana: University of Illinois Press, 1971); and John W. Blassingame, *The Slave Community: Plantation Life in the Antebellum South* (New York: Oxford University Press, 1972). Yet a growing number of current scholars and other authors have begun to argue that slavery did cause psychological problems across generations—sometimes known as posttraumatic slave syndrome. See, for example, Alma Carten, "How Slavery's Legacy Affects the Mental Health of Black Americans," *New Republic*, 27 July 2015. Another thread of the argument calls for more attention to the effects of slavery and racism on whites. Clinical psychologist Alvin Poussaint and a number of his colleagues petitioned the American Psychological Association (APA) in 1999 to classify racism as a mental disorder. The APA declined, arguing that racism was a cultural rather than an individual problem, and that if racists could rationalize their actions by saying they had no control over their behavior, they would be less vulnerable to prosecution. Alvin Poussaint, "They Hate. They Kill. Are They Insane?" *New York Times*, 26 August 1999.

18. Historian Walter Johnson is a prominent critic of slave "agency," admittedly

a hackneyed term these days. See "Slavery, Reparations, and the Mythic March of Freedom," *Raritan* 27, no. 2 (Fall 2007): 51–54, and esp. "On Agency," *Journal of Social History* 37, no. 1 (Fall 2003): 113–25.

19. Lawrence W. Levine, *Black Culture and Black Consciousness: Afro-American Folk Thought from Slavery to Freedom* (New York: Oxford University Press, 1977), xi, 440.

20. Some representative works, but by no means all, include Du Bois, *Black Reconstruction in America*; Merton L. Dillon, *Slavery Attacked: Southern Slaves and Their Allies, 1619–1865* (Baton Rouge: Louisiana State University Press, 1990); Ira Berlin and Philip D. Morgan, eds., *The Slaves' Economy: Independent Production by Slaves in the Americas* (London: Frank Cass, 1991); Ira Berlin, *Generations of Captivity: A History of African-American Slaves* (Cambridge, MA: Belknap Press, 2003); Wilma A. Dunaway, *The African-American Family in Slavery and Emancipation* (New York: Cambridge University Press, 2003); Glymph, *Out of the House of Bondage*; Dylan C. Penningroth, *The Claims of Kinfolk: African American Property and Community in the Nineteenth-Century South* (Chapel Hill: University of North Carolina Press, 2003); Jack Greene and Philip D. Morgan, eds., *Atlantic History: A Critical Appraisal* (New York: Oxford University Press, 2009); Nell Irvin Painter, *Southern History across the Color Line* (Chapel Hill: University of North Carolina Press, 2002); Benjamin Quarles, *The Negro in the Civil War* (New York: Russell and Russell, 1968); Willie Lee Rose, *Rehearsal for Reconstruction: The Port Royal Experiment* (Indianapolis, IN: Bobbs-Merrill, 1964); Leslie A. Schwalm, *A Hard Fight for We: Women's Transition from Slavery to Freedom in South Carolina* (Urbana: University of Illinois Press, 1997); Hahn, *Nation under Our Feet*; Douglas R. Egerton, *Gabriel's Rebellion: The Virginia Slave Conspiracies of 1800 and 1802* (Chapel Hill: University of North Carolina Press, 1993); Joseph T. Glatthaar, *Forged in Battle: The Civil War Alliance of Black Soldiers and White Officers* (New York: Free Press: Collier Macmillan, 1990); Edwin S. Redkey, ed., *A Grand Army of Black Men: Letters from African American Soldiers in the Union Army, 1861–1865* (New York: Cambridge University Press, 1992); Leon F. Litwack, *Been in the Storm So Long: The Aftermath of Slavery* (New York: Knopf, 1979); E. Foner, *Reconstruction*; Blight, *Race and Reunion*; W. R. Brock, *An American Crisis: Congress and Reconstruction, 1865–1877* (New York: St. Martin's Press, 1963); Kenneth Stampp, *The Era of Reconstruction, 1865–1877* (New York: Knopf, 1965); Stampp, *The Peculiar Institution: Slavery in the Ante-bellum South* (New York: Vintage Books, 1956); Nathan Huggins, *Black Odyssey: The Afro-American Ordeal in Slavery* (New York: Pantheon Books, 1977); James M. McPherson, "Who Freed the Slaves?" *Proceedings of the American Philosophical Society* 139 (March 1995): 1–10; Don E. Fehrenbacher, *The Dred Scott Case: Its Significance in American Law and Politics* (New York: Oxford University Press, 1978); Fehrenbacher, *The Slaveholding Republic: An*

Account of the United States Government's Relations to Slavery (New York: Oxford University Press, 2001); Adam Rothman, *Slave Country: American Expansion and the Origins of the Deep South* (Cambridge, MA: Harvard University Press, 2005); Patrick Rael, *Black Identity and Black Protest in the Antebellum North* (Chapel Hill: University of North Carolina Press, 2002). See also the volumes produced by the Freedmen and Southern Society Project hosted at the University of Maryland. See the publications under *Freedom: A Documentary History of Emancipation, 1861–1867,* at www.freedmen.umd.edu/fssppubs.htm. For recent reexaminations of the state of the field, see Steven Hahn, *The Political Worlds of Slavery and Freedom* (Cambridge, MA: Harvard University Press, 2009); and Randal L. Hall, ed., "Commemorating Seventy-Five Years of the *Journal of Southern History,*" special issue, *Journal of Southern History,* 75, no. 3 (August 2009), an issue that reconsiders key historical problems ranging from slavery's origins to the present.

21. Gomez, *Exchanging Our Country Marks*; Gwendolyn Midlo Hall, *Africans in Colonial Louisiana: The Development of Afro-Creole Culture in the Eighteenth Century* (Baton Rouge: Louisiana State University Press, 1992); G. Hall, *Slavery and African Ethnicities in the Americas: Restoring the Links* (Chapel Hill: University of North Carolina Press, 2005).

22. A notable exception to this historiographical pattern is Hahn, *Nation under Our Feet,* and *Political Worlds of Slavery and Freedom.*

23. Jacquelyn Dowd Hall, "The Long Civil Rights Movement and the Political Uses of the Past," *Journal of American History* 91, no. 4 (March 2005): 1233–63; Sue Thrasher, Jacquelyn Dowd Hall, and Bob Hall, "Learning from the Long Civil Rights Movement's First Generation," *Southern Cultures* 16, no. 2 (Summer 2010): 72–89; Peter F. Lau, *Democracy Rising: South Carolina and the Fight for Black Equality since 1865* (Lexington: University Press of Kentucky, 2006), 1–2. One historian pushes the movement toward the early twentieth century: see Nan Elizabeth Woodruff, *American Congo: The African American Freedom Struggle in the Delta* (Chapel Hill: University of North Carolina Press, 2003).

24. Stephanie J. Shaw, "Using the WPA Narratives to Study the Impact of the Great Depression," *Journal of Southern History* 69, no. 3 (August 2003): 623–58; John W. Blassingame, "Using the Testimony of Ex-Slaves: Approaches and Problems," *Journal of Southern History* 41, no. 4 (November 1975): 473–92.

25. Walter Johnson, *Soul by Soul: Life Inside the Antebellum Slave Market* (Cambridge, MA: Harvard University Press, 1999), 226 n. 24.

26. John Blassingame conducted an extensive analysis of the major antebellum editors of slave narratives and found them to be professionally responsible men with few ties to abolitionists. He also discovered that narrators carefully chose editors who had a reputation for integrity, and that the postwar narratives were the most dependable subset of the nineteenth-century narratives. His article also

provides an extensive discussion of the strengths and weaknesses of the WPA narratives. Blassingame, "Using the Testimony of Ex-Slaves," 474–78.

27. C. Vann Woodward, "History from Slave Sources: A Review Article," *American Historical Review* 79, no. 2 (April 1974): 470–81.

28. I have been especially influenced by Hahn, *Nation under Our Feet;* Hahn's work on rural black politics from slavery to the Great Migration treats pre-emancipation black political thought as central, rather than peripheral, to the history of the era. *Known for My Work* expands his findings into the realm of ethics and extends farther into the twentieth century in order to demonstrate the durability of that ethos. I also owe a substantial debt to the inspiration and insight of Mia Bay, author of *The White Image in the Black Mind: African-American Ideas about White People, 1830–1925* (New York: Oxford University Press, 2000).

29. Ira Berlin and Philip D. Morgan, eds., *Cultivation and Culture: Labor and the Shaping of Slave Life in the Americas* (Charlottesville: University of Virginia Press, 1993); Philip D. Morgan, *Slave Counterpoint: Black Culture in the Eighteenth-Century Chesapeake and Lowcountry* (Chapel Hill: University of North Carolina Press, 1998); Julie Saville, *The Work of Reconstruction: From Slave to Wage Laborer in South Carolina, 1860–1870* (New York: Cambridge University Press, 1994); Eric Foner, *Nothing but Freedom: Emancipation and Its Legacy* (Baton Rouge: Louisiana State University Press, 1983); E. Foner, *Forever Free: The Story of Emancipation and Reconstruction* (New York: Knopf, 2005).

30. Litwack, *Been in the Storm So Long;* Hahn, *Nation under Our Feet;* Ida B. Wells-Barnett, *Crusade for Justice: The Autobiography of Ida B. Wells,* ed. Alfreda M. Duster (Chicago: University of Chicago Press, 1972).

31. Du Bois, *Black Reconstruction in America,* 670.

32. Robert Reich, a political economist and former secretary of labor in the Clinton administration, reported in his 2013 documentary film, *Inequality for All* (72 Productions, Director Jacob Kornbluth), that since 2009, 95 percent of all economic gains have accrued to the top 1 percent of the population. The 400 richest Americans own more than the bottom 150 million combined. In 2012, the incomes of the richest 1 percent rose 20 percent, while the remaining 99 percent experienced a 1 percent rise. See also Paul Wiseman, "Richest 1 Percent Earn Biggest Share since '20s," *AP News,* 10 September 2013; Thomas Piketty, *Capital in the Twenty-First Century* (Cambridge, MA: Belknap Press, 2014). Piketty found, "In the United States, the most recent survey by the Federal Reserve, which covers [2010–11], indicates that the top decile own 72 percent of America's wealth, while the bottom half claim just 2 percent. Note, however, that this source, like most surveys in which wealth is self-reported, underestimates the largest fortunes" (257–58). In *The Price of Inequality* (New York: W. W. Norton, 2012), Joseph E. Stiglitz reported that in 2007, the year before the 2008 crash, "the top 0.1 percent of America's households

had an income that was 220 times larger than the *average* of the bottom 90 percent. Wealth was even more unequally distributed than income, with the wealthiest 1 percent owning more than a third of the nation's wealth" (2–3). See also Thomas Piketty and Emmanuel Saez, "Income Inequality in the United States, 1913–1998," *Quarterly Journal of Economics* 118, no. 1 (2003): 1–39.

These aggregate statistics, however, fail to capture the racial wealth gap that currently exists. In 2011, liquid wealth, or assets that are available for conversion to cash, amounted to $200 for African Americans, most of it in checking accounts, compared to $23,000 for whites, making the liquid wealth of whites one hundred times greater than for African Americans. Median total wealth for whites was fifteen times greater than that of blacks, at $111,740 versus $7,113; moreover African Americans were twice as likely to have no assets whatsoever. Whites were more likely to own homes and less likely to be underwater on their mortgages. Fifty-eight percent of whites have retirement accounts, whereas fewer than one-third of African Americans do. For every dollar of wealth whites possess, African Americans own five cents. Education does not eliminate these gaps. African American heads of household with college degrees possess 33 percent less wealth than their white counterparts. To close this gap, the median African American household would need to save 100 percent of its income for three years. Studies also show that white wealth is more likely to be boosted through inheritances. See Rebecca Tippett, Avis Jones-DeWeever, Maya Rockeymore, Darrick Hamilton, and William Darity Jr., *Beyond Broke: Why Closing the Racial Wealth Gap Is a Priority for National Economic Security* (Washington, DC: Center for Global Policy Solutions, 2014), 1–7, http://globalpolicysolutions.org/wp-content/uploads/2014/04/BeyondBroke_Exec_Summary.pdf; Darrick Hamilton, William Darity Jr., Anne E. Price, Vishnu Sridharan, and Rebecca Tippett, *Umbrellas Don't Make It Rain: Why Studying and Working Hard Isn't Enough for Black Americans* (Durham, NC: Duke Center for Social Equality, 2015), 1–10, www.insightcced.org/uploads/CRWG/Umbrellas-Dont-Make-It-Rain8.pdf.

33. Barbara J. Fields, "Slavery, Race, and Ideology in the United States of America," *New Left Review* 181 (May–June 1990): 95–118, addresses this interpretive problem.

34. Martha Biondi, "The Rise of the Reparations Movement," *Radical History Review* 87 (Fall 2003): 5.

35. Some key works on the reparations movement include Biondi, "Rise of the Reparations Movement"; Roy E. Finkenbine, "Historians and Reparations," *Organization of American Historians Newsletter*, 6 February 2006; Ronald W. Walters, *The Price of Racial Reconciliation* (Ann Arbor: University of Michigan Press, 2008), esp. chaps. 5–8; Randall Robinson, *The Debt: What America Owes to Blacks* (New York: Dutton, 2000); J. Angelo Corlett, *Race, Racism, and Reparations* (Ithaca,

NY: Cornell University Press, 2003); Raymond Winbush, ed., *Should America Pay?* (New York: HarperCollins, 2003); and Richard F. America, ed., *The Wealth of Races: The Present Value of Benefits from Past Injustices*, Contributions in Afro-American and African Studies no. 132 (New York: Greenwood Press, 1990).

Chapter 1. "There Will Be a Day of Reckoning": What Is a Slave?

1. Jourdon Anderson to Colonel P. H. Anderson, 7 August 1865, reprinted in Carter G. Woodson, ed., *The Mind of the Negro as Reflected in Letters Written during the Crisis, 1800–1860* (New York: Negro Universities Press, 1969; originally published 1929), 536–39.

2. Berlin and Morgan, *Cultivation and Culture*.

3. See Berlin and Morgan, *Slaves' Economy*, and *Cultivation and Culture*; Penningroth, *Claims of Kinfolk*; Hahn, *Nation under Our Feet*, 24–33.

4. For an analysis of just how foundational cotton production was to the development not only of the Cotton South but of capitalism on a global scale, see Sven Beckert, *Empire of Cotton: A Global History* (New York: Knopf, 2014), esp. chap. 5; and Baptist, *Half Has Never Been Told*, esp. chaps. 3 and 4.

5. Penningroth, *Claims of Kinfolk*, chap. 2. The literature on independent economies is substantial. It includes Philip D. Morgan, "Work and Culture: The Task System and the World of Lowcountry Blacks, 1700–1800," *William & Mary Quarterly*, 3rd. ser., 39, no. 4 (October 1982): 563–99; Morgan, "The Ownership of Property by Slaves in the Mid-Nineteenth-Century Low Country," *Journal of Southern History* 49 (August 1983): 399–420; Betty Wood, *Women's Work, Men's Work: The Informal Slave Economies of Lowcountry Georgia* (Athens: University of Georgia Press, 1995); Berlin and Morgan, *Slaves' Economy*; Lawrence T. McDonnell, "Money Knows No Master: Market Relations and the American Slave Community," in *Developing Dixie: Modernization in a Traditional Society*, ed. Winfred B. Moore Jr., Joseph Tripp, and Lyon G. Tyler Jr. (Westport, CT: Greenwood Press, 1988), 31–44; Loren Schweninger, "The Underside of Slavery: The Internal Economy, Self-Hire, and Quasi-Freedom in Virginia, 1780–1865," *Slavery and Abolition* 12 (September 1991): 1–22; Schweninger, "Slave Independence and Enterprise in South Carolina, 1780–1865," *South Carolina Historical Magazine* 93 (April 1992): 101–25; Schweninger, *Black Property Owners in the South, 1790–1915* (Urbana: University of Illinois Press, 1990).

6. Anne Farrow, Joel Lang, and Jenifer Frank, *Complicity: How the North Promoted, Prolonged, and Profited from Slavery* (New York: Ballantine Books, 2005), esp. chaps. 1 and 2.

7. Charles Nordhoff, "The Freedmen of South Carolina: Some Account of Their Appearance, Character, Condition, and Peculiar Customs," 20 March 1863,

in *From Slavery to Freedom: The African-American Pamphlet Collection, 1824–1909*, 7–8, Library of Congress: American Memory Collection, memory.loc.gov.

8. Quoted in Robert Ernst, "Negro Concepts of Americanism," *Journal of Negro History* 39, no. 3 (July 1954): 208–9. The American Colonization Society (ACS), founded in 1816, aimed to remove the free black population from the country and colonize them in Liberia and Sierra Leone, leaving slavery as the only status for black people remaining in the United States. The ACS established its office in Washington, DC, and its first president was Supreme Court justice Bushrod Washington, nephew of President George Washington. Members included prominent men from the North and South, though slaveholders dominated: Virginians Charles Fenton Mercer, John Tyler, and John Randolph; New Jersey minister Robert Finley; Francis Scott Key; future president Andrew Jackson; Kentucky senator Henry Clay; and Massachusetts senator Daniel Webster were among them.

9. David Walker, *David Walker's Appeal to the Coloured Citizens of the World*, ed. and intro. Peter P. Hinks (University Park: Pennsylvania State University Press, 2000 [1829]), 65; see also Peter P. Hinks, *To Awaken My Afflicted Brethren: David Walker and the Problem of Antebellum Slave Resistance* (University Park: Pennsylvania State University Press, 1997), chap. 4 and passim.

10. H. Bibb to Mr. Albert G. Sibley, 4 November and 2 December 1852, in John W. Blassingame, ed., *Slave Testimony: Two Centuries of Letters, Speeches, Interviews, and Autobiographies* (Baton Rouge: Louisiana State University Press, 1977), 52–57.

11. Edward E. Baptist has also identified theft as a central component of slaves' evaluations of their condition, chiefly for those who fell victim to the internal slave trade and were thereby separated from family members, who often spoke of people having been stolen. Baptist, *Half Has Never Been Told*, 187–213.

12. John Brown, *Slave Life in Georgia: A Narrative of the Life, Sufferings, and Escape of John Brown, A Fugitive Slave*, ed. F. N. Boney (Savannah, GA: Beehive Press, 1972 [1855]), 166.

13. Austin Steward, *Twenty-Two Years a Slave, and Forty Years a Freeman* (Syracuse, NY: Syracuse University Press, 2002 [1857]), 51.

14. See the discussion in, for example, John Hope Franklin and Loren Schweninger, *Runaway Slaves: Rebels on the Plantation* (New York: Oxford University Press, 1999), 42–48, 216–19.

15. William Craft and Ellen Craft, *Running a Thousand Miles for Freedom: The Escape of William and Ellen Craft from Slavery*, intro. Barbara McCaskill (Athens: University of Georgia Press, 1999 [1860]), 3.

16. Douglass, "What Is a Slave?" in Brotz, *African-American Social and Political Thought*, 216.

17. For detailed statistics on the scope and operations of the internal slave trade, see Baptist, *Half Has Never Been Told*, 158–84.

18. Julia Brown and Sarah Byrne quoted in George Rawick, ed., *The American Slave: A Composite Autobiography*, vol. 12, *Georgia Narratives*, pt. 1 (Greenwood, CT: Greenwood Press, 1972), 143 and 168, respectively; Cornelia Andrews, Charity Austin, and Lizzie Baker quoted in vol. 14, pt. 1, *North Carolina Narratives*, 29, 59, and 69, respectively. Phebe Brownrigg to My dear daughter, 13 September 1835, and James Phillips to Mary Phillips, 20 June 1852, both in Blassingame, *Slave Testimony*, 22, 95–96.

19. J. Brown, *Slave Life in Georgia*, 8–11.

20. Louis Hughes, *Thirty Years a Slave: From Bondage to Freedom*, ed. William L. Andrews (Montgomery, AL: NewSouth Books, 2002 [1897]), 64–65.

21. J. Brown, *Slave Life in Georgia*, 166, 169–70; see also Julie Roy Jeffrey, *The Great Silent Army of Abolitionism: Ordinary Women in the Antislavery Movement* (Chapel Hill: University of North Carolina Press, 1998), 20–22, 48, 257 n. 76, for examples of how difficult it was for grassroots antislavery women to persuade people of these points and to organize successful boycotts, particularly against cotton goods. See also Lawrence B. Glickman, "'Buy for the Sake of the Slave': Abolitionism and the Origins of American Consumer Action," *American Quarterly* 56, no. 4 (2004): 889–912.

22. Hughes, *Thirty Years a Slave*, 13, 151.

23. Economic historians of the 1970s—the cliometricians—argued that this interpretation of slavery's economic and social consequences was ahistorical in the sense that unsubstantiated arguments were employed to underscore the deleterious effects of slavery on the national economy and thus to bolster the argument for war. Slavery's quantifiable profitability meant that in "pure" economic terms it constituted no threat to the national economy—and, indeed, was essential to it. Many correctly stressed that the slave economy was intimately integrated into the national economy and that northern business and commercial elites—in particular, men who marketed and shipped slave-produced products—overwhelmingly supported slavery, were hostile toward the northern free black population, became charter members of the American Colonization Society, were staunch Democrats, and resolutely opposed the abolitionist movement. Thus, from a strictly economic standpoint, these historians argued, the Republican arguments used to prosecute the Civil War, while effective propaganda, were demonstrably erroneous about macroeconomic realities. Slavery and the emerging free labor economy were not necessarily at odds. Numerous other threads of inquiry evolved from this debate, many of them concerning how hard various groups—mistresses, masters, yeomen, and slaves—worked or did not work. The reputations of women and even more so slaveholding women, along with yeomen, were rehabilitated as a consequence. There were even debates about slave work ethics in the 1970s, somewhat odd pieces that dealt chiefly with slaveholders' views, economic theory, and the observations of

the emerging northern working class. Strangely enough, in an era when "doing history from the bottom up" was de rigueur, the thoughts of the enslaved themselves were considered only tangentially. In a recent reevaluation John Ashworth argues, "It is no exaggeration to say that Republicans fought the Civil War primarily because they deplored the economic effects of slavery," and that while the antislavery critique of the negative economic effects of slavery on the national economy could wax rhetorical, dismissal of these views has "been pushed too far. The northern critique was closer to the mark than is generally recognized." Ashworth's analysis of urban-industrial development in the antebellum South led him to conclude that the well-documented gulf between free and slave states' infrastructural development in fact reflected the baleful effects of slavery, as well as a recognition by most slaveholders that urban industrial development should remain in check since it posed real threats to master-slave relations. "The overriding point is that it is dangerous to generalize about human behavior in a slave society on the basis of unconscious assumptions drawn from experience of a wage labor economy," Ashworth underscores. This corrective refreshes the debates about labor conflicts, slavery, capitalism, and politics in the antebellum era. Nonetheless, Ashworth's analysis still unfolds from the documents of the powerful and well known. John Ashworth, *Slavery, Capitalism, and Politics in the Antebellum Republic*, vol. 1, *Commerce and Compromise, 1820–1860* (Cambridge: Cambridge University Press, 1995).

Chief among the cliometricians were Robert W. Fogel and Stanley L. Engerman, *Time on the Cross: The Economics of American Negro Slavery*, 2 vols. (Boston: Little, Brown, 1974). Fogel added to the argument in 1989 in *Without Consent or Contract: The Rise and Fall of American Slavery* (New York: Norton, 1989). Herbert Gutman criticized these works in *Slavery and the Numbers Game: A Critique of Time on the Cross* (Urbana: University of Illinois Press, 1975). Howard Temperley, "Capitalism, Slavery, and Ideology," *Past and Present* 75 (1977): 94–118, concurred with Gutman. Though not a cliometrician, Eugene D. Genovese made similar arguments in *The World the Slaveholders Made: Two Essays in Interpretation*, 2nd ed. (Middletown, CT: Wesleyan University Press, 1988). The history of Republican economic ideology against slavery can be found in E. Foner, *Free Soil, Free Labor, Free Men*; and Ashworth, *Slavery, Capitalism, and Politics*, 80–85, 501.

Currently, a new wave of research on the relationship between slavery and capitalism has emerged. Walter Johnson, in *River of Dark Dreams: Slavery and Empire in the Cotton Kingdom* (Cambridge, MA: Belknap Press, 2013), has argued that slavery itself was a capitalistic system, but he arrives at this conclusion chiefly by focusing on the economic ties between slaveholders and the emerging capitalist markets in the Atlantic world, New York, London, and Liverpool. Such an approach discounts the social relations of production within slavery itself; that is, between slaves and masters, which were decidedly not market-based. Earlier,

Barbara J. Fields, in "Slavery, Race, and Ideology in the United States," stressed that excising the master-slave economic relationship from analyses of capitalist development promoted an incomplete and thus inaccurate view of economic changes in the nineteenth century. Another recent work, Baptist, *Half Has Never Been Told*, esp. 312–42 and 352–54, falls in between these two authors, although it shares some of the views of both. Baptist makes the same argument that slaves and free African Americans did: that slave labor created the enormous profits that were then deployed in the service of capitalist development, not just in North America but in Great Britain and France as well. These works and others like them have circled back to Eric Williams's classic work, *Capitalism and Slavery* (Chapel Hill: University of North Carolina Press, 1944). Williams, who became the prime minister of Trinidad and Tobago in the 1960s, argued that profits from slavery were of central importance in the era of developing capitalism. His work centered on the economic relationships between the Caribbean and Great Britain, although he did give some attention to U.S. and British economic similarities.

24. Henry Watson, *Narrative of Henry Watson, a Fugitive Slave* (Boston: Bela Marsh, 1848), 26, in *From Slavery to Freedom: The African-American Pamphlet Collection, 1824–1909*, 7–8, Library of Congress: American Memory Collection, memory.loc.gov.

25. C. L. Innes, ed., *Slave Life in Virginia and Kentucky: A Narrative by Francis Fedric, Escaped Slave* (Baton Rouge: Louisiana State University Press, 2010 [1860]), 61.

26. Frederick Douglass, "The Self-Made Man: Address before the Students of the Indian Industrial School," p. 24, undated manuscript, Frederick Douglass Papers, Library of Congress.

27. Frederick Douglass, "What Are the Colored People Doing For Themselves?" in Brotz, *African-American Social and Political Thought*, 203–4.

28. Harriet Jacobs, *Incidents in the Life of a Slave Girl: Written by Herself*, ed. Jean Fagan Yellin (Cambridge, MA: Harvard University Press, 1987 [1861]), 26.

29. *Antislavery Almanac for 1840* (New York: S. W. Benedict; Boston: Isaac Knapp, 1840), 29; also in Jacobs, *Incidents in the Life of a Slave Girl*, 265 n. 14.

30. John S. Rock, "What If the Slaves Are Emancipated?" in *Lift Every Voice: African American Oratory, 1787–1900*, ed. Philip S. Foner and Robert James Branham (Tuscaloosa: University of Alabama Press, 1998), 363.

31. J. Brown, *Slave Life in Georgia*, 170–72.

32. Adams, *Narrative of the Life of John Quincy Adams*, 12.

33. James W. C. Pennington, *The Fugitive Blacksmith; or, Events in the History of James W. C. Pennington, Pastor of a Presbyterian Church, New York, Formerly a Slave in the State of Maryland, United States*, 2nd ed. (London: Charles Gilpin, 1849),

reprinted in *Five Slave Narratives: A Compendium* (New York: Arno Press, 1968), 56–57 (all page numbers refer to the modern edition).

34. Hughes, *Thirty Years a Slave*, 143.

35. Frederick Douglass, *My Bondage and My Freedom*, intro. Philip S. Foner (New York: Dover, 1969 [1855]), 161; emphasis added.

Chapter 2. "I Found That There Were Puzzling Exceptions": The Economic Foundations of Race during Slavery and Jim Crow

1. Some representative works on slave resistance and rebellion include James Sidbury, *Becoming African in America: Race and Nation in the Early Black Atlantic* (New York: Oxford University Press, 2007); Eugene D. Genovese, *From Rebellion to Revolution: Afro-American Slave Revolts in the Making of the Modern World* (Baton Rouge: Louisiana State University Press, 1979); Morgan, *Slave Counterpoint*; Egerton, *Gabriel's Rebellion*; Egerton, *He Shall Go Out Free: The Lives of Denmark Vesey* (Madison: University of Wisconsin Press, 1999); Edgerton, ed., *Rebels, Reformers, and Revolutionaries: Collected Essays and Second Thoughts* (New York: Routledge, 2002); Julius S. Scott III, "The Common Wind: Currents of Afro-American Communication in the Age of the Haitian Revolution" (PhD diss., Duke University, 1986); Sylvia R. Frey, *Water from the Rock: Black Resistance in a Revolutionary Age* (Princeton, NJ: Princeton University Press, 1991); Emilia Viotti da Costa, *Crowns of Glory, Tears of Blood: The Demerara Slave Rebellion of 1823* (New York: Oxford University Press, 1994); Alfred N. Hunt, *Haiti's Influence on Antebellum America: Slumbering Volcano in the Caribbean* (Baton Rouge: Louisiana State University Press, 1988); Franklin and Schweninger, *Runaway Slaves*; Hugo Prosper Learning, *Hidden Americans: Maroons of Virginia and the Carolinas* (New York: Garland, 1995); Fergus M. Bordewich, *Bound for Canaan: The Underground Railroad and the War for the Soul of America* (New York: Amistad, 2005); Hinks, *To Awaken My Afflicted Brethren*; Herbert Aptheker, ed., *American Negro Slave Revolts*, 5th ed., foreword by John H. Bracey (New York: International, 1983 [1943]); Winthrop D. Jordan, *Tumult and Silence at Second Creek: An Inquiry into a Civil War Slave Conspiracy* (Baton Rouge: Louisiana State University Press, 1993); Wendall Addington, "Slave Insurrections in Texas," *Journal of Negro History* 35 (October 1950): 408–54; Harvey Wish, "American Slave Insurrections before 1861," *Journal of Negro History* 22 (July 1937): 299–320; Baptist, *Half Has Never Been Told*, 56–65, covers the Deslondes revolt in Louisiana in 1811.

2. Bay, *White Image in the Black Mind*, 113–83; Jacqueline Jones, *A Dreadful Deceit: The Myth of Race from the Colonial Era to Obama's America* (New York: Basic Books, 2013).

3. Douglass, *My Bondage and My Freedom*, 90.

4. Ibid., 158–59.

5. Franklin and Schweninger, *Runaway Slaves*, 213–16.

6. Douglass, *My Bondage and My Freedom*, 60.

7. See, for example, the speech of Lewis Clarke in Blassingame, *Slave Testimony*, 151–64; account is on 155.

8. Douglass, *My Bondage and My Freedom*, 59–60.

9. Craft and Craft, *Running a Thousand Miles for Freedom*, 4–6; similar evidence of poor European children being sold into slavery appears in Baptist, *Half Has Never Been Told*, 83.

10. Lewis Clarke, "Leaves from a Slave's Journal of Life," in Blassingame, *Slave Testimony*, 155.

11. A historical novel examined this reality brilliantly; see David Anthony Durham, *A Walk through Darkness* (New York: Doubleday, 2002).

12. Solomon Northup, *Twelve Years a Slave*, eds. Sue Eakin and Joseph Logsdon (Baton Rouge: Louisiana State University Press, 1968 [1853]), 188–89.

13. David Walker, "The Necessity of a General Union," in Foner and Branham, *Lift Every Voice*, 113.

14. Walker, *David Walker's Appeal*, 23–25.

15. Egerton, *Gabriel's Rebellion*, 204.

16. "A. Philip Randolph Oral History, 1972," in Andrew E. Kersten, *A. Philip Randolph: A Life in the Vanguard* (Lanham, MD: Rowman & Littlefield, 2007), 124.

17. Jacobs, *Incidents in the Life of a Slave Girl*, 98–104.

18. Douglass, *My Bondage and My Freedom*, 310–12; see also Karen E. Fields and Barbara J. Fields, *Racecraft: The Soul of Inequality in American Life* (New York: Verso Books, 2012), 82–84 and passim.

19. Douglass, *My Bondage and My Freedom*, 159, 320.

20. Ibid., 221.

21. Hinks, *To Awaken My Afflicted Brethren*, esp. chap. 7; see Malcolm X's Harlem speeches in documentary footage in Orlando Bagwell, prod., *Malcolm X: Make It Plain* (Blackside/Roja Productions for American Experience, 1994).

22. Charles Ball, *Fifty Years in Chains; or, The Life of an American Slave* (Detroit: Negro History Press, 1971 [1859]), 150–51; Herbert Aptheker reached similar conclusions about 1950s and '60s activists in "Afro-American Superiority: A Neglected Theme in the Literature," *Phylon* 31, no. 4 (1970): 336–43.

23. Steward, *Twenty-Two Years a Slave*.

24. Daniel A. Payne, "Slavery Brutalizes Man," in Foner and Branham, *Lift Every Voice*, 174.

25. Craig Steven Wilder, *Ebony and Ivy: Race, Slavery, and the Troubled History of America's Universities* (New York: Bloomsbury Press, 2013), esp. pt. 2.

26. See the discussion of Darwinian theory in Carole Emberton, *Beyond Redemption: Race, Violence, and the American South after the Civil War* (Chicago: University of Chicago Press, 2013), 66–67.

27. George Washington Albright, "Mississippi Narratives," *Daily Worker*, 18 June 1937, and *Daily World*, 11 July 1975, reprinted in Rawick, *American Slave*, supp. ser. 1, vol. 6, pt. 1, p. 19.

28. Susie King Taylor, *A Black Woman's Civil War Memoirs: Reminiscences of My Life in Camp with the 33rd U.S. Colored Troops, Late the 1st South Carolina Volunteers*, ed. Patricia W. Romero, intro. Willie Lee Rose (New York: Marcus Weiner, 1988 [1902]), 111–12, 140–41.

29. Thomas E. Miller, "A Plea against the Disfranchisement of the Negro," in Foner and Branham, *Lift Every Voice*, 808–9, 811. Between 1889 and 1891 Miller served in the U.S. House of Representatives.

Chapter 3. In a Cage of Obscene Birds: Slavery's Consequences for Slaveholders and the Nation

1. Johnson, *Soul by Soul*; Steven Deyle, *Carry Me Back: The Domestic Slave Trade in American Life* (New York: Oxford University Press, 2005); Michael Tadman, *Speculators and Slaves: Masters, Traders, and Slaves in the Old South* (Madison: University of Wisconsin Press, 1989); Richard J. Follett, *The Sugar Masters: Planters and Slaves in Louisiana's Cane World, 1820–1860* (Baton Rouge: Louisiana State University Press, 2005).

2. Heather Andrea Williams, *Self-Taught: African American Education in Slavery and Freedom* (Chapel Hill: University of North Carolina Press, 2005); Paul Finkelman, ed. and intro., *Slavery and the Law*, 2 vols. (Madison: University of Wisconsin Press, 1996); Finkelman, *Statutes on Slavery: The Pamphlet Literature*, 2 vols. (New York: Garland, 1988); Finkelman, *The Law of Freedom and Bondage: A Casebook* (New York: Oceana, 1986).

3. Frederick Douglass, "Address before the Tennessee Colored Agricultural and Mechanical Association," September 18, 1873, in Brotz, *African-American Social and Political Thought*, 291; Douglass, *My Bondage and My Freedom*, 68.

4. H. Bibb to Mr. Albert G. Sibley, 7 October and 4 November 1852, in Blassingame, *Slave Testimony*, 52–55.

5. Jackson Whitney to William Riley, 18 March 1859, in Blassingame, *Slave Testimony*, 114–15.

6. Hughes, *Thirty Years a Slave*, 151.

7. *Light and Truth of Slavery, Aaron's History* (Worcester, MA, 1845), 25, available from *Documenting the American South*, http://docsouth.unc.edu/neh/aaron/aaron.html.

8. Sam Aleckson, *Before the War, and after the Union: An Autobiography* (Boston: Gold Mind, 1929), 99, available from *Documenting the American South*, http://docsouth.unc.edu/neh/aleckson/aleckson.html.

9. Jacobs, *Incidents in the Life of a Slave Girl*, 52.

10. Steward, *Twenty-Two Years a Slave*, 26; see Glymph, *Out of the House of Bondage*, esp. chaps. 1 and 2, for an extended analysis of slave mistresses' violence toward female slaves.

11. J. Brown, *Slave Life in Georgia*, 47.

12. Northup, *Twelve Years a Slave*, 157.

13. Thomas Jefferson, *Notes on the State of Virginia*, ed. William Peden (New York: W. W. Norton, 1982 [1787]), 162–63.

14. Douglass, *My Bondage and My Freedom*, 80, 83.

15. Pennington, *Fugitive Blacksmith*, 69–73.

16. Douglass, *My Bondage and My Freedom*, 141–46, 151–54, 161.

17. Watson, *Narrative of Henry Watson*.

18. Douglass, *My Bondage and My Freedom*, 131–32.

19. Jacobs, *Incidents in the Life of a Slave Girl*, 15.

20. J. Sella Martin, speech in the *Nonconformist* (London), 8 November 1865, reprinted in C. Peter Ripley, Jeffrey S. Rossbach et al., eds., *The Black Abolitionist Papers*, 5 vols. (Chapel Hill: University of North Carolina Press, 1985–92), 1:565–67; also see Ripley et al., ed., *Witness for Freedom: African American Voices on Race, Slavery, and Emancipation* (Chapel Hill: University of North Carolina Press, 1993), 80.

21. Charles L. Perdue Jr., Thomas E. Barden, and Robert K. Phillips, eds., *Weevils in the Wheat: Interviews with Virginia Ex-Slaves* (Bloomington: Indiana University Press, 1980), 273.

22. Pennington, *Fugitive Blacksmith*, xii.

23. J. Brown, *Slave Life in Georgia*, 166.

24. Jacobs, *Incidents in the Life of a Slave Girl*, 50.

25. Hughes, *Thirty Years a Slave*, 136–37, 151.

26. Douglass, *My Bondage and My Freedom*, 263, 272–73.

27. Isaac Mason, *Life of Isaac Mason as a Slave* (1910; reprint, Miami, FL: Mnemosyne, 1969), 49, available from *Documenting the American South*, http://docsouth.unc.edu/fpn/mason/mason.html.

28. William Mallory, "Old Plantation Days" (Hamilton, Ont.[?]: n.p., n.d. 1902[?]), 3, available from *Documenting the American South*, http://docsouth.unc.edu/neh/mallory/mallory.html.

29. Jacobs, *Incidents in the Life of a Slave Girl*, 12, 101.

30. *Light and Truth of Slavery, Aaron's History* (Worcester, MA: n.p., 184[?]), 24, http://docsouth.unc.edu/neh/aaron/aaron.html.

31. Ball, *Fifty Years in Chains*, 216.

32. Aristotle, *Politics*, trans. Ernest Barker (Oxford: Oxford University Press, 1995), Book VI, 265. The perception of laziness itself changed in all societies undergoing industrial revolutions, as the United States was in the post–Civil War decades. Prior to industrialization, most elites regarded labor as a curse rather than a virtue. Work had to take place in order for higher civilization to exist. As Hannah Arendt underscored, a central feature of the modern work ethic "is its glorification of labor," a historical phenomenon that for the majority of free people in the United States dated back only to the emancipation era. Hannah Arendt and Peter R. Baehr, eds., *The Portable Hannah Arendt* (New York: Penguin, 2000), 169–70. See also Rodgers, *Work Ethic in Industrial America*.

33. William Wells Brown, *From Fugitive Slave to Free Man: The Autobiographies of William Wells Brown*, 2nd ed., ed. and intro. William L. Andrews (Columbia: University of Missouri Press, 2003 [1848]), 107–8; emphasis in the original.

34. Hughes, *Thirty Years a Slave*, 137.

35. Walker, "Necessity of a General Union," in Foner and Branham, *Lift Every Voice*, 131.

36. Henry Highland Garnet, "The Past and Present Condition, and the Destiny of the Colored Race: A Discourse Delivered on the Fifteenth Anniversary of the Female Benevolent Society of Troy, New York (Troy, NY: Steamer Press of J. C. Kneeland, 1848), 27, available from Digital Commons at the University of Nebraska–Lincoln, http://digitalcommons.unl.edu/etas/13/.

37. James Mellon, ed., *Bullwhip Days: The Slaves Remember* (New York: Weidenfeld & Nicolson, 1988), 115.

38. William Wells Brown, "A Lecture Delivered before the Female Anti-slavery Society of Salem: at Lyceum Hall," 14 November 1847, 4–5, 7. Reported by Henry M. Parkhurst. Rare Book Room Manuscript and Special Collections Library, Duke University.

39. J. Brown, *Slave Life in Georgia*, 167–69.

Chapter 4. "Cruelty Is Inseparable from Slavery": Violence, Rape, and the Right of Self-Defense

1. By and large, studies of violence against slaves are limited to an analysis of the acts perpetrated against them, as opposed to the social and psychological consequences borne by the victims. Some exceptions include Nell Irvin Painter, "Soul Murder and Slavery: Toward a Fully Loaded Cost Accounting," in *Southern History across the Color Line*, 15–39; Saidiya V. Hartman, *Scenes of Subjection: Terror, Slavery, and Self-Making in Nineteenth-Century America* (New York: Oxford University Press, 1997); for the Reconstruction era, see Emberton, *Beyond Redemption*; Rosen, *Terror in the Heart of Freedom*; Kidada Williams, *They Left Great Marks on Me:*

African American Testimonies of Racial Violence from Emancipation to World War I (New York: New York University Press, 2012).

2. As Edward E. Baptist has aptly noted, historians have fallen victim to slaveholder rationales about violence as well, being on the whole reluctant to use the term "torture" when they discuss violence.

> Even white abolitionist critics of slavery and their heirs among the ranks of historians were reluctant to say that it was torture to beat a bound victim with a weapon until the victim bled profusely, did what was wanted, or both. Perhaps one unspoken reason why many have been so reluctant to apply the term "torture" to slavery is that even though they denied slavery's economic dynamism, they knew that slavery on the cotton frontier made a lot of product. No one was willing, in other words, to admit that they lived in an economy whose bottom gear was torture. Yet we should call torture by its name. . . . you can find at one point or another almost every product sold in New Orleans stores converted into an instrument of torture: carpenters' tools, chains, cotton presses, hackles, handsaws, hoe handles, irons for branding livestock, nails, pokers, smoothing irons, singletrees, steelyards, tongs. Every modern method of torture was used at one time or another: sexual humiliation, mutilation, electric shocks, solitary confinement in "stress positions," burning, even waterboarding.

Baptist, *Half Has Never Been Told*, 139, 141. His chapter 4 is devoted to issues of violence and torture in the cotton South, where steadily escalating cotton production was a direct consequence of increased levels of torture, which Baptist recognizes as a factor of production.

3. Walker, *David Walker's Appeal*, 65–66.

4. Ibid., 69.

5. J. Brown, *Slave Life in Georgia*, 165–66.

6. Douglass, *My Bondage and My Freedom*, 90.

7. Baptist, *Half Has Never Been Told*, 141.

8. Henry Bibb, *Narrative of the Life and Adventures of Henry Bibb, An American Slave, Written by Himself* (New York, 1850); reprinted in Gilbert Osofsky, ed., *Puttin' on Ole Massa* (New York: Harper & Row, 1969), 119–20.

9. J. Brown, *Slave Life in Georgia*, 58.

10. Bibb, *Narrative of the Life and Adventures*, in Osofsky, *Puttin' on Ole Massa*, 132–34.

11. J. Brown, *Slave Life in Georgia*, 110–11.

12. Hughes, *Thirty Years a Slave*, 27–28.

13. Ibid., 25–28, 42.

14. Edward E. Baptist observed that many cotton planters and overseers attacked their best pickers in order to force them to produce higher daily quotas. Baptist, *Half Has Never Been Told*, 140.

15. J. Brown, *Slave Life in Georgia*, 32–39.

16. Ibid., 40–42. For more information on this topic see Todd Savitt, *Medicine and Slavery: The Diseases and Health Care of Blacks in Antebellum Virginia* (Urbana: University of Illinois Press, 1978), chap. 9; and Harriet A. Washington, *Medical Apartheid: The Dark History of Medical Experimentation on Black Americans from Colonial Times to the Present* (New York: Anchor Books, 2007).

17. James Williams, *The Narrative of James Williams, an American Slave* (New York: American Anti-Slavery Society, 1838), 79, available from *Documenting the American South*, http://docsouth.unc.edu/fpn/williams/williams.html.

18. Ball, *Fifty Years in Chains*, 388–91, 407–12.

19. J. Brown, *Slave Life in Georgia*, 58–59.

20. Solomon Bradley, interview, 1863, and Robert Smalls, interview, 1863, in Blassingame, *Slave Testimony*, 372, 379; Marie Harvey quoted in Rawick, *American Slave, Arkansas Narratives*, vol. 2, pt. 3, 231.

21. Steward, *Twenty-Two Years a Slave*, 338.

22. Douglass, *My Bondage and My Freedom*, 85–88.

23. On 26 July 1864 the *New Orleans Tribune* ran an article, "The Treatment of Women," which observed that "the tortures sometimes inflicted on these helpless favorites of the husband by the infuriated wife in order to render them less attractive to the husband, are not to be described."

24. Northup, *Twelve Years a Slave*, 142–43, 194–201.

25. Follett, *Sugar Masters*, 46–89. Some key works on women and slavery include Norrece T. Jones Jr., "Rape in Black and White: Sexual Violence in the Testimony of Enslaved and Free Americans," in *Slavery and the American South*, ed. Winthrop Jordan (Jackson: University of Mississippi Press, 2003), 93–108, see also commentary by Jan Lewis on 108–16; Darlene Clark Hine, "Rape and the Inner Lives of Southern Black Women: Thoughts on the Culture of Dissemblance," in Virginia Bernhard et al., eds., *Southern Women: Histories and Identities* (Columbia: University of Missouri Press, 1992), 177–79; Deborah Gray White, *A'rn't I a Woman? Female Slaves in the Plantation South*, 2nd ed. (New York: W. W. Norton, 1999); Brenda E. Stevenson, *Life in Black and White: Family and Community in the Slave South* (New York: Oxford University Press, 1996); Blassingame, *Slave Community*, 154–56, 172–73; Catherine Clinton, "Caught in the Web of the Big House: Women and Slavery," in *The Web of Southern Social Relations: Women, Family, and Education*, ed. Walter J. Fraser Jr., R. Frank Saunders Jr., and Jon L. Wakelyn (Athens: University of Georgia Press, 1985); Clinton, *The Plantation Mistress: Women's World in the Old South* (New York: Pantheon, 1982); Martha Hodes, *White Women, Black Men: Illicit Sex in the Nineteenth-Century South* (New Haven, CT: Yale University Press, 1997), 1–9; Adele Logan Alexander, *Ambiguous Lives: Free Women of Color in Rural Georgia, 1789–1879* (Fayetteville: University of Arkansas

Press, 1991), 63–66, 78–79, 86–89; Carolyn Powell, "In Remembrance of Mira," in *Discovering the Women in Slavery: Emancipating Perspectives on the American Past*, ed. Patricia Gordon (Athens: University of Georgia Press, 1996), 47–60; Marie Jenkins Schwartz, *Born in Bondage: Growing Up Enslaved in the Antebellum South* (Cambridge, MA: Harvard University Press, 2000); Victoria E. Bynum, "Misshapen Identity: Memory, Folklore, and the Legend of Rachel Knight," in Gordon, *Discovering the Women in Slavery*, 29–46; Thelma Jennings, "'Us Colored Women Had to Go through a Plenty': Sexual Exploitation of African-American Slave Women," *Journal of Women's History* 1, no. 3 (Winter 1990): 45–74; Jacobs, *Incidents in the Life of a Slave Girl*; Johnson, *Soul by Soul*; Painter, "Soul Murder and Slavery," 125–46; Hartman, *Scenes of Subjection*, 79–112; Hartman, *Lose Your Mother: A Journey along the Atlantic Slave Route* (New York: Farrar, Straus and Giroux, 2007); Elizabeth Fox-Genovese, *Within the Plantation Household: Black and White Women in the Old South* (Chapel Hill: University of North Carolina Press, 1988); Edward E. Baptist, "'Cuffy,' 'Fancy Maids,' and 'One-Eyed Men'": Rape, Commodification, and the Domestic Slave Trade in the United States," *American Historical Review* 106, no. 5 (December 2001): 1619–50; Stephanie M. H. Camp, *Closer to Freedom: Enslaved Women and Everyday Resistance in the Plantation South* (Chapel Hill: University of North Carolina Press, 2004); Glymph, *Out of the House of Bondage*, esp. chaps. 1 and 2.

26. See also the evidence in Baptist, *Half Has Never Been Told*, 233–44.

27. Baptist, *Half Has Never Been Told*, 118–43, provides an extended analysis of this phenomenon.

28. Watson, *Narrative of Henry Watson*, Library of Congress, 12–15, 19, 21–26, 31, 35–38.

29. Adams, *Narrative of the Life of John Quincy Adams*, 43.

30. Benjamin Drew, ed., *North-Side View of Slavery* (New York: Negro Universities Press, 1968 [1856]), 73–74.

31. Franklin and Schweninger, *Runaway Slaves*, 210–13, 216–19.

32. For an extended development of this observation see David Barry Gaspar, *Bondmen and Rebels: A Study of Master-Slave Relations in Antigua, with Implications for Colonial British America* (Baltimore: Johns Hopkins University Press, 1985), 255–58.

33. Henry Irving Tragle, ed., *The Southampton Slave Revolt of 1831: A Compilation of Source Material* (Amherst: University of Massachusetts Press, 1971), 17.

34. Bibb, *Narrative of the Life and Adventures*, in Osofsky, *Puttin' on Ole Massa*, 66.

35. As Walter Johnson has noted, "The withering difficulty of organizing a revolution in the midst of an active and powerful campaign of slaveholding counterinsurgency and the long odds of its success, might have led even fully self-realized

psychological independents to resist without revolting." Johnson, "Clerks All! Or, Slaves with Cash," *Journal of the Early Republic* 26 (Winter 2006): 646.

36. Josiah Henson, *The Life of Josiah Henson, Formerly a Slave, Now an Inhabitant of Canada, As Narrated by Himself* (Boston: Arthur D. Phelps, 1849), 40–58, available from *Documenting the American South*, http://docsouth.unc.edu/neh/henson49/henson49.html.

37. Jacobs, *Incidents in the Life of a Slave Girl*, 196.

38. Perdue et al., eds., *Weevils in the Wheat*, 128, 93.

39. Douglass, *My Bondage and My Freedom*, 269–70.

40. Adams, *Narrative of the Life of John Quincy Adams*, 45, 48.

41. Sam Aleckson, *Before the War, and after the Union*, in *Documenting the American South*.

42. Jeff Hamilton, *My Master: The Inside Story of Sam Houston and His Times*, as told to Lenoir Hunt (Austin: State House Press, 1992 [1940]), 2.

43. Henry Bibb to William Gatewood, 23 March 1844, in Blassingame, *Slave Testimony*, 48–49.

44. James L. Smith, *Autobiography of James L. Smith, Including, Also, Reminiscences of Slave Life, Recollections of the War, Education of the Freedmen, Causes of the Exodus, etc.* (Norwich: Press of the Bulletin Co., 1881), 100, available from *Documenting the American South*, http://docsouth.unc.edu/neh/smithj/smithj.html.

45. Drew, *North-Side View of Slavery*, 270.

46. Walker, *David Walker's Appeal*, 66.

47. Douglass, *My Bondage and My Freedom*, 205–49.

48. Walker, *David Walker's Appeal*, 26.

Chapter 5. Democracy Meets the Industrial Revolution: Reconstruction Achievements and the Counterrevolution against Them

1. Karl Marx, *The Eighteenth Brumaire of Louis Bonaparte* (New York: International, 1963 [1852]), 13.

2. E. Foner, *Reconstruction*, chap. 5; Hahn, *Nation under Our Feet*, 116–59.

3. Hahn, *Nation under Our Feet*, 146–54; E. Foner, *Reconstruction*, 195–212.

4. William H. Barnes, *History of the Thirty-Ninth Congress of the United States* (New York: Negro Universities Press, 1969 [1868]), 97–98.

5. E. Foner, *Reconstruction*, 239–61.

6. Ibid., 314–15; Hahn, *Nation under Our Feet*, 164–65.

7. Hahn, *Nation under Our Feet*, 177–98; Michael W. Fitzgerald, *The Union League Movement in the Deep South: Politics and Agricultural Change during Reconstruction* (Baton Rouge: Louisiana State University Press, 1989).

8. Elsa Barkley Brown, "Negotiating and Transforming the Public Sphere: African American Political Life in the Transition from Slavery to Freedom," *Public*

Culture 7, no. 1 (Fall 1994): 107–46; Hahn, *Nation under Our Feet*, 175; Schwalm, *Hard Fight for We*, 190–94.

9. Kathleen Ann Clark, *Defining Moments: African American Commemoration and Political Culture in the South, 1863–1913* (Chapel Hill: University of North Carolina Press, 2005), 33–38; Blight, *Race and Reunion*, 67.

10. E. Foner, *Reconstruction*; Foner, *Freedom's Lawmakers: A Directory of Black Officeholders during Reconstruction* (New York: Oxford University Press, 1993); Hahn, *Nation under Our Feet*; Fitzgerald, *Union League Movement*.

11. The Emancipation Proclamation, issued on 1 January 1863, declared all slaves behind Confederate lines free, but that status was contingent upon the outcome of the war. In reality, the proclamation freed not a single person. Lincoln exempted slaves in Union-occupied districts and in the four loyal slave states of Maryland, Missouri, Delaware, and Kentucky. The proclamation also legitimized African American entry into the Union Army, which ultimately resulted in the enlistment of some 200,000 black soldiers, the majority of them former slaves. In the proclamation's aftermath, slave resistance on farms and plantations escalated and the addition of much-needed manpower tipped the advantage in the war to the Union.

12. Frederick Douglass, "The Mission of the War," in Foner and Branham, *Lift Every Voice*, 420–21; emphasis added.

13. Henry Highland Garnet, "Let the Monster Perish," excerpted from *A Memorial Discourse by Rev. Henry Highland Garnet, Delivered in the Hall of the House of Representatives, Washington, D.C., on Sabbath, February 12, 1865, with an Introduction by James McCune Smith* (Philadelphia, 1865), in Foner and Branham, *Lift Every Voice*, 432–43; quotation on 443.

14. B. K. Sampson, "To My White Fellow Citizens," in Foner and Branham, *Lift Every Voice*, 467–69; quotation on 469.

15. Speech of Martin R. Delany, reported in the letter of Lt. Edward M. Stoeber to Brt. Maj. S. M. Taylor, Asst. Adj't Gen'l, 24 July 1865, in Foner and Branham, *Lift Every Voice*, 446–51.

16. Frances Ellen Watkins Harper, "We Are All Bound Up Together: Proceedings of the Eleventh Women's Rights Convention" (May 1866), in Foner and Branham, *Lift Every Voice*, 456–60.

17. Garnet, "Let the Monster Perish," 440–41.

18. "Proceedings of the Convention of the Colored People of Va., Held in the City of Alexandria, Aug. 2, 3, 4, 5, 1865," in *Proceedings of the Black State Conventions, 1840–1865*, ed. Philip S. Foner and George E. Walker (Philadelphia, PA: Temple University Press, 1980), 262.

19. Rev. Henry McNeal Turner, "I Claim the Rights of a Man," in Foner and Branham, *Lift Every Voice*, 480–81. The editors note that "Turner's speech has been preserved in Ethel Maude Christler's 'Participation of Negroes in the Government

of Georgia, 1867–1870' (master's thesis, Atlanta University, June 1932), 82–96. Christler copied the speech from a pamphlet she reportedly obtained from Bishop J. S. Flipper of Atlanta."

20. James Lynch, *A Few Things about the Educational Work among Freedmen of South Carolina and Georgia, Also, Addresses Delivered at Augusta and Nashville* (Baltimore, MD: William K. Boyle, Printer, 1865), 21–22.

21. Henry McNeal Turner, "On the Anniversary of Emancipation," *Augusta Colored American*, 6 January 1866, reprinted in Edwin S. Redkey, ed., *Respect Black: The Writings and Speeches of Henry McNeal Turner* (New York: Arno Press, 1971), 5–7.

22. *New Orleans Tribune*, 19 April 1865. The Battle of Fort Pillow, often called the Massacre of Fort Pillow, occurred in April 1864 in Tennessee, upriver from Memphis. Confederates savagely attacked black troops, shooting them in the back, burning them, and burying them alive. Confederate policy treated black Union soldiers as slave insurrectionists.

23. "Let There Be Light: Important Facts Concerning the Negro," in *Facts Concerning the Freedmen: Their Capacity and Their Destiny*, Collected and Published by the Emancipation League (Boston: Press of Commercial Printing House, 1863), 12, 10, 7, 4, in Library of Congress, American Memory Collection, memory.loc.gov.

24. Capt. Andw. Geddes to Colonel C. Cadle Jr., 6 Oct. 1865, in *Freedom: A Documentary History of Emancipation, 1861–1867,* ed. Steven Hahn et al., 813; see also the editor's introduction to chap. 9; and Hahn, *Nation under Our Feet,* chap. 6.

25. Hahn, *Nation under Our Feet,* 263; Emberton, *Beyond Redemption,* chap. 3.

26. *The struggle between the civilization of slavery and that of freedom, recently and now going on in Louisiana: An address delivered by Edward C. Billings, Esq., of New Orleans, at Hatfield, Mass., Oct. 20, 1873* (Northampton, MA: Gazette Printing Co.'s Steam Press, 1873), 17–18, in Library of Congress, American Memory Collection, memory.loc.gov.

27. For two recent analyses of the massacre see Charles Lane, *The Day Freedom Died: The Colfax Massacre, the Supreme Court, and the Betrayal of Reconstruction* (New York: Henry Holt, 2008); and Leanna Keith, *The Colfax Massacre: The Untold Story of Black Power, White Terror and the Death of Reconstruction* (New York: Oxford University Press, 2008). The perpetrators' federal convictions were appealed to the Supreme Court in *United States v. Cruikshank* (1876), which held that the Fourteenth Amendment applied only to state governments and not to individuals who violated civil rights, thus ushering in a specious argument that informed a number of later decisions, including the 1883 declaration of the 1875 Civil Rights Act as unconstitutional and the intellectual bedrock of *Plessy v. Ferguson* in 1896.

28. For a recent analysis of this process in one state, see Christopher M. Span,

African American Education in Mississippi, 1862–1875 (Chapel Hill: University of North Carolina Press, 2009).

29. Litwack, *Been in the Storm So Long*; E. Foner, *Reconstruction*; Hahn, *Nation under Our Feet*; James Dance Cawthon, "A Caddo Parish Sheriff during Reconstruction Times," *Northern Louisiana Historical Journal* 20, no. 1 (1989): 3–19.

30. Jane Elizabeth Dailey, *Before Jim Crow: The Politics of Race in Postemancipation Virginia* (Chapel Hill: University of North Carolina Press, 2000).

31. E. Foner, *Reconstruction*, 364–79; Hahn, *Nation under Our Feet*, 259–64.

32. Quoted in Hahn, *Nation under Our Feet*, 448.

33. Joseph Rainey, "We Did Not Discriminate," *Congressional Globe*, 1872, reprinted in *In Their Own Words: A History of the American Negro, 1865–1916*, ed. Milton Meltzer (New York: Thomas Y. Crowell, 1965), 39–42.

34. George Washington Albright, "Mississippi Narratives," in Rawick, *American Slave*, supp. ser. 1, vol. 6, pt. 1, 12–18.

35. T. Thomas Fortune, "Between Two Fires," *New York Globe*, 27 October 1883, in *T. Thomas Fortune, The Afro-American Agitator: A Collection of Writings, 1880–1928*, ed. Shawn Leigh Alexander (Gainesville: University Press of Florida, 2008), 20–21.

36. Perdue et al., *Weevils in the Wheat*, 213.

37. Janet Sharp Hermann, *The Pursuit of a Dream* (New York: Oxford University Press, 1981); E. Foner, *Reconstruction*, 58–59; Hahn, *Nation under Our Feet*, 79–82, 167.

38. Isaac Myers, "Uniting Workingmen," in Foner and Branham, *Lift Every Voice*, 483–85; W.E.B. Du Bois, *Economic Co-operation among Negro Americans: Report of a Study Made by Atlanta University* (1907), in *Documenting the American South*, 152–54, http://docsouth.unc.edu/church/dubois07/dubois.html.

39. Adams, *Narrative of the Life of John Quincy Adams*, 16–17, 21–22.

40. "Proceedings of the California State Convention of the Colored Citizens, Held in Sacramento on the 25th, 27th, and 28th of October, 1865," in Foner and Walker, *Proceedings of the Black State Conventions*, 191.

41. Berlin, *Generations of Captivity*, 266; E. Foner, *Reconstruction*, 102–10.

42. Berlin et al., eds., *Freedom: A Documentary History of Emancipation, 1861–1867, Selected from the Holdings of the National Archives of the United States*, ser. 1, vol. II: *The Wartime Genesis of Free Labor: The Upper South* (New York: Cambridge University Press, 1993), 426–29.

43. Hahn et al., *Freedom*, ser. 3, vol. 1, *Land and Labor*, 817.

44. Adams, *Narrative of the Life of John Quincy Adams*, 15.

45. Saville, *Work of Reconstruction*, 18–24; Emberton, *Beyond Redemption*, 74–75; Hahn, *Nation under Our Feet*, 135–46; "Minutes of an Interview between the Colored Ministers and Church Officers at Savannah with the Secretary of War

and Major-Gen. Sherman, City of Savannah, Ga., Jan. 12, 1865," in Berlin et al., *Free at Last: A Documentary History of Slavery, Freedom, and the Civil War* (New York: New Press, 1992), 312, 314.

46. William T. Sherman, *Memoirs of General W. T. Sherman* (New York: Library of America, 1990), 2:250–52.

47. The literature on lynching is substantial. An introduction would include Leon F. Litwack, *Trouble in Mind: Black Southerners in the Age of Jim Crow* (New York: Vintage, 1999), esp. chap. 6; K. Williams, *They Left Great Marks on Me*; Manfred Berg, *Popular Justice: A History of Lynching in America* (Chicago: Ivan R. Dee, 2011); Evelyn M. Simien, ed., *Gender and Lynching: The Politics of Memory* (New York: Palgrave Macmillan, 2011); Mia Bay, *To Tell the Truth Freely: The Life of Ida B. Wells* (New York: Hill & Wang, 2010); Claude Andrew Clegg III, *Troubled Ground: A Tale of Murder, Lynching, and Reckoning in the New South* (Urbana: University of Illinois Press, 2010); Edwin T. Arnold, *"What Virtue There Is in Fire": Cultural Memory and the Lynching of Sam Hose* (Athens: University of Georgia Press, 2009); Christopher Waldrep, *African Americans Confront Lynching: Strategies of Resistance from the Civil War to the Civil Rights Era* (Lanham, MD: Rowman & Littlefield, 2009); Waldrep, ed., *Lynching in America: A History in Documents* (New York: New York University Press, 2006); Bruce E. Baker, *This Mob Will Surely Take My Life: Lynchings in the Carolinas, 1871–1947* (New York: Continuum, 2008); Paula J. Giddings, *Ida: A Sword among Lions: Ida B. Wells and the Campaign against Lynching* (New York: Amistad, 2008); Philip Drey, *At the Hands of Persons Unknown: The Lynching of Black America* (New York: Modern Library, 2003); W. Fitzhugh Brundage, *Under Sentence of Death: Lynching in the South* (Chapel Hill: University of North Carolina Press, 1997); Brundage, *Lynching in the New South: Georgia and Virginia, 1880–1930* (Urbana: University of Illinois Press, 1993); Stuart E. Tolney and E. M. Beck, *A Festival of Violence: An Analysis of Southern Lynching, 1881–1930* (Urbana: University of Illinois Press, 1995); Jacquelyn Dowd Hall, *Revolt against Chivalry: Jessie Daniel Ames and the Women's Campaign against Lynching* (New York: Columbia University Press, 1993); Paul Finkelman, ed., *Lynching, Racial Violence, and the Law* (New York: Garland, 1992).

48. Philip S. Foner, ed., *Life and Writings of Frederick Douglass*, 4 vols. (New York: International, 1950–55), 4:476.

49. Walter White, *Rope and Faggot: A Biography of Judge Lynch* (New York: Knopf, 1929), 11; see other examples of this view in Litwack, *Trouble in Mind*, 320–21, 540 n. 91–92. Ida B. Wells-Barnett, *On Lynching: Southern Horrors, a Red Record, Mob Rule in New Orleans* (New York: Arno Press, 1969 [1892]); Wells-Barnett, *Crusade for Justice*; see also Patricia Schecter, *Ida B. Wells-Barnett and American Reform, 1880–1930* (Chapel Hill: University of North Carolina Press, 2001). Wells's findings have been refined since their initial publication in the late

1890s, but the fundamental interpretations have remained the same. Between 1892 and 1951, 4,730 people were lynched, 3,437 of whom (70 percent) were African American. Litwack, *Trouble in Mind*, 93.

50. Pete Daniel, *The Shadow of Slavery: Peonage in the South, 1901–1969* (Urbana: University of Illinois Press, 1972); Douglas A. Blackmon, *Slavery by Another Name: The Reenslavement of Black Americans from the Civil War to World War II* (New York: Random House, 2008).

51. Koritha Mitchell, *Living with Lynching: African American Lynching Plays, Performance, and Citizenship, 1890–1930* (Urbana: University of Illinois Press, 2011), 17, 26, 37.

52. Paul Harvey, "'These Untutored Masses': The Campaign for Respectability among White and Black Evangelicals in the American South, 1870–1930," *Journal of Religious History* 21, no. 3 (October 1997): 303 and passim; E. Brown, "Negotiating and Transforming the Public Sphere."

53. Rev. Francis J. Grimké, "The Negro Will Never Acquiesce as Long as He Lives," 20 November 1898, in Foner and Branham, *Lift Every Voice*, 873–74. Grimké was the nephew of abolitionists Angelina and Sarah Grimké, the son of their brother Henry and a slave woman, Nancy Weston.

54. Gaines, *Uplifting the Race*, 6.

Chapter 6. Ethical Transmissions: Consultations with the Emancipation Generation

1. Eric Arnesen, "A. Philip Randolph and the New Black Politics," in *The Human Rights Tradition in the Civil Rights Movement*, ed. Susan M. Glisson (New York: Rowman & Littlefield, 2006), 80.

2. Ibid.

3. Kersten, "A. Philip Randolph Oral History, 1972," 123.

4. Benjamin J. Davis Jr., *Communist Councilman from Harlem: Autobiographical Notes Written in a Federal Penitentiary* (New York: International, 1969), 26, 28–29, emphasis added; see also Hahn, *Nation under Our Feet*, 3–4, 15–16.

5. Sterling Stuckey, "'I Want to Be an African': Paul Robeson and the Ends of Nationalist Theory and Practice, 1919–1945," *Massachusetts Review* 17, no. 1 (Spring 1976): 81–138.

6. Paul Robeson, *Here I Stand* (Boston: Beacon Press, 1958), 8–9.

7. Quoted in Stuckey, "I Want to Be an African," 81.

8. Robeson, *Here I Stand*, 10.

9. Ibid., 15.

10. Ibid., 11; Charles Payne observed that rural African Americans in Mississippi in the 1950s and 1960s still held these slave-based beliefs dear to heart. "If humanism is a belief in the essential oneness of human kind," Payne wrote,

"then one traditional strand of southern Black culture was a visceral humanism, a dearly bought, broad perspective on human behavior that militated against thinking about people in one-dimensional terms." Charles Payne, *I've Got the Light of Freedom: The Organizing Tradition and the Mississippi Freedom Struggle* (Berkeley: University of California Press, 1995), 314.

11. Robeson, *Here I Stand*, 20.

12. Ibid., 28, emphasis added.

13. Robert Russa Moton, *Finding a Way Out: An Autobiography* (Garden City, NY: Doubleday, 1921), 15.

14. Ida B. Wells, "Southern Horrors: Lynch Law in All Its Phases" (1892), in Jacqueline Jones Royster, ed., *Southern Horrors and Other Writings: The Anti-Lynching Campaign of Ida B. Wells, 1892–1900* (New York: Bedford Books, 1997), 70.

15. W.E.B. Du Bois, *Autobiography of W.E.B. Du Bois: A Soliloquy on Viewing My Life from the Last Decade of Its First Century* (New York: International, 1968), 286.

16. Nate Shaw, *All God's Dangers: The Life of Nate Shaw*, ed. Theodore Rosengarten (New York: Vintage, 1984), 555–56.

17. Timothy Tyson, "Robert F. Williams, 'Black Power,' and the Roots of the African American Freedom Struggle," *Journal of American History* 85, no. 2 (September 1998): 540–47, 570.

18. Bob Moses to Mary King, quoted in Payne, *I've Got the Light of Freedom*, 204.

19. Shaw, *All God's Dangers*, 26–31.

20. Ibid., 544, 552, 175.

21. Walter Johnson has described this attitude about greed as rejecting the "bourgeois notion of freedom as the right to possess" while embracing the "more radical notions of freedom achieved through the duty to contribute, and around notions of self and the care of the self framed not by independence but by belonging." Johnson, "Clerks All!," 648.

22. Zora Neale Hurston, *Their Eyes Were Watching God*, ed. Sherley Anne Williams (Urbana: University of Illinois Press, 1978 [1937]), 172.

23. Genna Rae McNeil, *Groundwork: Charles Hamilton Houston and the Struggle for Civil Rights* (Philadelphia: University of Pennsylvania Press, 1983), 84; Patricia Sullivan, *Lift Every Voice: The NAACP and the Making of the Civil Rights Movement* (New York: New Press, 2009), 159–62.

24. Charles W. Chesnutt, "The Courts and the Negro," in *Plessy v. Ferguson: A Brief History with Documents*, ed. Brook Thomas (Boston: Bedford Books, 1997), 156.

25. Erik S. Gellman, *Death Blow to Jim Crow: The National Negro Congress and the Rise of Militant Civil Rights* (Chapel Hill: University of North Carolina Press, 2012), 4–7.

26. Ibid., 234–39.

27. Barbara Ransby, *Ella Baker and the Black Freedom Movement: A Radical Democratic Vision* (Chapel Hill: University of North Carolina Press, 2003), chap. 1, 13–45.

28. Hahn, *Nation under Our Feet*, 465–66. In the 1920s, an additional 800,000 left, joined by 400,000 more during the Depression decade. Between 1940 and 1960, nearly another 3.5 million migrated.

29. Ibid., 465–76.

30. *Negro World*, 29 January 1927.

31. Manning Marable, *Malcolm X: A Life of Reinvention* (New York: Viking, 2011), 17–18.

32. Ibid., 19–21.

33. From documentary footage in Bagwell, prod., *Malcolm X*.

34. Ibid.

35. Ibid.; emphasis added.

36. Marable, *Malcolm X*, 20–36.

37. Hahn, *Political Worlds of Slavery and Freedom*, 155–57.

38. Marable, *Malcolm X*, 483–87.

Chapter 7. Ethical Legacies for the Twenty-First Century: Apologies, Regrets, Therapy, and Reparations

1. Franklin first made this statement in an 8 September 1968 *New York Times* article, "Rediscovering Black America: A Historical Roundup."

2. V. P. Franklin, "Introduction: African Americans and Movements for Reparations: From Ex-slave Pensions to the Reparations Superfund," *Journal of African American History* 97, nos. 1–2 (Winter–Spring 2012): 1–12.

3. Roy E. Finkenbine, "Belinda's Petition: Reparations for Slavery in Revolutionary Massachusetts," *William & Mary Quarterly* 64, no. 1 (January 2007): 95–104.

4. Frederick Law Olmsted, *The Cotton Kingdom: A Traveller's Observations on Cotton and Slavery in the American Slave States*, ed. Arthur M. Schlesinger Sr. and Lawrence N. Powell (New York: Random House, 1984 [1861]), 83; see also Johnson, *River of Dark Dreams*, 213.

5. Thomas C. Buchanan, "Rascals on the Antebellum Mississippi: African American Steamboat Workers and the St. Louis Hanging of 1841," *Journal of Social History* 34, no. 4 (Summer 2001): 797–817.

6. Walker, *David Walker's Appeal*, 70–71.

7. Hosea Easton, "Treatise on the Intellectual Character and Civil and Political Condition of the Colored People," in *To Heal the Scourge of Prejudice: The Life and Writings of Hosea Easton*, ed. George R. Price and James Brewer Stewart (Amherst: University of Massachusetts Press, 1999), 118–19.

8. Quoted in Finkenbine, "Belinda's Petition," 104.

9. Roy E. Finkenbine, "We Need to Include Reparations in the Story of Solomon Northup," *History News Network*, 20 January 2014, http://hnn.us/article/154463#sthash.fYN9xEo9.dpuf.

10. Thaddeus Stevens, speech on Section 4 of H.R. 29, *Congressional Globe*, 40th cong., 1st sess., March 1867, pp. 203, 205.

11. John David Smith, "The Enduring Myth of 'Forty Acres and a Mule,'" *Chronicle of Higher Education*, 21 February 2003, B11; Mary Frances Berry, "When Education Was Seen as Proper Reparations for Slavery," *Journal of Blacks in Higher Education* 48 (Summer 2005): 102–3.

12. Lawrie Balfour, "Unreconstructed Democracy: W.E.B. Du Bois and the Case for Reparations," *American Political Science Review* 97, no. 1 (February 2003): 33–44; T. Thomas Fortune, "Civil Rights and Social Privileges," *AME Church Review* 2 (1886), reprinted in Shawn Leigh Alexander, ed., *T. Thomas Fortune, the Afro-American Agitator: A Collection of Writings, 1880–1928* (Gainesville: University Press of Florida, 2008), 123–24.

13. Mary Frances Berry, *My Face Is Black Is True: Callie House and the Struggle for Ex-Slave Reparations* (New York: Knopf, 2005), 200–11.

14. Mitchell and his colleagues formed the National Liberty Party in 1903 and nominated a presidential ticket in 1904. The presidential candidate was George Edwin Taylor from Alabama and his running mate was Virginian W. C. Payne. James M. Davidson, "Encountering the Ex-Slave Reparations Movement from the Grave: The National Industrial Council and National Liberty Party, 1901–1907," *Journal of African American History* 97, nos. 1–2 (Winter–Spring 2012): 13–38.

15. James Forman, "Black Manifesto," reprinted in Michael T. Martin and Marilyn Yaquinto, eds., *Redress for Historical Injustices in the United States: On Reparations for Slavery, Jim Crow, and Their Legacies* (Durham, NC: Duke University Press, 2007), 593–99. See also Johnson, "Slavery, Reparations, and the Mythic March of Freedom," 56–59; and Elaine Allen Lechtreck, "'We Are Demanding $500 Million for Reparations': The Black Manifesto, Mainline Religious Denominations, and Black Economic Development," *Journal of African American History* 97, nos. 1–2 (Winter–Spring 2012): 39–71.

16. "National Black Political Agenda: The Gary Declaration," 1972, reprinted in Martin and Yaquinto, *Redress for Historical Injustices*, 600–5. For more information on the movement in the twentieth century, see Berry, *My Face Is Black Is True*, epilogue; Martin and Yaquinto, *Redress for Historical Injustices*; V. P. Franklin, ed., "African Americans and Movements for Reparations: Past, Present, and Future," special issue, *Journal of African American History* 97, nos. 1–2 (2012); James T. Campbell, "Settling Accounts? An Americanist Perspective on Historical Reconciliation," *American Historical Review* 114, no. 4 (October 2009): 963–77.

Campbell's work focuses on truth and reconciliation efforts, which fall into the therapeutic category of redress initiatives. The article was part of an international forum on reconciliation initiatives and whether accurate historical accounts of abuses could reduce social conflicts. Campbell argued that such efforts could "at least narrow the range of permissible lies,'" which he regarded as "no small achievement" (977).

17. *National Coalition of Blacks for Reparations in America* (newsletter), ncobra. org; see also "National Coalition of Blacks for Reparations in America (2000): The Reparations Campaign," in Martin and Yaquinto, *Redress for Historical Injustices*, 625–28; Robert L. Allen, "Past Due: The African American Quest for Reparations," *Black Scholar* 28, no. 2 (Summer 1998): 2–17.

18. Charles J. Ogletree, "Repairing the Past: New Efforts in the Reparations Debate," *Proteus* 24, no. 2 (2007): 3–22; Ogletree, "Tulsa Reparations: The Survivors' Story," in Martin and Yaquinto, *Redress for Historical Injustices*, 452–68.

19. Hilary McD. Beckles, *Britain's Black Debt: Reparations for Caribbean Slavery and Native Genocide* (Kingston, Jamaica: University of West Indies Press, 2013), 168–70.

20. See www.congress.gov/bill/114th-congress/house-bill/40/all-info.

21. See the summary in Joe R. Feagin, "Documenting the Costs of Slavery, Segregation, and Contemporary Racism: Why Reparations Are in Order for African Americans," *Harvard BlackLetter Law Journal* 20 (2004): 49–81; William Darity Jr., "Forty Acres and a Mule: Placing a Price Tag on Oppression," in America, *Wealth of Races*, 3–13; Larry Neal, "A Calculation and Comparison of the Current Benefits of Slavery and an Analysis of Who Benefits," in ibid., 91–106; James Marketti, "Estimated Present Value of Income Diverted during Slavery," in ibid., 107–24.

22. Darrell J. Gaskin, Alvin E. Heaten, and Shelley I. White-Means, "Racial Disparities in Health and Wealth: The Effects of Slavery and Past Discrimination," *Review of Black Political Economy* 32, nos. 3–4 (Winter 2005): 95–110.

23. National Urban League, "The State of Black America, 2015," soba.iamempowered.com; Pew Research Center, "Wealth Inequality Has Widened along Racial, Ethnic Lines since the End of the Great Recession," 12 December 2014, pewresearch.org.

24. Ta-Nehisi Coates, "The Case for Reparations," *Atlantic*, 21 June 2014, 54–72. For a positive evaluation of Coates's article, see Manuel Roig Franzia, "With *Atlantic* Article on Reparations, Ta-Nehisi Coates Sees Payoff for Years of Struggle," *Washington Post*, 18 June 2014. For negative responses, see Kevin D. Williamson, "The Case against Reparations," *National Review*, 24 May 2014; and David Frum, "The Impossibility of Reparations," *Atlantic*, 3 June 2014. Coates responded in "The Radical Practicality of Reparations: A Reply to David Frum," *Atlantic*, 4 June 2014. See also Don Rojas, "Will the CARICOM Reparations Initiative Inspire a Revitalization of the U.S. Movement?" *Nation*, 24 May 2014.

25. David Smith, "Blair: Britain's 'Sorrow' for Shame of Slave Trade," *Guardian*, 25 November 2006.

26. Charles J. Ogletree, "Litigating the Legacy of Slavery," *New York Times*, 31 March 2002; "U.S. Opens Spigot after Farmers Claim Discrimination," *New York Times*, 25 April 2013.

27. In April 2012 Democratic governor Bev Perdue initially recommended $11 million in reparations. A total of 7,600 people were sterilized through the eugenics program. The legislature complied with the request, but reduced the amount to $10 million, in July 2013. "Truth and Atonement in North Carolina," *New York Times*, 29 April 2012; "N.C. Legislature Approves $10 Million for Victims of Forced Sterilization," upi.com, 26 July 2013; "Eugenics Compensation Amendment Continues to Leave Some Victims Out," *North Carolina Health News*, 29 May 2015, northcarolinahealthnews.org.

28. Biondi, "Rise of the Reparations Movement," 8–9.

29. Ginger Thompson, "South Africa to Pay $3,900 to Each Family of Apartheid Victims," *New York Times*, 16 April 2003.

30. Feagin, "Documenting the Costs of Slavery," 64.

31. Alan Cowell, "Britain to Compensate Kenyan Victims of Colonial-Era Torture," *New York Times*, 6 June 2013.

32. Beckles, *Britain's Black Debt*, xi–xiv, esp. chap. 13; V. P. Franklin, "Commentary—Reparations as a Development Strategy: The CARICOM Reparations Commission," *Journal of African American History* 98 (Summer 2013): 363–66; Laurent Dubois, "Confronting the Legacies of Slavery," *New York Times*, 28 October 2013.

33. John Torpey, *Making Whole What Has Been Smashed: On Reparations Politics* (Cambridge, MA: Harvard University Press, 2006), 107–8, 110, 123–24, 125. Also named in the suit were Brown Brothers Harriman and Co., New York Life Insurance Co., Norfolk Southern Corp., Lehman Brothers Corp., Lloyd's of London, Union Pacific Railroad, J. P. Morgan Chase, R. J. Reynolds Tobacco Co., Brown and Williamson, Liggett Group Inc., Canada National Railway, Southern Mutual Insurance Co., American International Group (AIG), and Loews Corp. Numerous investigations into the actual monetary value of uncompensated slave labor exist, some ranging as high as $24 trillion, with hundreds of millions in interest annually. See, for example, Feagin, "Documenting the Costs of Slavery."

34. Ken Magill, "From J. P. Morgan Chase, An Apology and $5 Million in Slavery Reparations," *New York Sun*, 1 February 2005; Baptist, *Half Has Never Been Told*, 274, found that one of these predecessor banks, Citizen's Bank of Louisiana, left inventories of more than five hundred mortgaged slaves in the years leading up to the Panic of 1837, a practice the bank followed for the remainder of the antebellum era.

35. "Remarks by the President in Apology for Study Done in Tuskegee," White House Press Release, 16 May 1997, http://www.cdc.gov/tuskegee/clintonp.htm; "Clinton Regrets 'Clearly Racist' U.S. Study," *New York Times*, 14 May 1997; Henry Louis Gates Jr., "The Future of Slavery's Past," *New York Times*, 29 July 2001; "Florida Legislature Apologizes for State's History of Slavery," *New York Times*, 27 March 2008; "A Slavery Apology, but the Debate Continues," *New York Times*, 13 January 2008; "Slavery Marks University's Past," TuscaloosaNews.com, 7 April 2006; *UVA Today*, 24 April 2007; "Senate Backs Apology for Slavery," *Washington Post*, 19 June 2009.

36. General Assembly of North Carolina, 2007 session, House Bill 751, "Wilmington Race Riot Acknowledgement," 1–2. See www.ah.dcr.state.nc.us/1898-wrrc for the full commission report. For information on the riot see David Cecelski and Timothy Tyson, eds., *Democracy Betrayed: The Wilmington Race Riot of 1898 and Its Legacy* (Chapel Hill: University of North Carolina Press, 1998).

37. Harriet A. Washington, "Apology Shines Light on Racial Schism in Medicine," *New York Times*, 29 July 2008.

38. Andy Guess, "Facing Up to a Role in Slavery," *Inside Higher Education*, 25 April 2007; *Slavery-and-Universities*, wikispaces.com/Harvard; "Slave Traders in Yale's Past Fuel Debates on Restitution," *New York Times*, 13 August 2001; *Slavery and Justice: Report of the Brown University Steering Committee on Slavery and Justice*, 2003, www.brown.edu/Research/Slavery_Justice; Johnson, "Slavery, Reparations, and the Mythic March"; Adolph Reed, "The Case against Reparations," *Progressive Magazine* 64, no. 12 (December 2000): 15–18. Reed deems such approaches "a politics of psychobabble" and argues that class-based "access to quality health care, the right to a decent and dignified livelihood, affordable housing, [and] quality education for all" is the only possible way to redress historical grievances. Race-based solutions, according to Reed, only undermine the chances of multiracial solidarity. See a similar argument in Torpey, *Making Whole What Has Been Smashed*. "Slavery and the University: Histories and Legacies" conference, Emory University, 3–6 February 2001; program and podcasts available at https://slavery-and-universities.wikispaces.com/Conference2011.

39. Wilder, *Ebony and Ivy*, 10–11, 289–90, and passim.

40. olufunke moses, "John Hope Franklin: Apologies Aren't Enough," *Indy-Week*, 18 April 2007, indyweek.com.

41. Ibid. David Horowitz presented a particularly vitriolic and ahistorical case against reparations in "Ten Reasons Why Reparations for Blacks Is a Bad Idea for Blacks—and Racist Too," *Front Page Magazine* 3 (January 2001). Horowitz even argued that blacks owed America a debt for having emancipated them. For a rebuttal, see Ernest Allen Jr. and Robert Chrisman, "Ten Reasons: A Response to David Horowitz," *Black Scholar* 31, no. 2 (2001): 49.

42. See, for example, the findings summarized in William Darity Jr., "Forty Acres and a Mule in the 21st Century," *Social Science Quarterly* 89, no. 3 (September 2008): 658–60.

43. Charles J. Ogletree, "Litigating the Legacy of Slavery," *New York Times*, 31 March 2002.

44. Today, even political influence has come under attack with the Supreme Court's assault on the Voting Rights Act of 1965. In 2013, the Court struck down the preclearance requirement of the act, permitting nine states and numerous counties and municipalities to change election laws without prior federal approval. In the wake of that decision, gerrymandering, stricter voter identification laws, and suspension of early voting have occurred with growing regularity, demonstrating that black political power remains a threat to the ruling elite. "John Lewis and Others React to the Supreme Court's Voting Rights Act Ruling," *Washington Post*, 25 June 2013.

45. Beckles, *Britain's Black Debt*, 22.

Bibliography

Primary Sources

Alexander, Shawn Leigh, ed. *T. Thomas Fortune, The Afro-American Agitator: A Collection of Writings, 1880–1928*. Gainesville: University Press of Florida, 2008.

Antislavery Almanac for 1840. New York: S. W. Benedict; Boston: Isaac Knapp, 1840.

Aptheker, Herbert, ed. *American Negro Slave Revolts*. 5th ed. Foreword by John H. Bracey. New York: International, 1983; originally published 1943.

Ball, Charles. *Fifty Years in Chains; or, The Life of an American Slave*. Detroit: Negro History Press, 1971; originally published 1859.

Barnes, William H. *History of the Thirty-Ninth Congress of the United States*. New York: Negro Universities Press, 1969; originally published 1868.

Berlin, Ira, Barbara J. Fields, Steven F. Miller, Joseph P. Reidy, and Leslie S. Rowland, eds. *Free at Last: A Documentary History of Slavery, Freedom, and the Civil War*. New York: New Press, 1992.

Berlin, Ira, Steven F. Miller, Joseph P. Reidy, and Leslie S. Rowland, eds. *Freedom: A Documentary History of Emancipation, 1861–1867, Selected from the Holdings of the National Archives of the United States*. Ser. 1, vol. II: *The Wartime Genesis of Free Labor: The Upper South*. New York: Cambridge University Press, 1993.

Blassingame, John W., ed. *Slave Testimony: Two Centuries of Letters, Speeches, Interviews, and Autobiographies*. Baton Rouge: Louisiana State University Press, 1977.

Brotz, Howard, ed. *African-American Social and Political Thought, 1850–1920*. New Brunswick, NJ: Transaction, 1996.

Brown, John. *Slave Life in Georgia: A Narrative of the Life, Sufferings, and Escape of John Brown, A Fugitive Slave*. Edited by F. N. Boney. Savannah, GA: Beehive Press, 1972; originally published 1855.

Brown, William Wells. *From Fugitive Slave to Free Man: The Autobiographies of William Wells Brown*. 2nd ed. Edited and with an introduction by William L.

Andrews. Columbia: University of Missouri Press, 2003; originally published 1848.

Chesnutt, Charles W. "The Courts and the Negro." In *Plessy v. Ferguson: A Brief History with Documents*, edited by Brook Thomas. Boston: Bedford Books, 1997.

Congressional Globe, 40th cong., 1st sess. Washington, DC: Congressional Globe Office: 1867.

Craft, William, and Ellen Craft. *Running a Thousand Miles for Freedom: The Escape of William and Ellen Craft from Slavery*. Intro. Barbara McCaskill. Athens: University of Georgia Press, 1999; originally published 1860.

Davis, Benjamin J. Jr. *Communist Councilman from Harlem: Autobiographical Notes Written in a Federal Penitentiary*. New York: International, 1969.

Documenting the American South. University Library, University of North Carolina–Chapel Hill, 2004. http://docsouth.unc.edu.

Douglass, Frederick. *My Bondage and My Freedom*. Intro. Philip S. Foner. New York: Dover, 1969; originally published 1855.

Drew, Benjamin, ed. *North-Side View of Slavery*. New York: Negro Universities Press, 1968; originally published 1856.

Du Bois, W.E.B. *Autobiography of W.E.B. Du Bois: A Soliloquy on Viewing My Life from the Last Decade of Its First Century*. New York: International, 1968.

Finkelman, Paul, ed. and intro. *Statutes on Slavery: The Pamphlet Literature*. 2 vols. New York: Garland, 1988.

Foner, Philip S., ed. *Life and Writings of Frederick Douglass*. 4 vols. New York: International, 1950–55.

Foner, Philip S., and Robert James Branham, eds. *Lift Every Voice: African American Oratory, 1787–1900*. Tuscaloosa: University of Alabama Press, 1998.

Foner, Philip S., and George E. Walker, eds. *Proceedings of the Black State Conventions, 1840–1865*. Philadelphia: Temple University Press, 1980.

Frederick Douglass Papers, Library of Congress.

Garnet, Henry Highland. "The Past and Present Condition, and the Destiny of the Colored Race: A Discourse Delivered on the Fifteenth Anniversary of the Female Benevolent Society of Troy, New York, February 14, 1848." Troy, NY: Steamer Press of J. C. Kneeland, 1848. Available at the Digital Commons at the University of Nebraska–Lincoln, http://digitalcommons.unl.edu/cgi/viewcontent.cgi?article=1012&context=etas.

Hahn, Steven, Steven F. Miller, Susan E. O'Donovan, John C. Rodrigue, and Leslie S. Rowland, eds. *Freedom: A Documentary History of Emancipation, 1861–1867, Selected from the Holdings of the National Archives of the United States*. Ser. 3, vol. 1, *Land and Labor, 1865*. Chapel Hill: University of North Carolina Press, 2008.

Hamilton, Jeff. *My Master: The Inside Story of Sam Houston and His Times*, as Told to Lenoir Hunt. Austin: State House Press, 1992; originally published 1940.

Hughes, Louis. *Thirty Years a Slave: From Bondage to Freedom: The Institution of Slavery as Seen on the Plantation in the Home of the Planter*. Edited by William L. Andrews. Montgomery, AL: NewSouth Books, 2002; originally published 1897.

Hurston, Zora Neale. *Their Eyes Were Watching God*. Edited by Sherley Anne Williams. Urbana: University of Illinois Press, 1978; originally published 1937.

Innes, C. L., ed. *Slave Life in Virginia and Kentucky: A Narrative by Francis Fedric, Escaped Slave*. Baton Rouge: Louisiana State University Press, 2010; originally published 1860.

Jacobs, Harriet. *Incidents in the Life of a Slave Girl: Written by Herself*. Edited by Jean Fagan Yellin. Cambridge, MA: Harvard University Press, 1987; originally published 1861.

Jefferson, Thomas. *Notes on the State of Virginia*. Edited by William Peden. New York: W. W. Norton, 1982; originally published 1787.

Kersten, Andrew E. "A. Philip Randolph Oral History, 1972." In *A. Philip Randolph: A Life in the Vanguard*. Lanham, MD: Rowman & Littlefield, 2007.

Library of Congress, American Memory Collection. *From Slavery to Freedom: The African-American Pamphlet Collection, 1824–1909*. http://memory.loc.gov/ammem/aapchtml/aapchome.html.

Lynch, James. *A Few Things about the Educational Work among Freedmen of South Carolina and Georgia, Also, Addresses Delivered at Augusta and Nashville*. Baltimore, MD: William K. Boyle, Printer, 1865.

Martin, Michael T., and Marilyn Yaquinto, eds. *Redress for Historical Injustices in the United States: On Reparations for Slavery, Jim Crow, and Their Legacies*. Durham, NC: Duke University Press, 2007.

Marx, Karl. *The Eighteenth Brumaire of Louis Bonaparte*. New York: International, 1963; originally published 1852.

Mellon, James, ed. *Bullwhip Days: The Slaves Remember*. New York: Weidenfeld & Nicolson, 1988.

Meltzer, Milton, ed. *In Their Own Words: A History of the American Negro, 1865–1916*. New York: Thomas Y. Crowell, 1965.

Moton, Robert Russa. *Finding a Way Out: An Autobiography*. Garden City, NY: Doubleday, 1921.

North Carolina Office of Archives and History. *1898 Wilmington Race Riot Commission*. www.ah.dcr.state.nc.us/1898-wrrc.

Northup, Solomon. *Twelve Years a Slave*. Edited by Sue Eakin and Joseph Logsdon. Baton Rouge: Louisiana State University Press, 1968; originally published 1853.

Olmsted, Frederick Law. *The Cotton Kingdom: A Traveller's Observations on Cotton and Slavery in the American Slave States*. Edited by Arthur M. Schlesinger Sr.

and Lawrence N. Powell. New York: Random House, 1984; originally published 1861.

Osofsky, Gilbert, ed. *Puttin' on Ole Massa*. New York: Harper & Row, 1969.

Pennington, James W. C. *The Fugitive Blacksmith; or, Events in the History of James W. C. Pennington, Pastor of a Presbyterian Church, New York, Formerly a Slave in the State of Maryland, United States*. 2nd ed. London: Charles Gilpin, 1849; reprinted in *Five Slave Narratives: A Compendium*. New York: Arno Press, 1968.

Perdue, Charles L. Jr., Thomas E. Barden, and Robert K. Phillips, eds. *Weevils in the Wheat: Interviews with Virginia Ex-Slaves*. Bloomington: Indiana University Press, 1980.

Price, George R., and James Brewer Stewart, eds. *To Heal the Scourge of Prejudice: The Life and Writings of Hosea Easton*. Amherst: University of Massachusetts Press, 1999.

Rawick, George, ed. *The American Slave: A Composite Autobiography*. 44 vols. plus supplement series. Greenwood, CT: Greenwood Press, 1972.

Redkey, Edwin S., ed. *A Grand Army of Black Men: Letters from African American Soldiers in the Union Army, 1861–1865*. New York: Cambridge University Press, 1992.

———. *Respect Black: The Writings and Speeches of Henry McNeal Turner*. New York: Arno Press, 1971.

Ripley, C. Peter, Roy E. Finkenbine, Michael F. Hembree, and Donald Yacovone, eds. *Witness for Freedom: African American Voices on Race, Slavery, and Emancipation*. Chapel Hill: University of North Carolina Press, 1993.

Ripley, C. Peter, Jeffrey S. Rossbach, et al., eds. *The Black Abolitionist Papers*. 5 vols. Chapel Hill: University of North Carolina Press, 1985–92.

Robeson, Paul. *Here I Stand*. Boston: Beacon Press, 1958.

Royster, Jacqueline Jones, ed. *Southern Horrors and Other Writings: The Anti-Lynching Campaign of Ida B. Wells, 1892–1900*. New York: Bedford Books, 1997.

Shaw, Nate. *All God's Dangers: The Life of Nate Shaw*. Edited by Theodore Rosengarten. New York: Vintage, 1984.

Sherman, William T. *Memoirs of General W. T. Sherman*. 2 vols. New York: Library of America, 1990.

Steward, Austin. *Twenty-Two Years a Slave, and Forty Years a Freeman*. Intro. Graham Russell Hodges. Syracuse, NY: Syracuse University Press, 2002; originally published 1857.

Taylor, Susie King. *A Black Woman's Civil War Memoirs: Reminiscences of My Life in Camp with the 33rd U.S. Colored Troops, Late the 1st South Carolina Volunteers*. Edited by Patricia W. Romero. Intro. Willie Lee Rose. New York: Marcus Weiner, 1988; originally published 1902.

Tragle, Henry Irving, ed. *The Southampton Slave Revolt of 1831: A Compilation of Source Material*. Amherst: University of Massachusetts Press, 1971.

Waldrep, Christopher, ed. *Lynching in America: A History in Documents*. New York: New York University Press, 2006.

Walker, David. *David Walker's Appeal to the Coloured Citizens of the World*. Edited and with an introduction by Peter P. Hinks. University Park: Pennsylvania State University Press, 2000; originally published 1829.

Wells-Barnett, Ida B. *Crusade for Justice: The Autobiography of Ida B. Wells*. Edited by Alfreda M. Duster. Chicago: University of Chicago Press, 1972.

Woodson, Carter G., ed. *The Mind of the Negro as Reflected in Letters Written during the Crisis, 1800–1860*. New York: Negro Universities Press, 1969; originally published 1929.

Secondary Sources

Addington, Wendall. "Slave Insurrections in Texas." *Journal of Negro History* 35 (October 1950): 408–54.

Alexander, Adele Logan. *Ambiguous Lives: Free Women of Color in Rural Georgia, 1789–1879*. Fayetteville: University of Arkansas Press, 1991.

Allen, Ernest Jr., and Robert Chrisman. "Ten Reasons: A Response to David Horowitz." *Black Scholar* 31, no. 2 (2001): 49–56.

Allen, Robert L. "Past Due: The African American Quest for Reparations. *Black Scholar* 28, no. 2 (Summer 1998): 2–17.

America, Richard F., ed. *The Wealth of Races: The Present Value of Benefits from Past Injustices*. Contributions in Afro-American and African Studies no. 132. New York: Greenwood Press, 1990.

Aptheker, Herbert. "Afro-American Superiority: A Neglected Theme in the Literature." *Phylon* 31, no. 4 (1970): 336–43.

Arendt, Hannah, and Peter R. Baehr, eds. *The Portable Hannah Arendt*. New York: Penguin, 2000.

Aristotle. *Politics*. Trans. Ernest Barker. Oxford: Oxford University Press, 1995.

Arnold, Edwin T. *"What Virtue There Is in Fire": Cultural Memory and the Lynching of Sam Hose*. Athens: University of Georgia Press, 2009.

Ashworth, John. *Slavery, Capitalism, and Politics in the Antebellum Republic*. Vol. 1, *Commerce and Compromise, 1820–1860*. Cambridge: Cambridge University Press, 1995.

Bagwell, Orlando, producer. *Malcolm X: Make It Plain*. Blackside/Roja Productions for American Experience, 1994.

Baker, Bruce E. *This Mob Will Surely Take My Life: Lynchings in the Carolinas, 1871–1947*. New York: Continuum, 2008.

Balfour, Lawrie. "Unreconstructed Democracy: W.E.B. Du Bois and the Case for Reparations." *American Political Science Review* 97, no. 1 (February 2003): 33–44.

Baptist, Edward E. "'Cuffy,' 'Fancy Maids,' and 'One-Eyed Men': Rape, Commodification, and the Domestic Slave Trade in the United States." *American Historical Review* 106, no. 5 (December 2001): 1619–50.

———. *The Half Has Never Been Told: Slavery and the Making of American Capitalism*. New York: Basic Books, 2014.

Bay, Mia. *To Tell the Truth Freely: The Life of Ida B. Wells*. New York: Hill & Wang, 2010.

———. *The White Image in the Black Mind: African-American Ideas about White People, 1830–1925*. New York: Oxford University Press, 2000.

Beckert, Sven. *Empire of Cotton: A Global History*. New York: Knopf, 2014.

Beckles, Hilary McD. *Britain's Black Debt: Reparations for Caribbean Slavery and Native Genocide*. Kingston, Jamaica: University of West Indies Press, 2013.

Berg, Manfred. *Popular Justice: A History of Lynching in America*. Chicago: Ivan R. Dee, 2011.

Berlin, Ira. *Generations of Captivity: A History of African-American Slaves*. Cambridge, MA: Belknap Press, 2003.

Berlin, Ira, and Philip D. Morgan, eds. *Cultivation and Culture: Labor and the Shaping of Slave Life in the Americas*. Charlottesville: University of Virginia Press, 1993.

———. *The Slaves' Economy: Independent Production by Slaves in the Americas*. London: Frank Cass, 1991.

Berry, Mary Frances. *My Face Is Black Is True: Callie House and the Struggle for Ex-Slave Reparations*. New York: Knopf, 2005.

———. "When Education Was Seen as Proper Reparations for Slavery." *Journal of Blacks in Higher Education* 48 (Summer 2005): 102–3.

Biondi, Martha. "The Rise of the Reparations Movement." *Radical History Review* 87 (Fall 2003): 5–18.

Blackmon, Douglas A. *Slavery by Another Name: The Reenslavement of Black Americans from the Civil War to World War II*. New York: Random House, 2008.

Blassingame, John W. *The Slave Community: Plantation Life in the Antebellum South*. New York: Oxford University Press, 1972.

———. "Using the Testimony of Ex-Slaves: Approaches and Problems." *Journal of Southern History* 41, no. 4 (November 1975): 473–92.

Blight, David W. *Race and Reunion: The Civil War in American Memory*. Cambridge, MA: Belknap Press, 2001.

Blum, Edward J., and W. Scott Poole, eds. *Vale of Tears: New Essays on Religion and Reconstruction*. Macon, GA: Mercer University Press, 2005.

Bordewich, Fergus M. *Bound for Canaan: The Underground Railroad and the War for the Soul of America*. New York: Amistad, 2005.

Boxill, Bernard R. *Blacks and Social Justice*. Totowa, NJ: Rowman & Allanheld, 1984.

Brock, W. R. *An American Crisis: Congress and Reconstruction, 1865–1877.* New York: St. Martin's Press, 1963.

Brown, Elsa Barkley. "Negotiating and Transforming the Public Sphere: African American Political Life in the Transition from Slavery to Freedom." *Public Culture* 7, no. 1 (Fall 1994): 107–46.

Brundage, W. Fitzhugh. *Lynching in the New South: Georgia and Virginia, 1880–1930.* Urbana: University of Illinois Press, 1993.

———. *Under Sentence of Death: Lynching in the South.* Chapel Hill: University of North Carolina Press, 1997.

Buchanan, Thomas C. "Rascals on the Antebellum Mississippi: African American Steamboat Workers and the St. Louis Hanging of 1841." *Journal of Social History* 34, no. 4 (Summer 2001): 797–817.

Camp, Stephanie M. H. *Closer to Freedom: Enslaved Women and Everyday Resistance in the Plantation South.* Chapel Hill: University of North Carolina Press, 2004.

Campbell, James T. "Settling Accounts? An Americanist Perspective on Historical Reconciliation." *American Historical Review* 114, no. 4 (October 2009): 963–77.

Cawthon, James Dance. "A Caddo Parish Sheriff during Reconstruction Times." *Northern Louisiana Historical Journal* 20, no. 1 (1989): 3–19.

Cecelski, David, and Timothy Tyson, eds. *Democracy Betrayed: The Wilmington Race Riot of 1898 and Its Legacy.* Chapel Hill: University of North Carolina Press, 1998.

Clark, Kathleen Ann. *Defining Moments: African American Commemoration and Political Culture in the South, 1863–1913.* Chapel Hill: University of North Carolina Press, 2005.

Clegg, Claude Andrew III. *Troubled Ground: A Tale of Murder, Lynching, and Reckoning in the New South.* Urbana: University of Illinois Press, 2010.

Clinton, Catherine. *The Plantation Mistress: Women's World in the Old South.* New York: Pantheon, 1982.

Coates, Ta-Nehisi. "The Case for Reparations." *Atlantic,* 21 June 2014: 54–72.

———. "The Radical Practicality of Reparations: A Reply to David Frum." *Atlantic,* 4 June 2014.

Corlett, J. Angelo. *Race, Racism, and Reparations.* Ithaca, NY: Cornell University Press, 2003.

Da Costa, Emilia Viotti. *Crowns of Glory, Tears of Blood: The Demerara Slave Rebellion of 1823.* New York: Oxford University Press, 1994.

Dailey, Jane Elizabeth. *Before Jim Crow: The Politics of Race in Postemancipation Virginia.* Chapel Hill: University of North Carolina Press, 2000.

Daniel, Pete. *The Shadow of Slavery: Peonage in the South, 1901–1969.* Urbana: University of Illinois Press, 1972.

Darity, William, Jr. "Forty Acres and a Mule in the 21st Century." *Social Science Quarterly* 89, no. 3 (September 2008): 656–64.

Davidson, James M. "Encountering the Ex-Slave Reparations Movement from the Grave: The National Industrial Council and National Liberty Party, 1901–1907." *Journal of African American History* 97, nos. 1–2 (Winter–Spring 2012): 13–38.

Deyle, Steven. *Carry Me Back: The Domestic Slave Trade in American Life.* New York: Oxford University Press, 2005.

Dillon, Merton L. *Slavery Attacked: Southern Slaves and Their Allies, 1619–1865.* Baton Rouge: Louisiana State University Press, 1990.

Drey, Philip. *At the Hands of Persons Unknown: The Lynching of Black America.* New York: Modern Library, 2003.

Dubois, Laurent. "Confronting the Legacies of Slavery." *New York Times,* 28 October 2013.

Du Bois, W.E.B. *Black Reconstruction in America: An Essay Toward a History of the Part Which Black Folk Played in the Attempt to Reconstruct Democracy in America, 1860–1880.* New York: Meridian Books, 1964; originally published 1935.

———. *The Gift of Black Folk: The Negroes in the Making of America.* Introduction by Glenda Carpio. Oxford W.E.B. Du Bois Series, series editor Henry Louis Gates Jr. Oxford: Oxford University Press, 2007; originally published 1924.

Dunaway, Wilma A. *The African-American Family in Slavery and Emancipation.* New York: Cambridge University Press, 2003.

Durham, David Anthony. *A Walk through Darkness.* New York: Doubleday, 2002.

Egerton, Douglas R. *Gabriel's Rebellion: The Virginia Slave Conspiracies of 1800 and 1802.* Chapel Hill: University of North Carolina Press, 1993.

———. *He Shall Go Out Free: The Lives of Denmark Vesey.* Madison: University of Wisconsin Press, 1999.

———. *The Wars of Reconstruction: The Brief, Violent History of America's Most Progressive Era.* New York: Bloomsbury Press, 2014.

Egerton, Douglas R., ed. *Rebels, Reformers, and Revolutionaries: Collected Essays and Second Thoughts.* New York: Routledge, 2002.

Elkins, Stanley M. *Slavery: A Problem in American Institutional and Cultural Life.* Chicago: University of Chicago Press, 1959.

Emberton, Carole. *Beyond Redemption: Race, Violence, and the American South after the Civil War.* Chicago: University of Chicago Press, 2013.

Ernst, Robert. "Negro Concepts of Americanism." *Journal of Negro History* 39, no. 3 (July 1954): 206–19.

Farrow, Anne, Joel Lang, and Jenifer Frank. *Complicity: How the North Promoted, Prolonged, and Profited from Slavery.* New York: Ballantine Books, 2005.

Feagin, Joe R. "Documenting the Costs of Slavery, Segregation, and Contemporary Racism: Why Reparations Are in Order for African Americans." *Harvard BlackLetter Law Journal* 20 (2004): 49–81.

Fehrenbacher, Don E. *The Dred Scott Case: Its Significance in American Law and Politics.* New York: Oxford University Press, 1978.

———. *The Slaveholding Republic: An Account of the United States Government's Relations to Slavery.* New York: Oxford University Press, 2001.

Fields, Barbara J. "Slavery, Race, and Ideology in the United States of America." *New Left Review* 181 (May–June 1990): 95–118.

Fields, Karen E., and Barbara J. Fields. *Racecraft: The Soul of Inequality in American Life.* New York: Verso Books, 2012.

Finkelman, Paul. *The Law of Freedom and Bondage: A Casebook.* New York: Oceana, 1986.

———. *Slavery and the Law.* 2 vols. Madison: University of Wisconsin Press, 1996.

Finkelman, Paul., ed. *Lynching, Racial Violence, and the Law.* New York: Garland, 1992.

Finkenbine, Roy E. "Belinda's Petition: Reparations for Slavery in Revolutionary Massachusetts." *William & Mary Quarterly* 64, no. 1 (January 2007): 95–104.

———. "We Need to Include Reparations in the Story of Solomon Northup." *History News Network,* 20 January 2014. http://hnn.us/article/154463#sthash.fYN9xE09.dpuf.

Fitzgerald, Michael W. *The Union League Movement in the Deep South: Politics and Agricultural Change during Reconstruction.* Baton Rouge: Louisiana State University Press, 1989.

Fogel, Robert W. *Without Consent or Contract: The Rise and Fall of American Slavery.* New York: Norton, 1989.

Fogel, Robert W., and Stanley L. Engerman. *Time on the Cross: The Economics of American Negro Slavery.* 2 vols. Boston: Little, Brown, 1974.

Follett, Richard J. *The Sugar Masters: Planters and Slaves in Louisiana's Cane World, 1820–1860.* Baton Rouge: Louisiana State University Press, 2005.

Foner, Eric. *Forever Free: The Story of Emancipation and Reconstruction.* New York: Knopf, 2005.

———. *Free Soil, Free Labor, Free Men: The Ideology of the Republican Party before the Civil War.* 2nd ed. New York: Oxford University Press, 1995.

———. *Freedom's Lawmakers: A Directory of Black Officeholders during Reconstruction.* New York: Oxford University Press, 1993.

———. *Nothing but Freedom: Emancipation and Its Legacy.* Baton Rouge: Louisiana State University Press, 1983.

———. *Reconstruction: America's Unfinished Revolution.* New York: Harper & Row, 1988.

Fox-Genovese, Elizabeth. *Within the Plantation Household: Black and White Women in the Old South.* Chapel Hill: University of North Carolina Press, 1988.

Franklin, John Hope, and Loren Schweninger. *Runaway Slaves: Rebels on the Plantation*. New York: Oxford University Press, 1999.

Franklin, V. P., ed. "African Americans and Movements for Reparations: Past, Present, and Future." Special issue, *Journal of African American History* 97, nos. 1–2 (2012).

————. "Commentary—Reparations as a Development Strategy: The CARICOM Reparations Commission." *Journal of African American History* 98 (Summer 2013): 363–66.

————. "Introduction: African Americans and Movements for Reparations: From Ex-slave Pensions to the Reparations Superfund." *Journal of African American History* 97, nos. 1–2 (Winter–Spring 2012): 1–12.

Franzia, Manuel Roig. "With *Atlantic* Article on Reparations, Ta-Nehisi Coates Sees Payoff for Years of Struggle." *Washington Post*, 18 June 2014.

Fraser, Walter J. Jr., R. Frank Saunders Jr., and Jon L. Wakelyn, eds. *The Web of Southern Social Relations: Women, Family and Education*. Athens: University of Georgia Press, 1985.

Frazier, E. Franklin. *The Negro Family in the United States*. Chicago: University of Chicago Press, 1939.

Frey, Sylvia R. "The Visible Church: Historiography of African American Religion since Raboteau." *Slavery and Abolition* 29, no. 1 (March 2008): 83–110.

————. *Water from the Rock: Black Resistance in a Revolutionary Age*. Princeton, NJ: Princeton University Press, 1991.

Frey, Sylvia R., and Betty Wood. *Come Shouting to Zion: African American Protestantism in the American South and British Caribbean to 1830*. Chapel Hill: University of North Carolina Press, 1998.

Frum, David. "The Impossibility of Reparations." *Atlantic*, 3 June 2014.

Gaines, Kevin. *Uplifting the Race: Black Leadership, Culture, and Politics in the Twentieth Century*. Chapel Hill: University of North Carolina Press, 1996.

Gaskin, Darrell J., Alvin E. Heaten, and Shelley I. White-Means. "Racial Disparities in Health and Wealth: The Effects of Slavery and Past Discrimination." *Review of Black Political Economy* 32, nos. 3–4 (Winter 2005): 95–110.

Gaspar, David Barry. *Bondmen and Rebels: A Study of Master-Slave Relations in Antigua, with Implications for Colonial British America*. Baltimore: Johns Hopkins University Press, 1985.

Gellman, Erik S. *Death Blow to Jim Crow: The National Negro Congress and the Rise of Militant Civil Rights*. Chapel Hill: University of North Carolina Press, 2012.

Genovese, Eugene D. *From Rebellion to Revolution: Afro-American Slave Revolts in the Making of the Modern World*. Baton Rouge: Louisiana State University Press, 1979.

———. "Rebelliousness and Docility in Negro Slavery: A Critique of the Elkins Thesis." *Civil War History* 13, no. 4 (December 1967): 293–314.

———. *The World the Slaveholders Made: Two Essays in Interpretation.* 2nd ed. Middletown, CT: Wesleyan University Press, 1988.

Giddings, Paula J. *Ida: A Sword among Lions: Ida B. Wells and the Campaign against Lynching.* New York: Amistad, 2008.

Gilroy, Paul. *The Black Atlantic: Modernity and Double Consciousness.* Cambridge, MA: Harvard University Press, 1993.

Gin, Kathryn. "'The Heavenization of Earth': African American Visions and Uses of the Afterlife, 1863–1901." *Slavery and Abolition* 31 (June 2010): 207–31.

Glatthaar, Joseph T. *Forged in Battle: The Civil War Alliance of Black Soldiers and White Officers.* New York: Free Press: Collier Macmillan, 1990.

Glickman, Lawrence B. "'Buy for the Sake of the Slave': Abolitionism and the Origins of American Consumer Action." *American Quarterly* 56, no. 4 (2004): 889–912.

Glisson, Susan M., ed. *The Human Rights Tradition in the Civil Rights Movement.* New York: Rowman & Littlefield, 2006.

Glymph, Thavolia. *Out of the House of Bondage: The Transformation of the Plantation Household.* Cambridge: Cambridge University Press, 2008.

Gomez, Michael A. *Exchanging Our Country Marks: The Transformation of African Identities in the Colonial and Antebellum South.* Chapel Hill: University of North Carolina Press, 1998.

———, ed. *Diasporic Africa: A Reader.* New York: New York University Press, 2006.

Gordon, Patricia, ed. *Discovering the Women in Slavery: Emancipating Perspectives on the American Past.* Athens: University of Georgia Press, 1996.

Greene, Jack, and Philip D. Morgan, eds. *Atlantic History: A Critical Appraisal.* New York: Oxford University Press, 2009.

Guess, Andy. "Facing Up to a Role in Slavery." *Inside Higher Education,* 25 April 2007.

Gutman, Herbert. *Slavery and the Numbers Game: A Critique of* Time on the Cross. Urbana: University of Illinois Press, 1975.

Hahn, Steven. *A Nation under Our Feet: Black Political Struggles in the Rural South, from Slavery to the Great Migration.* Cambridge, MA: Belknap Press, 2003.

———. *The Political Worlds of Slavery and Freedom.* Cambridge, MA: Harvard University Press, 2009.

Hall, Gwendolyn Midlo. *Africans in Colonial Louisiana: The Development of Afro-Creole Culture in the Eighteenth Century.* Baton Rouge: Louisiana State University Press, 1992.

———. *Slavery and African Ethnicities in the Americas: Restoring the Links.* Chapel Hill: University of North Carolina Press, 2005.

Hall, Jacquelyn Dowd. "The Long Civil Rights Movement and the Political Uses of the Past." *Journal of American History* 91, no. 4 (March 2005): 1233–63.

———. *Revolt against Chivalry: Jessie Daniel Ames and the Women's Campaign against Lynching.* New York: Columbia University Press, 1993.

Hall, Randal L., ed. "Commemorating Seventy-Five Years of the *Journal of Southern History.*" Special issue, *Journal of Southern History* 75, no. 3 (August 2009).

Hartman, Saidiya V. *Lose Your Mother: A Journey along the Atlantic Slave Route.* New York: Farrar, Straus, and Giroux, 2007.

———. *Scenes of Subjection: Terror, Slavery, and Self-Making in Nineteenth-Century America.* New York: Oxford University Press, 1997.

Harvey, Paul. "'These Untutored Masses': The Campaign for Respectability among White and Black Evangelicals in the American South, 1870–1930." *Journal of Religious History* 21, no. 3 (October 1997): 302–17.

Hermann, Janet Sharp. *The Pursuit of a Dream.* New York: Oxford University Press, 1981.

Herskovits, Melville J. *The Myth of the Negro Past.* Boston: Beacon Press, 1941.

Hine, Darlene Clark. "Rape and the Inner Lives of Southern Black Women: Thoughts on the Culture of Dissemblance." In *Southern Women: Histories and Identities,* edited by Virginia Bernhard, Betty Brandon, Elizabeth Fox-Genovese, and Theda Perdue. Columbia: University of Missouri Press, 1992.

Hinks, Peter P. *To Awaken My Afflicted Brethren: David Walker and the Problem of Antebellum Slave Resistance.* University Park: Pennsylvania State University Press, 1997.

Hodes, Martha. *White Women, Black Men: Illicit Sex in the Nineteenth-Century South.* New Haven, CT: Yale University Press, 1997.

Holloway, Joseph E., ed. *Africanisms in American Culture.* Bloomington: Indiana University Press, 1990.

Horowitz, David. "Ten Reasons Why Reparations for Blacks Is a Bad Idea for Blacks—and Racist Too." *Front Page Magazine* 3 (January 2001).

Huggins, Nathan. *Black Odyssey: The Afro-American Ordeal in Slavery.* New York: Pantheon Books, 1977.

Hunt, Alfred N. *Haiti's Influence on Antebellum America: Slumbering Volcano in the Caribbean.* Baton Rouge: Louisiana State University Press, 1988.

Jeffrey, Julie Roy. *The Great Silent Army of Abolitionism: Ordinary Women in the Antislavery Movement.* Chapel Hill: University of North Carolina Press, 1998.

Jennings, Thelma. "'Us Colored Women Had to Go through a Plenty': Sexual Exploitation of African-American Slave Women." *Journal of Women's History* 1, no. 3 (Winter 1990): 45–74.

Johnson, Walter. "Clerks All! Or, Slaves with Cash." *Journal of the Early Republic* 26 (Winter 2006): 641–51.

————. "On Agency." *Journal of Social History* 37, no. 1 (Fall 2003): 113–25.

————. *River of Dark Dreams: Slavery and Empire in the Cotton Kingdom.* Cambridge, MA: Belknap Press, 2013.

————. "Slavery, Reparations, and the Mythic March of Freedom." *Raritan* 27, no. 2 (Fall 2007): 41–67.

————. *Soul by Soul: Life Inside the Antebellum Slave Market.* Cambridge, MA: Harvard University Press, 1999.

Jones, Jacqueline. *A Dreadful Deceit: The Myth of Race from the Colonial Era to Obama's America.* New York: Basic Books, 2013.

Jones, Norrece T. Jr. "Rape in Black and White: Sexual Violence in the Testimony of Enslaved and Free Americans." In *Slavery and the American South*, edited by Winthrop Jordan. Jackson: University of Mississippi Press, 2003.

Jordan, Winthrop D. *Tumult and Silence at Second Creek: An Inquiry into a Civil War Slave Conspiracy.* Baton Rouge: Louisiana State University Press, 1993.

Kachun, Mitch. *Festivals of Freedom: Memory and Meaning in African American Emancipation Celebrations, 1808–1915.* Amherst: University of Massachusetts Press, 2003.

Keith, Leanna. *The Colfax Massacre: The Untold Story of Black Power, White Terror and the Death of Reconstruction.* New York: Oxford University Press, 2008.

King, Richard H. "Domination and Fabrication: Re-thinking Stanley Elkins's *Slavery*." *Slavery and Abolition* 22, no. 2 (August 2001): 1–28.

Lane, Anne J., ed. *Stanley Elkins and His Critics.* Urbana: University of Illinois Press, 1971.

Lane, Charles. *The Day Freedom Died: The Colfax Massacre, the Supreme Court, and the Betrayal of Reconstruction.* New York: Henry Holt, 2008.

Lau, Peter F. *Democracy Rising: South Carolina and the Fight for Black Equality since 1865.* Lexington: University Press of Kentucky, 2006.

Learning, Hugo Prosper. *Hidden Americans: Maroons of Virginia and the Carolinas.* New York: Garland, 1995.

Lechtreck, Elaine Allen. "'We Are Demanding $500 Million for Reparations': The Black Manifesto, Mainline Religious Denominations, and Black Economic Development." *Journal of African American History* 97, nos. 1–2 (Winter–Spring 2012): 39–71.

Levine, Lawrence W. *Black Culture and Black Consciousness: Afro-American Folk Thought from Slavery to Freedom.* New York: Oxford University Press, 1977.

Litwack, Leon F. *Been in the Storm So Long: The Aftermath of Slavery.* New York: Knopf, 1979.

————. *Trouble in Mind: Black Southerners in the Age of Jim Crow.* New York: Vintage, 1999.

Logan, Rayford. *The Negro in American Life and Thought: The Nadir, 1877–1901.* London: Dial Press, 1954.

Lott, Tommy L., and John P. Pittman, eds. *A Companion to African-American Philosophy*. Malden, MA: Blackwell, 2003.

Marable, Manning. *Malcolm X: A Life of Reinvention*. New York: Viking, 2011.

McDonnell, Lawrence T. "Money Knows No Master: Market Relations and the American Slave Community," in *Developing Dixie: Modernization in a Traditional Society*, edited by Winfred B. Moore Jr., Joseph Tripp, and Lyon G. Tyler Jr. Westport, CT: Greenwood Press, 1988.

McNeil, Genna Rae. *Groundwork: Charles Hamilton Houston and the Struggle for Civil Rights*. Philadelphia: University of Pennsylvania Press, 1983.

McPherson, James M. "Who Freed the Slaves?" *Proceedings of the American Philosophical Society* 139 (March 1995): 1–10.

Meier, August. *Negro Thought in America, 1880–1915: Racial Ideologies in the Age of Booker T. Washington*. Ann Arbor: University of Michigan Press, 1963.

Mitchell, Koritha. *Living with Lynching: African American Lynching Plays, Performance, and Citizenship, 1890–1930*. Urbana: University of Illinois Press, 2011.

Morgan, Philip D. "The Ownership of Property by Slaves in the Mid-Nineteenth-Century Low Country." *Journal of Southern History* 49 (August 1983): 399–420.

———. *Slave Counterpoint: Black Culture in the Eighteenth-Century Chesapeake and Lowcountry*. Chapel Hill: University of North Carolina Press, 1998.

———. "Work and Culture: The Task System and the World of Lowcountry Blacks, 1700–1800." *William & Mary Quarterly*, 3rd ser., 39, no. 4 (October 1992): 563–99.

Nembhard, Jessica Gordon. *Collective Courage: A History of African American Cooperative Economic Thought and Practice*. University Park: Pennsylvania State University Press, 2014.

Newman, Richard. *Freedom's Prophet: Bishop Richard Allen, the AME Church, and the Black Founding Fathers*. New York: New York University Press, 2008.

Ogletree, Charles J. "Litigating the Legacy of Slavery." *New York Times*, 31 March 2002.

———. "Repairing the Past: New Efforts in the Reparations Debate." *Proteus* 24, no. 2 (2007): 3–22.

Painter, Nell Irvin. "Soul Murder and Slavery: Toward a Fully Loaded Cost Accounting." In *Southern History across the Color Line*. Chapel Hill: University of North Carolina Press, 2002.

———. *Southern History across the Color Line*. Chapel Hill: University of North Carolina Press, 2002.

Payne, Charles M. *I've Got the Light of Freedom: The Organizing Tradition and the Mississippi Freedom Struggle*. Berkeley: University of California Press, 1995.

Payne, Charles M., and Adam Green, eds. *Time Longer Than Rope: A Century of African American Activism, 1850–1950*. New York: New York University Press, 2003.

Penningroth, Dylan C. *The Claims of Kinfolk: African American Property and Community in the Nineteenth-Century South*. Chapel Hill: University of North Carolina Press, 2003.

Piketty, Thomas. *Capital in the Twenty-First Century*. Cambridge, MA: Belknap Press, 2014.

Piketty, Thomas, and Emmanuel Saez. "Income Inequality in the United States, 1913–1998." *Quarterly Journal of Economics* 118, no. 1 (2003): 1–39.

Pinn, Anthony B., ed. *By These Hands: A Documentary History of African American Humanism*. New York: New York University Press, 2001.

Pittman, John P., ed. *African-American Perspectives and Philosophical Traditions*. New York: Routledge, 1997.

Quarles, Benjamin. *The Negro in the Civil War*. New York: Russell and Russell, 1968.

Raboteau, Albert J. *A Fire in the Bones: Reflections on African-American Religious History*. Boston: Beacon Press, 1995.

Rael, Patrick. *Black Identity and Black Protest in the Antebellum North*. Chapel Hill: University of North Carolina Press, 2002.

Ransby, Barbara. *Ella Baker and the Black Freedom Movement: A Radical Democratic Vision*. Chapel Hill: University of North Carolina Press, 2003.

Reed, Adolph. "The Case against Reparations." *Progressive Magazine* 64, no. 12 (December 2000): 15–18.

Reich, Robert. *Inequality for All* [documentary film]. Director Jacob Kornbluth. 72 Productions, 2013.

Robinson, Randall. *The Debt: What America Owes to Blacks*. New York: Dutton, 2000.

Rodgers, Daniel T. *The Work Ethic in Industrial America, 1850–1920*. Chicago: University of Chicago Press, 1978.

Roediger, David. *Wages of Whiteness: Race and the Making of the American Working Class*. 2nd ed. London: Verso, 2007.

Rojas, Don. "Will the CARICOM Reparations Initiative Inspire a Revitalization of the U.S. Movement?" *Nation*, 24 May 2014.

Rose, Willie Lee. *Rehearsal for Reconstruction: The Port Royal Experiment*. Indianapolis, IN: Bobbs-Merrill, 1964.

Rosen, Hannah. *Terror in the Heart of Freedom: Citizenship, Sexual Violence, and the Meaning of Race in the Postemancipation South*. Chapel Hill: University of North Carolina Press, 2008.

Rothman, Adam. *Slave Country: American Expansion and the Origins of the Deep South*. Cambridge, MA: Harvard University Press, 2005.

Saville, Julie. *The Work of Reconstruction: From Slave to Wage Laborer in South Carolina, 1860–1870*. New York: Cambridge University Press, 1994.

Savitt, Todd. *Medicine and Slavery: The Diseases and Health Care of Blacks in Ante-bellum Virginia.* Urbana: University of Illinois Press, 1978.

Schecter, Patricia. *Ida B. Wells-Barnett and American Reform, 1880–1930.* Chapel Hill: University of North Carolina Press, 2001.

Schwalm, Leslie A. *A Hard Fight for We: Women's Transition from Slavery to Free-dom in South Carolina.* Urbana: University of Illinois Press, 1997.

Schwartz, Marie Jenkins. *Born in Bondage: Growing Up Enslaved in the Antebellum South.* Cambridge, MA: Harvard University Press, 2000.

Schweninger, Loren. *Black Property Owners in the South, 1790–1915.* Urbana: University of Illinois Press, 1990.

————. "Slave Independence and Enterprise in South Carolina, 1780–1865." *South Carolina Historical Magazine* 93 (April 1992): 101–25.

————. "The Underside of Slavery: The Internal Economy, Self-Hire, and Quasi-Freedom in Virginia, 1780–1865." *Slavery and Abolition* 12 (September 1991): 1–22.

Scott, Daryl M. *Social Policy and the Image of the Damaged Black Psyche, 1880–1996.* Chapel Hill: University of North Carolina Press, 1997.

Scott, Julius S., III, "The Common Wind: Currents of Afro-American Communication in the Age of the Haitian Revolution." PhD diss., Duke University, 1986.

Shaw, Stephanie J. "Using the WPA Narratives to Study the Impact of the Great Depression." *Journal of Southern History* 69, no. 3 (August 2003): 623–58.

Sidbury, James. *Becoming African in America: Race and Nation in the Early Black Atlantic.* New York: Oxford University Press, 2007.

Simien, Evelyn M., ed. *Gender and Lynching: The Politics of Memory.* New York: Palgrave Macmillan, 2011.

Smith, John David. "The Enduring Myth of 'Forty Acres and a Mule.'" *Chronicle of Higher Education*, 21 February 2003, B11.

Sobel, Mechal. *Trabelin' On: The Slave Journey to an Afro-Baptist Faith.* Westport, CT: Greenwood Press, 1979.

Span, Christopher M. *African American Education in Mississippi, 1862–1875.* Chapel Hill: University of North Carolina Press, 2009.

Stampp, Kenneth M. *The Era of Reconstruction, 1865–1877.* New York: Knopf, 1965.

————. *The Peculiar Institution: Slavery in the Ante-bellum South.* New York: Vintage Books, 1956.

————. "Rebels and the Search for the Negro's Personality in Slavery." *Journal of Southern History* 37, no. 3 (August 1970): 367–92.

Stevenson, Brenda E. *Life in Black and White: Family and Community in the Slave South.* New York: Oxford University Press, 1996.

Stevenson, Bryan. *Just Mercy: A Story of Justice and Redemption.* New York: Spiegel and Grau, 2014.

Stiglitz, Joseph E. *The Price of Inequality*. New York: W. W. Norton, 2012.

Stuckey, Sterling. "'I Want to Be an African': Paul Robeson and the Ends of Nationalist Theory and Practice, 1919–1945." *Massachusetts Review* 17, no. 1 (Spring 1976): 81–138.

Sullivan, Patricia. *Lift Every Voice: The NAACP and the Making of the Civil Rights Movement*. New York: New Press, 2009.

Tadman, Michael. *Speculators and Slaves: Masters, Traders, and Slaves in the Old South*. Madison: University of Wisconsin Press, 1989.

Temperley, Howard. "Capitalism, Slavery, and Ideology." *Past and Present* 75 (1977): 94–118.

Thompson, Robert Farris. *Flash of the Spirit: African and Afro-American Art and Philosophy*. New York: Vintage Books, 1981.

Thrasher, Sue, Jacquelyn Dowd Hall, and Bob Hall. "Learning from the Long Civil Rights Movement's First Generation." *Southern Cultures* 16, no. 2 (Summer 2010): 72–89.

Tolney, Stuart E., and E. M. Beck. *A Festival of Violence: An Analysis of Southern Lynching, 1881–1930*. Urbana: University of Illinois Press, 1995.

Torpey, John. *Making Whole What Has Been Smashed: On Reparations Politics*. Cambridge, MA: Harvard University Press, 2006.

Tyson, Timothy. "Robert F. Williams, 'Black Power,' and the Roots of the African American Freedom Struggle." *Journal of American History* 85, no. 2 (September 1998): 540–70.

Waldrep, Christopher. *African Americans Confront Lynching: Strategies of Resistance from the Civil War to the Civil Rights Era*. Lanham, MD: Rowman & Littlefield, 2009.

Walters, Ronald W. *The Price of Racial Reconciliation*. Ann Arbor: University of Michigan Press, 2008.

Washington, Harriet A. "Apology Shines Light on Racial Schism in Medicine." *New York Times*, 29 July 2008.

———. *Medical Apartheid: The Dark History of Medical Experimentation on Black Americans from Colonial Times to the Present*. New York: Anchor Books, 2007.

Webber, Thomas L. *Deep Like the Rivers: Education in the Slave Quarter Community, 1831–1865*. New York: Norton, 1978.

White, Deborah Gray. *Ar'n't I a Woman? Female Slaves in the Plantation South*. 2nd ed. New York: W. W. Norton, 1999.

White, Walter. *Rope and Faggot: A Biography of Judge Lynch*. New York: Knopf, 1929.

Wilder, Craig Steven. *Ebony and Ivy: Race, Slavery, and the Troubled History of America's Universities*. New York: Bloomsbury Press, 2013.

Williams, Eric E. *Capitalism and Slavery*. Chapel Hill: University of North Carolina Press, 1944.

Williams, Heather Andrea. *Self-Taught: African American Education in Slavery and Freedom*. Chapel Hill: University of North Carolina Press, 2005.

Williams, Kidada. *They Left Great Marks on Me: African American Testimonies of Racial Violence from Emancipation to World War I*. New York: New York University Press, 2012.

Williamson, Kevin D. "The Case against Reparations." *National Review*, 24 May 2014.

Winbush, Raymond, ed. *Should America Pay?* New York: HarperCollins, 2003.

Wish, Harvey. "American Slave Insurrections before 1861." *Journal of Negro History* 22 (July 1937): 299–320.

Wood, Betty. *Women's Work, Men's Work: The Informal Slave Economies of Low-country Georgia*. Athens: University of Georgia Press, 1995.

Woodruff, Nan Elizabeth. *American Congo: The African American Freedom Struggle in the Delta*. Chapel Hill: University of North Carolina Press, 2003.

Woodward, C. Vann. "History from Slave Sources: A Review Article." *American Historical Review* 79, no. 2 (April 1974): 470–81.

Index

Lynda Morgan is professor of history at Mount Holyoke College. Her teaching and research focus on nineteenth-century African American history, particularly the emancipation era.

CPSIA information can be obtained
at www.ICGtesting.com
Printed in the USA
BVHW030759280821
615510BV00006B/169